200+ SHOCKING TRUTHS ABOUT KRISHNA

Researched From All Ancient Scriptures

AF540073

DEEP TRIVEDI

Author of the Bestsellers 'I am Krishna' & 'I am The Mind'

Also available in Hindi, Marathi and Gujarati

First Edition: 2022
Price: Rs 349/-

Printed in India

Concept, Illustration and Design:

www.aatmaninnovations.com

Publisher: Aatman Innovations Pvt. Ltd.
Place of Publication: Mumbai

ISBN 978-93-84850-24-1

All Rights Reserved.

No part of this publication may be reproduced, stored in a retrieval system or transmitted in any form or by any means, electronic, mechanical, photocopying, recording or otherwise, without the prior written permission of the publisher.

Copyright © Aatman Innovations Pvt. Ltd.

DEEP TRIVEDI

Deep Trivedi is a renowned author, speaker and pioneer in spiritual psychodynamics. He writes and conducts workshops with an all-pervasive perspective, guiding individuals towards the achievement of their full potential. To date, he has led millions of people onto the path of success and happiness through his works.

In his voluminous works, Deep Trivedi has extensively explained Nature, its laws, its behaviour, its psychology and the effect it has on human life. No aspect of life and human psychology has been left untouched by him. He states that lack of psychological knowledge and understanding is the sole reason for all the sorrows and failures that pervade human life.

He has authored the bestsellers 'I am The Mind', 'I am Krishna', '101 All Time Great Stories with Life-Changing Philosophies', '3 Easy Steps To Win At Life' and many more. His bestseller 'I am The Mind' has been published in several national and international languages. He has been awarded the Times Power Men Award 2018 for his immense contribution to society.

His command over the biggest psychologies of life can be gauged by the fact that he holds the record for 'Maximum Workshops on Human Life', 'Maximum Workshops on Psychological Aspects of Tao Te Ching', 'Maximum Workshops on Ashtavakra Gita' and 'Maximum Workshops on Bhagavad Gita', spanning 168 hours, 28 minutes, 50 seconds in 58 days in different National and International record books. He also holds the record for 'Maximum Number of Quotations on Human Life' (about 12038) on subjects such as Soul, Human Life, Psychology, Laws of Nature, Destiny and many more. He has also been awarded an Honorary Doctorate for his works on the psychology of Bhagavad Gita. His interactive workshops have brought about a revolutionary transformation in people's lives by addressing their day-to-day concerns. These workshops have been conducted in front of live audiences across India.

He is known for his special ability to touch upon the deepest aspects of life and explain them by using lucid language, leaving no scope for ambiguity. The distinct spiritual-psychological language and expression in his writings and workshops begin to have an instant effect on the mind of the reader or listener, which makes Deep Trivedi a pioneer in this field.

To know more about Deep Trivedi, visit www.deeptrivedi.com

DEEP TRIVEDI

The Speaker

Deep Trivedi uses a unique combination of psycho-spiritual content, voice, language and expression, which effectuates an instantaneous transformation in his viewers and listeners. Millions of lives have been transformed just by listening to him.

His interactive workshops have brought about a revolutionary transformation in people's lives by addressing their day-to-day concerns. Deep Trivedi sheds light on every aspect of human life and mind and he has extensively spoken on The Bhagavad Gita, Tao Te Ching, Ashtavakra Gita, Secrets of Nature, Mind, Soul, Time, Destiny, and numerous other topics such as:

- **Ego**
- **God**
- **Guilt**
- **Love**
- **Anger**
- **Future**
- **Wealth**
- **Phobias**
- **Religion**
- **Complex**
- **Marriage**
- **Freedom**
- **Partiality**
- **Day-Sleep**
- **DNA-Genes**
- **Path of Life**
- **Personality**
- **Expectation**
- **Acceptance**
- **Hypocrisy**
- **Creativity**
- **Confusion**
- **Good-Bad**
- **Involvement**
- **Concentration**
- **Laws of Nature**
- **Time and Space**
- **Mind and Brain**
- **Self-Confidence**
- **Joy and Happiness**
- **Natural Intelligence**
- **Power of Transformation**

DVDs and Audio CDs of his workshops on the above topics and many more are available on **aatmanestore.com** and other leading e-commerce sites.

From the Author's Desk

The enigmatic personality that Krishna is, he has invariably been the subject of detailed, animated and sometimes even heated discussions. He is also the star of the Indian pantheon, so to speak, with perhaps the largest number of admirers across the length and breadth of India. Some exalt him to the status of the God of Gods, while others consider him to be larger than life, possessing an exceptionally majestic personality. Indubitably, down the ages, Krishna has remained an enigma, and this very peculiarity of his continues to spark curiosity in one and all. But the big question remains, what is Krishna all about? What kind of a life did he lead? Why is Krishna and his life discussed at such great length? Another paramount question lingering over the years is, are the details about Krishna's life readily available, or the stories about him merely a figment of someone's imagination?

Well, in this context, it is vital for everyone to apprehend a few points. The majority of details about Krishna's life, if not all of it, are certainly available in the scriptures. Unfortunately, however, not a single scripture chronicles his entire life, and therein lies the crux of the problem. Instead, fragmented information and discussions pertaining to his life can be found across a number of ancient Sanskrit scriptures. And it is by linking these smatterings of information from diverse sources that we are able to piece together Krishna's life.

This method, however, presents another problem. The details about Krishna's life are mentioned in only two kinds of scriptures; the first are the primeval ones, and the second are the ones chronicled at a much later date. Details about Krishna's real life are available only in the older scriptures, while the newer ones contain a fervid account of his life, wherein the imagination of the authors has traversed a wildly colourful domain. These scriptures have been embellished with a variety of fanciful details, and interestingly, this tinkering with Krishna's life did not cease there. In today's communication age, marked by revolutionary advancements, the tampering has increased exponentially. People, especially those depicting Krishna's life and the

Mahabharata in TV shows, have acted most irresponsibly by glossing over the factual details of Krishna's life. Without taking the trouble to delve into thorough research, the makers are having a field day, portraying Krishna's story in the manner that panders to their whims and fancies. For instance, one of the recently aired TV series has depicted Kansa, the king of Mathura and Krishna's uncle, as a bald man! Now, this completely contradicts the scriptures which state that he had long, flowing hair. As a matter of fact, after slaying Kansa, Krishna had dragged him by his hair to the middle of the court. Similarly, Krishna's adoptive parents, Nanda and Yashoda, are often portrayed as a young, good-looking couple, whereas in reality, both of them were past their prime when Krishna was placed in their care. In the same vein, Krishna's biological father, Vasudeva, had also crossed the wellspring of youth, and was well into the latter years of midlife at the time of Krishna's birth. And as for the portrayal of Krishna himself, well, people do not even bother to enquire into the details of his personal life. The wheels of imagination spin at a rapid pace, churning out a slew of fictitious stories; but even this does not suffice, as the stories are also liberally peppered with accounts of his so-called 'miracles'. Interestingly, these stories revolve either around his childhood or the period of the Mahabharata war; but these constitute just ten per cent of Krishna's life, which was far greater and more expansive. Unfortunately, there is a complete lack of discussion about this illustrious and phenomenal part of his life. This mockery of Krishna's life has been prevalent for quite some time, and one can ascribe it to several reasons, the foremost being, lack of exhaustive research. After all, comprehending a person's life from the numerous details spread out across several diverse scriptures is not an easy task. Such an effort requires the application of deep psychological knowledge. Moreover, Krishna's life was marked by all the complexities that are characteristic of every individual's life; but discussing them is not easy, for, the so-called society and community gloss over them for what they feel are unpalatable truths. Perhaps, they fear this would erode Krishna's divine, miraculous image!

However, in my opinion, Krishna is the supreme hero; and if you exalt someone to the stature of a hero, then you ought to comprehend every aspect of his life. A personality like Krishna has never been born again, nor will such a personality ever take birth in the future. Therefore, it is essential for everyone to become well acquainted with his complete personality. It is with this objective in mind that I have penned a first-person account of Krishna's life titled 'I am Krishna'. This book, published in six volumes, is an exhaustive account of Krishna's life, from the cradle to the grave, with meticulous details written sequentially in an interesting and exciting format. Apart from chronicling the entire life of Krishna, the book also sheds light on all his actions throughout his life, the circumstances under which he took them, and the reasons behind them. It is my firm opinion that we can glean a lot from our hero's life and personality, because after all, Krishna is a superhero. My book 'I am Krishna' is the culmination of an in-depth and thorough research panning all the scriptures related to his life. The book introduces us to our superhero, and enables us to fathom every aspect of his life that is worth inculcating.

Well, the objective behind the present book is to enable you to arm yourself with thorough knowledge about your superhero Krishna and his life, and to liberate you from the clutter of fictitious narratives that abound about him. In this endeavour of mine, I have presented before you all the evidence from the scriptures, along with references. And mind you, these details from the scriptures have either been suppressed for centuries or they have been deliberately ignored; or people simply haven't had access to them. However, I am of the opinion that once people are acquainted with the factual details about Krishna, they will also make an effort to fathom him in entirety. And the prime motive of this book is to inspire people to make that effort. For, Krishna's life was lived on an epic scale; a life that encompassed love as well as art, the exquisite enunciation of the Bhagavad Gita as well as numerous assassinations, marriages and children. His life was punctuated by the enjoyment of pleasures as well as renunciation, deception as well as divine truth. It was marked by conflict at home in addition to the struggles outside, with no dearth of friends and foes. And Krishna's specialty lies in the fact that in spite of all this, he remained undefeated in every battle of life! And this is precisely what all of us need to learn from him. However, for that purpose, you will first have to acquaint yourselves with the truth about his life. This book contains scores of questions pertaining to Krishna's life, and it also provides answers to those questions with the help of evidence gathered from various scriptures. Additionally, the book clarifies several facts and explains them at the required juncture. Let me also make it clear that hurting people's beliefs, sentiments and faith is not the motive of this book. The sole aim of this book is to wipe away the multiple layers of dust and patina that have been covering this pure gold i.e. Krishna's life, for centuries—a mammoth goal indeed. The main aim verily is to introduce your Krishna to you. I hope this endeavour of mine, penned in an interesting format, will enlighten you about Krishna's real life to a great extent.

Deep Trivedi

Questions Related to Krishna's Life

1. When was Krishna born?

Generally, one does not find an accurate account of the birth of any ancient saint or legendary personality in the scriptures. Even if it was available at some point, the anthropomorphists[1] of later eras have destroyed those testimonies, and have instead made the birth of those great beings appear as mysterious as possible. And this tendency can be noticed in the devotees and followers across all countries. Of course, this disease has dug its tentacles a bit too deep in India, not sparing even a colossus like Krishna. In fact, the history of Krishna has been subjected to the greatest number of embellishments. But since the present question is related to the time of Krishna's birth, let us first consider the testimony available in the Bhagavat Purana. This Purana only mentions the Rohini constellation and the monsoon season. According to the scripture, at the time of Krishna's birth, the sun was in the Rohini constellation, and it was raining.

अथ सर्वगुणोपेतः कालः परमशोभनः।
यर्हि एव अजनजन्मर्क्षं शान्तर्क्षग्रहतारकम्॥

Shukdeva said: "O Parikshit! Then, the beautiful moment arrived, endowed with all the auspicious qualities. The constellation of Rohini was rising, and all the other planets, constellations and stars were in a favourable position."

मघोनि वर्षत्यसकृत् यमानुजा
गंभीर तोयौघ जवोर्मि फेनिला।
भयानकावर्त शताकुला नदी
मार्गं ददौ सिन्धुरिव श्रियः पतेः॥

Shukdeva said: "During those days, there were frequent showers, because of which Yamuna river was in full spate. It was gushing forth fiercely and due to the unrelenting surge, the surface of the river was covered in foam. Terrible whirlpools were also forming in it. But just as the ocean had given way to Rama, the Yamuna gave way to him."

(Bhagavat Purana, Skandha–10, Chapter–3, Shloka–1, 50)

---

1. Adherents of the avatar theory who believe that deities descend on the earth in an incarnate form or some manifest shape (an incarnation of a god)

In both the shlokas of the Bhagavat Purana quoted above, there is no mention of date, month or year. However, in the Harivansha Purana, which is older than the Bhagavat Purana and is considered to be more authoritative, it is mentioned that it was night time and the eighth day of the month.

यामेव रजनीं कृष्णो जज्ञे वृष्णिकलोद्वहः।
तामेव रजनीं कन्यां यशोदापि व्यजायत।।

Vaishampayan said: "O Janamejaya! On the very day that Krishna, the scion of the Vrishni clan, took birth, Yashoda gave birth to a girl."

अभिजिन्नाम नक्षत्रं जयन्ती नाम शर्वरी।
मुहूर्तो विजयो नाम यत्र जातो जनार्दनः।।

He continued: "When Krishna was born, the Nakshatra was Abhijit, and due to the confluence of Rohini constellation, the night was called Jayanti, and the *muhurta*[2] at that time was Vijay."

(Harivansha Purana, Vishnu Parva, Chapter–4, Shloka–12, 17)

Even in the Brahmavaivarta Purana *(Shri Krishna Janma Khanda, Chapter–7, Shlokas–62-65)*, one can find a similar description. However, the time of Krishna's birth as mentioned in the Garga Samhita is different from all the previously quoted scriptures and is described as clearly as possible.

भाद्रे बुधे कृष्णेपक्षे धात्रर्क्षे हर्षणे वृषे।
कर्णे अष्टम्यामर्द्धरात्रे नक्षत्रेश महोदये।।

Narada said: "O Bahulashva! In the month of Bhadrapad, in the dark fortnight, under the Rohini constellation, under the Harshan Yoga, with Taurus as the ascendant on the eighth day of the month, at midnight, when the moon becomes visible in the sky, Krishna was born to Devaki in the house of Vasudeva."

(Garga Samhita, Goloka Khanda, Chapter–11, Shloka–23)

Therefore, based on the evidence presented above, one has to accept that Krishna was born at midnight on the eighth day of the dark fortnight in the month of Bhadrapad (August–September). But it is unclear when he was born, that is, how many years ago? Well, hundreds of books have been written on this subject based on the astronomical calculations of the *muhurtas, yogas,* ascendant planets and constellations mentioned in the scriptures quoted above. And all these books debunk each

2. an ancient unit of time equal to 48 minutes

other's claims. It will not be possible to dwell upon them here, nor is it appropriate, because all these calculations have been made only in the past 100–150 years. But the subject being discussed is an event that occurred 5,000 years ago. Even the scriptures, whose shlokas you have read above, have been written between 200 B.C.E. and 1500 C.E. Therefore, it cannot be said that the dates mentioned in them are indisputable either.

2. What was the background of Krishna's parents?

Krishna's parents, Devaki and Vasudeva, were the residents of the sovereign kingdom of Mathura. In those days, there was no permanent royal lineage of the Yadavas due to a traditional belief, which points at King Yayati, who had expelled his eldest son, Yadu, from the royal clan.

एवमुक्त्वा यदुं तात शसापैनं स मन्युमान्।
अराज्या ते प्रजा मूढ़ भवित्रिति नराधम।।

Vaishampayan said: "Respected One! Saying this, King Yayati, furious with his son Yadu, cursed him with these words, 'You despicable fool! Your progeny will always remain deprived of kingdom!'"

(Harivansha Purana, Harivansha Parva, Chapter–30, Shloka–29)

Therefore, the descendants of Yadu used to establish kingdoms as sovereign regimes and rule them. Later on, Vrishni and Andhak who were born in this Yadu clan, established Mathura and other territories as sovereign kingdoms and ruled them.

माद्र्याः पुत्रस्य जज्ञाते सुतौ वृष्ण्यन्धकावुभौ।
जज्ञाते तनयौ वृष्णेः श्वफल्कश्चित्रकस्तथा।।

Vaishampayan said: "Madri's son, Yudhajit had two sons, Vrishni and Andhak, and Vrishni had two sons Shvafalka and Chitrak."

(Harivansha Purana, Harivansha Parva, Chapter–34, Shloka–3)

In Vrishni's clan, there was Shursen, who was elected the king of Mathura. He had ten sons, among whom Vasudeva was the eldest. In Andhak's clan, there was Ahuka, who became a king and had two sons, Devaka and Ugrasen.

आहुकस्यतुकाश्यायां द्वौ पुत्रौ सम्बभूवतुः।।
देवकश्चोग्रसेनश्च देवपुत्रसमावुभौ।

Vaishampayan said: "Ahuka was married to the daughter of the king of

Kashi, and they had two sons, Devaka and Ugrasen."

(Harivansha Purana, Harivansha Parva, Chapter–38, Shloka–26-27)

From the history presented in the religious scriptures, it becomes evident that in those days, there were no taboos of descent or community in marital relationships. This is proven by the marital relationships between the descendants of the Vrishni and Andhak clans. For instance, Devaka had married off all his seven daughters to Vasudeva, the eldest son of Shursen.

कुमार्यः सप्त चाप्यासन् वसुदेवाय ता ददौ॥
देवकी शान्तिदेवा च सुदेवा देवरक्षिता।
वृकदेव्युपदेवी च सुनासी चैव सप्तमी॥

Vaishampayan said: "Devaka had seven daughters: Devaki, Shantideva, Sudeva, Devarakshita, Vrikadevi, Upadevi and Sunasi. Devaka had married them all to Vasudeva."

(Harivansha Purana, Harivansha Parva, Chapter–38, Shloka–28-29)

When Vasudeva was married, Ugrasen was ruling Mathura instead of Shursen, and the latter was living in Mathura with his entire family as one of the Yadava elites of the kingdom. From this scriptural evidence, it becomes clear that even though Krishna's parents were not the king and queen of any kingdom at that time, his family and relatives were certainly part of royal families. This is also proven by the fact that even Krishna's five aunts were married to kings of different kingdoms.

3. How many stepmothers did Krishna have?

Well, the scriptures do not seem to be unanimous in their opinion in answer to the above question. The reason being, in ancient times, when the art of writing had not developed much, history was orally transmitted from one generation to the next through folklore. When the writing began, scholars from different regions started writing down these folk tales at different periods of time. So, it was natural for them to differ from one another. Therefore, it is essential to thoroughly study all the scriptures to find information about Krishna's mothers. And on this basis, it can be said that he had 14 mothers: Rohini, Indira, Vaishakhi, Bhadra and Sunamni (all of them were granddaughters of Bahleek, the elder brother of King Shantanu of Hastinapur), Sahadeva, Shantideva,

Shreedeva, Devarakshita, Vrikadevi, Upadevi and Devaki (these were the daughters of Devaka, the younger brother of Mathura's reigning king, Ugrasen), Sutanu and Badava (both of them were Vasudeva's maidservants as well as his concubines). Devaki had given birth to Krishna, and the rest were his stepmothers:

या पत्न्यो वसुदेवस्य चतुर्दश वरांगना।
पौरवी रोहिणी नाम इन्दिरा च तथा वरा।।
वैशाखी च तथा भद्रा सुनाम्नी चैव पंचमी।
सहदेवा शान्तिदेवा श्रीदेवा देवरक्षिता।।
वृकदेव्युपदेवी च देवकी चैव सप्तमी।
सुतनुर्वडवा चैव द्वे एते परिचारिके।।

Vaishampayan said: "Janamejaya! Out of the 14 beautiful wives of Vasudeva, Rohini, her younger sisters, Indira, Vaishakhi, Bhadra and the fifth, Sunamni, were from the Paurava clan; while Sahadeva, Shantideva, Shreedeva, Devarakshita, Vrikadevi, Upadevi and the seventh, Devaki, were daughters of Devaka. Sutanu and Badava were two women in his service."

(Harivansha Purana, Harivansha Parva, Chapter–35, Shloka–1-3)

पौरवी रोहिणी भद्रा मदिरा रोचना इला।
देवकी प्रमुखाश्चासन्पत्न्य आनकदुन्दुभेः।।

Shukdeva said: "Anakadundubhi Vasudeva had several wives from the Puru clan such as Rohini, Bhadra, Madira, Rochana, Ila, Devaki and others."

(Bhagavat Purana, Skandha–9, Chapter–24, Shloka–45)

However, in a later chapter in the Bhagavat Purana itself, only two wives of Vasudeva are mentioned. When Krishna's entire family had gone on a pilgrimage to Samanta Panchaka on the occasion of solar eclipse, a large number of cowherds from Vrindavan, including Nanda and Yashoda, also reached there. They all mingled with each other. Vasudeva then performed an oblation at Samanta Panchaka, but on this occasion, only two wives of Vasudeva have been mentioned, which was against the prevalent Hindu tradition. Among the 14 wives, Rohini was Vasudeva's eldest wife and Devaki was the youngest. At this point, these are the only two that are mentioned.

रोहिणी देवकी चाथ परिष्वज्य व्रजेश्वरीम्।
स्मरन्त्यौ तत्कृतां मैत्रीं बाष्पकण्ठ्यौ समूचतुः॥

"Rohini and Devaki took Yashoda in their arms. They were overwhelmed with emotion on recalling the friendly and endearing behaviour of Yashoda towards them."

(Bhagavat Purana, Skandha–10, Chapter–82, Shloka–37)

Similar to the Bhagavat Purana, even Vishnu Purana and Brahmavaivarta Purana mention only two wives of Vasudeva: Devaki and Rohini.

(Vishnu Purana, Part–5, Chapter–1-2)

(Brahmavaivarta Purana, Shri Krishna Janma Khanda, Chapter–7)

On the other hand, there is no mention of these details in the Mahabharata. Another significant fact that deserves attention here is, when Kansa had imprisoned Vasudeva and Devaki, Vasudeva's second wife, Rohini was staying in Gokul under the protection of Nanda. But not a single scripture mentions where the other 12 wives were staying, and with whom they were staying at the time. The reason behind this could be that since Krishna and Balarama totally dominate all the scriptures, the authors must have chosen to focus only on the mothers of those two. However, these very scriptures mention the names of more than 63 siblings of Krishna. Therefore, their claim that Vasudeva had 14 wives cannot be rejected either.

4. Was Balarama Krishna's biological brother?

All Puranas unanimously state that Balarama was the son of Krishna's stepmother, Rohini. None of the scriptures disagree on this point.

(Harivansha Purana, Harivansha Parva, Chapter–35, Shloka–5)

(Bhagavat Purana, Skandha–9, Chapter–24, Shloka–45)

(Vishnu Purana, Part–5, Chapter–5, Shloka–5)

The Mahabharata does not mention anything about this in an unambiguous manner. The voluminous epic mentions Krishna and Balarama as brothers at various points, but it does not mention anywhere that they were the sons of Devaki and Rohini respectively.

5. How many brothers did Krishna have?

The Mahabharata does not clearly discuss any siblings of Krishna, but at various points, the epic does mention Balarama, Gada, Angada, Sarana and others as his brothers *(South Indian Mahabharata, Sabha Parva, Chapter–38)*. Even the Puranas mention different details about it.

i) Bhagavat Purana – This Purana contains the following details about Krishna and his siblings. Here are the names of Krishna's mothers and their respective sons:

Krishna's mothers	Their respective sons
Rohini	Balarama, Gada, Sarana, Durmada, Vipul, Dhruva and Krita
Paurvi	12 sons including Bhoot, Subhadra, Bhadravaaha, Durmada, Bhadra and others
Indira	Nanda, Upananda, Krituka, Shura and others
Kaushalya	Keshi
Rochana	Hasta and Hemaangada
Ila	Ulvalka
Shrutadeva	Viprishtha
Shantideva	Shrama, Pratishruta and others
Upadeva	10 sons including Kalpavarsha and others
Shreedeva	6 sons including Vasu, Hansa, Suvansha and others
Devarakshita	9 sons including Gada and others
Sahadeva	8 sons including Puruvishruta and others
Devaki	Krishna

This Purana mentions 63 brothers of Krishna, but since it says 'others' after these names, the number of brothers could possibly be more, which is not known.

(Bhagavat Purana, Skandha–9, Chapter–24, Shloka–46-54)

ii) Harivansha Purana – According to this Purana, here are the names of Krishna's mothers and their respective children:

Rohini: The sons were Balarama, Saarana, Shatha, Durdama, Damana,

Shvabhra, Pindaaraka and Ushinara. There were two daughters, Chitra and Subhadra, out of which Chitra died in her childhood.

(Harivansha Purana, Harivansha Parva, Chapter–35, Shloka–5-6)

In this Purana, only Rohini's children have been mentioned separately. Otherwise, it is only Krishna who is mentioned as Devaki's son everywhere. Precise details pertaining to this are not available in other Puranas either.

6. Was Subhadra Krishna's sister?

Subhadra is a major character in the Mahabharata, whose importance has been depicted unambiguously in the epic. King Parikshit, who carried forward the name of the Kuru dynasty, was the grandson of Subhadra. That is why Subhadra has been mentioned in all the relevant Puranas and the Mahabharata. According to one of them—Harivansha Purana—Subhadra was Balarama's sister:

चित्रां नाम कुमारीं च रोहिणीतनया दश।
चित्रा सुभद्रेति पुनर्विख्याता कुरुनन्दन।।

"Chitra and Subhadra were Rohini's daughters, meaning, the sisters of Balarama."

(Harivansha Purana, Harivansha Parva, Chapter–35, Shloka–6)

The Mahabharata mentions Subhadra as the biological sister of Saarana:

ममैषा भगिनी पार्थ सारणस्य सहोदरा।
सुभद्रा नाम भद्रं ते पितुर्मे दयिता सुता।
यदि ते वर्तते बुद्धिर्वक्ष्यते पितरं स्वयं।।

At one point in the Mahabharata, Krishna tells Arjuna, "O Arjuna, son of Kunti! She is mine and Saarana's biological sister; may you always prosper, her name is Subhadra. She is the beloved daughter of my father. If you are thinking of marrying her, I will myself take the proposal to my father."

(Mahabharata, Adi Parva, Chapter–218, Shloka–17; Neelkantha's Commentary)

Both Bhagavat Purana and Harivansha Purana mention Saarana as Balarama's brother or Rohini's son; that is why, according to the Mahabharata too, Subhadra was the biological sister of Balarama. However, according to the Bhagavat Purana, Subhadra was Devaki's daughter, meaning Krishna's biological sister:

अष्टमस्तु तयोरासीत्स्वयमेव हरिः किल।
सुभद्रा च महाभागा तव राजन्पितामही॥

Shukdeva said: "O Parikshit! Your supremely fortunate grandmother, Subhadra too was the daughter of Devaki."

(Bhagavat Purana, Skandha–9, Chapter–24, Shloka–55)

Comment: But since the Bhagavat Purana has been written much later, it is wiser to accept what the older scriptures state.

7. What is the truth about Radha?

Radha's significance in Krishna's life is immense, for, whether it is a short tale or a detailed story of Krishna, it is considered incomplete without the mention of Radha. However, ancient scriptures do not mention her at all. The Sabha Parva of the Mahabharata provides a brief description of Krishna's birth and childhood, but Radha is not mentioned in it *(South Indian Mahabharata, Sabha Parva, Chapter–38)*. There is no mention of Radha in the Harivansha Purana either. There is another scripture, Padma Purana, which is considered to have been written around 200 B.C.E. In this Purana, Chapter 72 of the Uttara Khanda has the Vishnu Sahastranaam Stotram, which has various names of Krishna based on all his feats; but Radha's name has not been mentioned in it at all. Even the Bhagavat Purana, which presents an exaggerated account of Krishna's life, does not mention Radha. It is mainly the Brahmavaivarta Purana in which Radha is discussed. This Purana depicts Radha and Krishna as Nature and the Supreme Being (or Spirit); and even Brahma, Vishnu and Mahesh (Shiva) have been depicted as being subservient to them. This Purana has crossed all social boundaries in discussing the love between Radha and Krishna.

In Chapter 2 of Shri Krishna Janma Khanda of the Brahmavaivarta Purana, Krishna's character has been depicted in such a manner that it has crossed all limits of decency. According to this Purana, Radha was the wife of a person called Rayaana from the Vaishya community, who was the brother of Krishna's foster mother, Yashoda. This means that Radha was Krishna's aunt *(Brahmavaivarta Purana, Shri Krishna Janma Khanda, Chapter–2)*. Apart from this Purana, the Garga Samhita also lends great importance to Radha. According to this scripture, Radha was the daughter of Vrishabhanu and Kirti Kumari, who lived near Vrindavan, and the marriage between Radha and Krishna was fixed in their childhood *(Garga Samhita, Goloka Khanda, Chapter–15)*. The words 'Radha' and 'Krishna' have also been mentioned in the Skandha Purana *(Chapter 28 of Vasudeva Mahatmaya in the Vaishnava Khanda)*. So, ancient scriptures do not mention Radha at all, while the relatively new scriptures are replete with all kinds of details about the relationship between Radha and Krishna. On the basis of these scriptures, readers will have to use their own prudence and decide what the truth could be.

8. How many wives of Krishna do the scriptures mention?

According to the scriptures, Krishna had eight wives—Rukmini, Satyabhama, Jambavati, Bhadra, Mitravinda, Satya, Lakshmana and Kalindi. Collectively, they were called Ashtabharya (eight wives).

महिषीरष्ट कल्याणीस्ततोऽन्या मधुसूदनः।
उपयेमे महाबाहुर्गुणोपेताः कुलोद्भवाः।।

"Madhusudana, the Mighty Armed One, married eight high-born, virtuous princesses who were the epitome of auspiciousness."

(Harivansha Purana, Vishnu Parva, Chapter–60, Shloka–40)

Apart from these, there were 16,000 women, whom Krishna had rescued from Narakasura's captivity. They certainly cannot be called Krishna's queens.

स्त्रीसहस्राणि चान्यानि षोडशातुलविक्रमः।

The point to be noted here is, in the shloka quoted above, the word 'women' is used instead of 'wives'. In the commentary on Mahabharata by Neelkantha, which is popular in north India, there is no mention of Krishna's marriage with the women imprisoned by Narakasura. However, the popular South Indian version of the Mahabharata states the following shloka related to this:

गांधर्वेन विवाहेन विवाहं कुरु नः प्रियम्।
ततोऽस्मत्प्रियकामार्थे भगवान् मारुतोऽब्रवीत्।।

"Marry us according to the Gandharva tradition and gratify us."

(South Indian Mahabharata - Gita Press - Sabha Parva, Chapter–38)

The evidence available in two ancient scriptures shows that no one doubts the fact that Krishna had eight wives. However, the stories about the fate of the 16,100 women rescued by Krishna from Narakasura's captivity differ from scripture to scripture. Apart from these two scriptures, the Bhagavat Purana, Vishnu Purana, Brahmavaivarta Purana, Garga Samhita and others depict these 16,100 women as Krishna's wives, and also include various kinds of stories woven around them. Another point to be noted here is, the Saamba Purana and the Matsya Purana even have negative stories about them. Therefore, it depends entirely on the prudence of the readers whether they choose to remain grounded to the reality and accept that Krishna had eight wives, or whether they wish to enter the imaginary, Puranic world and grapple with the idea that Krishna had 16,108 wives.

9. Have the Puranic scriptures ridiculed Krishna's conduct?
Almost all Puranic scriptures are replete with contradictory statements about Krishna, and that too having crossed all boundaries of exaggeration. On one hand, a seer and great personage like him has been called the Creator of the Universe, and on the other, even his simple, personal life has been presented in a repugnant manner. It is not possible to reproduce all such descriptions as an answer to a single question, because it is a subject that requires extensive deliberation. Therefore, I am briefly pointing towards a few shlokas as proof of this, so that readers can understand the real agenda of the authors of such works. Let us take a look at this shloka from the Bhagavat Purana, which obliquely hints at Krishna's relationship with other women.

कामयामह एतस्य श्रीमत्पादरजः श्रियः।
कुचकुंकुम गंधाढ्यं मूर्ध्ना वोढुं गदाभृत्तः॥

Rohini, who is one of the many women rescued from the clutches of Narakasura, says: "We do not desire any enjoyment or position. All we wish for is to be showered by the dust of the saffron applied on the breasts of Krishna's paramours that is stuck on his feet."

व्रजस्त्रियो यद्वाञ्छन्ति पुलिन्द्यस्तृणवीरुधः।
गावश्चारयतो गोपाः पदस्पर्शं महात्मनः॥

"We merely wish to touch those lotus feet of Shri Krishna, which the milkmaids, the tribal women, the grass, the straw and the creepers yearn to touch."

(Bhagavat Purana, Skandha–10, Chapter–83, Shloka–43)

Essentially, it can be said that the other 16,000 women mentioned in various accounts of Krishna's life had a one-sided affair with him. A book titled 'Gopal Sahastranaam Stotram' which ostensibly glorifies Krishna, has left no stone unturned in tarnishing the character of Krishna in the name of devotion. In this book, Krishna has been called the illegitimate husband of the wives of the cowherds, and has also been called the leader of thieves and lustful men.

गोपालः कामिनी जारः चौर जार शिखामणिः।

(Gopal Sahastranaam Stotram – 138)

In Chapter 72 of the Uttara Khanda of the Padma Purana, there appears the Vishnu Sahastranaam Stotram in which Krishna has been called by names such as Kamadeva – 830, Ratipati – 831, Manmatha – 832, Kameshwaripriya – 840 and others. Meaning, Krishna was a sensualist according to this Purana too.

Comment: The evidence from the scriptures mentioned above makes it unambiguous that diverse opinions about Krishna abound even in the scriptures. It is not that all of them considered him to be decent and valiant only, for, he has been denigrated at various points in several of them. The Jain scriptures, in fact, have sent him to 'hell' on account of several of his deeds. And honestly speaking, it is this very uniqueness of Krishna's personality that attracts everyone.

10. Many people have labelled Krishna as a betrayer; what do the scriptures say about this?

All the available scriptures that give a detailed account of Krishna and his life are replete with contradictions and chicanery in equal measure. For instance, the Gopal Sahastranaam Stotram will leave a layperson totally perplexed, as the text in this Stotram is bound to make him wonder whether it is a prayer to Krishna or his character assassination. In this book, Krishna has been called the illegitimate husband of the wives of the cowherds, and has also been called the leader of thieves and lustful men.

गोपालः कामिनी जारः चौर जार शिखामणिः।

(Gopal Sahastranaam Stotram – 138)

In the Mahabharata, Shishupala calls Krishna immoral:

को हि धर्मच्युते पूजामेवं युक्तां नियोजयेत्।

Shishupala said: "Which virtuous person will ever worship an immoral person like Krishna?"

(Mahabharata, Sabha Parva, Chapter–38, Shloka–22)

Krishna has also been called ungrateful, because he had killed Kansa:

यस्य चानेन धर्मज्ञः भुक्तमन्नं बलीयशः।
स चानेन हतः कंसः इत्येतन्न महाद्भुतम्॥

Elaborating on the same point, Shishupala says: "O Bhishma, the one who knows what righteousness is! He killed the mighty Kansa, whose hospitality he and his family had enjoyed; it is not a big deal for an ungrateful person like him."

(Mahabharata, Sabha Parva, Chapter–41, Shloka–11)

Furthermore, Krishna has been called the killer of cattle and women:

गोघ्नः स्त्रीघ्नश्च सन् भीष्मपितामह तद्वाक्याद् यदि पूज्यते।

Speaking about this, Shishupala says: "O Bhishma! In spite of being the killer of cattle and women, this man called Krishna is being honoured only because of your orders; but how can someone who is guilty of killing these two be honoured as the principal guest?"

(Mahabharata, Sabha Parva, Chapter–41, Shloka–16)

At various points in the Mahabharata, Krishna has also been called a cheater and a liar:

येन धर्मात्मनाऽऽत्मानं ब्रह्मण्यमभिजानता।
प्रेषितं पाद्यमस्मै तद् दातुमग्रे दुरात्मने॥
भुज्यतामिति तेनोक्ताः कृष्णभीमधनंजयाः।
जरासंधेन कौरव्य कृष्णेन विकृतं कृतम्॥
यद्ययं जगतः कर्ता यथैनं मूर्ख मन्यसे।
कस्मान्न ब्राह्मणं सम्यगात्मानमवगच्छति॥

Shishupala said: "When Krishna, Arjuna and Bhima had visited Jarasandha disguised as Brahmins, and were welcomed as Brahmins and even served food that was fit for Brahmins, why did Krishna refuse to eat? Old man Bhishma! If, according to you, he is God, then why did he discriminate in this manner? Why did he not accept the hospitality extended to Brahmins? He did so because he is a rogue and he is duplicitous."

(Mahabharata, Sabha Parva, Chapter–42, Shloka–4-6)

In the Mahabharata, Krishna has also been accused of abducting and marrying a woman who was already betrothed to someone else:

मन्यमानो हि कः सत्सु पुरुषः परिकीर्तयेत्।
अन्यपूर्वां स्त्रियं जातु त्वदन्यो मधूसूदन॥

Shishupala lashed out at Krishna: "Shameless Krishna! Who else but you can declare in this assembly that your wife is actually a woman who was betrothed to someone else?"

(Mahabharata, Sabha Parva, Chapter–45, Shloka–19)

Comment: In short, the scriptures have roundly denounced Krishna's actions at various points, due to several reasons. And to be honest, this is precisely why it can be said that Krishna was a complete personality.

11. What is the truth behind Krishna's display of his colossal form in the battlefield of Kurukshetra?

This incident is described only in the Mahabharata, with no mention found in any other Purana; and this is something worth paying attention to. Actually, the shlokas of the Bhishma Parva in the Mahabharata, beginning from Chapter 23–40, have been published separately as the Bhagavad Gita, and it is the Chapter 11 of the Gita that includes the incident of Krishna displaying his colossal form. The Padma Purana and the Kurma Purana do speak about the greatness of the Bhagavad Gita, but there is no independent mention of Krishna assuming a colossal form in any of the Puranas. Incidentally, apart from the chapters included in the Bhagavad Gita, there is another occasion in the Mahabharata during which Krishna is said to have assumed a colossal form. Before the Mahabharata war, when Krishna visited Hastinapur as an envoy of peace and when Duryodhana attempted to arrest him, Krishna is said to have assumed a colossal form.

(Mahabharata, Udyoga Parva, Chapter–131)

In the Bhagavat Purana and the Garga Samhita, one can certainly find a description of Krishna showing his mother, Yashoda, the entire universe *(Bhagavat Purana, Skandha–10, Chapter–8, Shloka–32-39)*;

(Garga Samhita, Goloka Khanda, Chapter–15). But there is a problem here too. The Brahmavaivarta Purana, Harivansha Purana and others do not mention any such incident. So, the ancient scriptures say one thing, while the newer scriptures say something else altogether. This makes it quite evident that the latter scriptures have not only exaggerated several incidents of Krishna's life, but have also added copious imaginary stories in his name. That is why it is essential for readers to exercise caution while trying to fathom Krishna. They have to ensure at all times that their sense of discernment remains active while reading such works, because there are as many 'facts' about Krishna as there are scriptures.

12. Why did Krishna put an end to Indra's worship in Vrindavan?

Krishna's intelligence was incomparable and this becomes self-evident through several incidents of his life. In his childhood, he had proven the adage 'Coming events cast their shadows before.' He would not take long to discern right from wrong; and in this context, he also took the right decisions instantly. The incident of Indra's worship is another evidence of his active intelligence. The Bhagavat Purana describes the cessation of Indra's worship by Krishna in this manner:

तत्र तावत् क्रियायोगो भवतां किं विचारितः।
अथ वा लौकिकस्तन्मे पृच्छतः साधु भण्यताम्॥

Krishna asked his father Nanda: "Father! Why are you making all these arrangements? Have you applied your mind to it or are you just abiding by a worldly tradition?"

(Bhagavat Purana, Skandha–10, Chapter–24, Shloka–7)

In reply, Nanda said:

पर्जन्यो भगवान् इन्द्रो मेघास्तस्यात्ममूर्तयः।
तेऽभिवर्षन्ति भूतानां प्रीणनं जीवनं पयः॥
तं तात वयमन्ये च वार्मुचां पतिमीशरम्।
द्रव्यैस्तद् रेतसा सिद्धैः यजन्ते क्रतुभिर्नराः॥
तच्छेषेणोपजीवन्ति त्रिवर्गफलहेतवे।
पुंसां पुरुषकाराणां पर्जन्यः फलभावनः॥
य एनं विसृजेत् धर्मं परम्पर्यागतं नरः।
कामाल्लोभात् भयाद् द्वेषात् स वै नाप्नोति शोभनम्॥

"Son, Indra is the god of rain and these clouds are verily his forms. He showers rain to quench the thirst of the people on earth and to bless them with the boon of life. All the materials used in his worship are derived from water and all of us humans subsist on whatever remains after the worship. This has been our family tradition for long, and that is why, if one discontinues this traditional duty, one does not prosper."

(Bhagavat Purana, Skandha–10, Chapter–24, Shloka–8-11)

The intelligent Krishna found his father's explanation quite strange, and thus, interrupting his father, he said:

कर्मणा जायते जन्तुः कर्मणैव विलीयते।
सुखं दुःखं भयं क्षेमं कर्मणैवाभिपद्यते ॥

"A living being takes birth and dies in accordance with his *karma,* and it is through his *karma* alone that he attains happiness or sorrow, or fear or the sense of security."

(Bhagavat Purana, Skandha–10, Chapter–24, Shloka–13)

किमिन्द्रेणेह भूतानां स्वस्वकर्मानुवर्तिनाम्।
अनीशेनान्यथा कर्तुं स्वभावविहितं नृणाम्॥
स्वभावतन्त्रो हि जनः स्वभावमनुवर्तते।
स्वभावस्थमिदं सर्वं सदेवासुरमानुषम्॥

"When all living beings are reaping the fruits of their *karma*, how can Indra intervene? Father, when he cannot alter the fruits reaped by human beings based on their previously acquired disposition, why do we need him? A human being is governed by his disposition and that is what he follows. In fact, even this world that shelters Gods, demons, humans and others, is established in its own nature."

(Bhagavat Purana, Skandha–10, Chapter–24, Shloka–15-16)

सत्वं रजस्तम इति स्थित्युत्पत्त्यन्तहेतवः।
रजसोत्पद्यते विशं अन्योऽन्यं विविधं जगत्॥
रजसा चोदिता मेघा वर्षन्त्यम्बूनि सर्वतः।
प्रजास्तैरेव सिध्यन्ति महेन्द्रः किं करिष्यति॥

"The qualities of *Sattva* (purity), *Rajas* (activity) and *Tamas* (ignorance) are the causes behind the creation, sustenance and dissolution of this world, and it is because of the quality of *Rajas* that clouds shower rain all around. What does Indra have to do with this and what can he do?"

(Bhagavat Purana, Skandha– 10, Chapter–24, Shloka–22-23)

न नः पुरोजनपदा न ग्रामा न गृहा वयम्।
नित्यं वनौकसस्तात वनशैलनिवासिनः॥
तस्माद् गवां ब्राह्मणानां अद्रेश्चारभ्यतां मखः।
य इन्द्रयागसम्भाराः तैरयं साध्यतां मखः॥

Finally, explaining the futility of the conception of the demigod, Indra and his worship, Krishna advised his father, "We own neither a kingdom, city nor a village or house; we have always been and will be forest dwellers, and it is the Govardhana Hill which is our life support. So, we must worship the Govardhana Hill with the material that we have prepared for Indra's worship."

(Bhagavat Purana, Skandha–10, Chapter–24, Shloka–24-25)

Even according to the Harivansha Purana, Krishna advised his father to consider the worship of Indra as a futile exercise and instead worship the Govardhana Hill in view of their occupation *(Harivansha Purana, Vishnu Parva, Chapter–16, Shloka–2-3)*. The Mahabharata narrates the incident of Krishna lifting the Govardhana Hill, but does not mention anything about Indra's worship being stopped.

The Vishnu Purana *(Part–5, Chapter–10, Shloka–19-30)* has a combination of narratives from the Bhagavat Purana and Harivansha Purana, and the reasons it mentions behind Krishna's cessation of Indra's worship are the same as those mentioned in those two Puranas. The description of this incident in the Garga Samhita *(Giriraj Khanda, Chapter–1)* is similar to that of the Bhagavat Purana. As for the Brahmavaivarta Purana, that too mentions Krishna's cessation of Indra's worship on similar lines as the Bhagavat Purana.

Comment: From this explanation, one must comprehend that Krishna was intelligent and determined right from his childhood. He was not only able to recognise a wrong tradition, but he was also capable of strongly opposing it.

13. Did Krishna really have 16,108 marriages?

In general, all the Puranas and the Mahabharata provide a detailed account of Krishna's 16,100 marriages, apart from his eight main marriages. The Mahabharata version with Neelkantha's commentary, which is popular in north India, mentions Krishna's marriage with the women languishing in Narakasura's captivity in this manner:

अनेकयुगवर्षायुर्निहत्य नरकं मृधे।
नीत्वा कन्यासहस्राणि उपयेमे यथाविधि॥

Vidura said to Duryodhana: "After killing Narakasura, who had been living for several aeons and countless years, Krishna set out with thousands of princesses from Narakasura's palace and married them according to the prescribed rituals."

(Mahabharata, Udyoga Parva, Chapter–130, Shloka–58; Gita Press Edition–44)

The popular South Indian version of the Mahabharata has the following shloka:

गांधर्वेन विवाहेन विवाहं कुरु नः प्रियम्।
ततोऽस्मत्प्रियकामार्थे भगवान् मारुतोऽब्रवीत्॥

The women who were free from Narakasura's captivity said: "Marry us according to the Gandharva tradition and please us."

(Popular South Indian version of Mahabharata, Sabha Parva, Chapter–38)

The Harivansha Purana describes this marriage of Krishna in the following manner:

स्त्रीसहस्राणि चान्यानि षोडशातुलविक्रमः।

"Apart from them, there were 16,000 other women."

(Harivansha Purana, Vishnu Parva, Chapter–60, Shloka–43)

The Bhagavat Purana describes this incident in the following manner:

तं प्रविष्टं स्त्रियो वीक्ष्य नरवर्यं विमोहिताः।
मनसा वव्रिरेऽभीष्टं पतिं दैवोपसादितम्॥
भूयात् पतिरयं मह्यं धाता तदनुमोदताम्।
इति सर्वाः पृथक् कृष्णे भावेन हृदयं दधुः॥
ताः प्राहिणोद् द्वारवतीं सुमृष्टविरजोऽम्बराः।
नरयानैर्महाकोशान् रथोशान् द्रविणं महत्॥

Shukdeva said: "When those women saw Krishna in the gynaeceum, they were bowled over, and in their heart of hearts they accepted him as their husband. Then, Krishna gifted them beautiful jewellery and garments and made arrangements to send them to Dwarka on palanquins. He also sent heaps full of treasure, several horses and chariots with them."

(Bhagavat Purana, Skandha–10, Chapter–59, Shloka–34-36)

The Vishnu Purana describes it similarly:

रत्नानि नरकावासाज्जग्राह मुनिसत्तम।।
कन्यापुरे स कन्यानां षोडशातुलविक्रमः।
शताधिकानि ददृशे सहस्राणि महामते।।
चतुर्दन्तान् गजोशोग्रयान् षट्सहस्रान् स दृष्टवान्।
काम्बोजानां तथोशानां नियुतान्येकविंशतिम्।।
कन्यास्तोश तता नागांस्तानेशान् द्वारकां पुरीम्।
प्रषयामास गोविन्दः सद्यो नरककिंकरेः।।

Sage Parashar said to Sage Maitreya: "And then he took several kinds of precious stones from Narakasura's palace. Thereafter, Krishna went to Narakasura's gynaeceum and saw 16,100 young women, 6,000 four-tusked elephants and 21,000 horses of a superior breed from the kingdom of Kamboj. He then instructed Narakasura's servants to take those women, horses and elephants to Dwarka."

(Vishnu Purana, Part–5, Chapter–29, Shloka–30-33)

Chapter 16 of the Dwarka Khanda of the Garga Samhita also mentions the 16,000 women briefly. The Brahmavaivarta Purana describes this incident in the following manner:

निहत्य नरकं भूपं रणेन दारुणेन च।।
पत्नीषोडशसाहस्रं विहारं च चकार सः।।

Narayana said to Sage Narada: "After killing King Narak of Pragjyotishpura in a terrifying war, he accepted 16,000 women as his wives and went on a pleasure trip with them."

(Brahmavaivarta Purana, Shri Krishna Janma Khanda, Chapter–54, Shloka–16)

Comment: Out of all the testimonies mentioned above, the narration provided in the Harivansha Purana seems practical, because from Narakasura's palace, Krishna had acquired elephants, horses, precious stones as well as the women who were languishing in Narakasura's captivity. So, their one-sided love for Krishna is natural, as they were now under his refuge; but it seems well-nigh impossible that he would have married all of them.

14. Did Krishna really manifest the entire universe in his mouth?

This incident has been described only in the Bhagavat Purana in (*Skandha–10, Chapter–8*). When Krishna ate mud and Yashoda asked him to open his mouth in order to clean it, she saw the entire universe in his mouth. This incident has not been mentioned in any Purana except the Bhagavat Purana; the Mahabharata does not mention it either.

Comment: This is the problem with the scriptures that were penned later, as new incidents keep springing up in them. Therefore, if you wish to learn the truth about anything, it is better to rely on the ancient scriptures.

15. Did Krishna kill Putana?

The story of Krishna killing Putana is mentioned in all the scriptures including the Bhagavat Purana, Vishnu Purana, Brahma Purana, Brahmavaivarta Purana and the Mahabharata. According to the story mentioned in the Bhagavat Purana *(Skandha–10, Chapter–6)*, when Putana began breastfeeding Krishna, with poison applied to her breasts, he sucked with such force that she died instantly.

In the Mahabharata *(Sabha Parva, Chapter–41)*, Shishupala has been shown reviling Krishna, calling him 'the slayer of Putana', 'the slayer of women' and so on. The truth is, apart from Putana, Krishna never killed any woman and he never indulged in any act of violence against women. In the Vishnu Purana *(Part–5, Chapter–5),* Putana has been called a child-slayer or the one who hunts children and kills them. And this is the very reason Krishna had to kill a woman.

In the Harivansha Purana *(Vishnu Parva, Chapter–6)*, Putana is described as Kansa's servitor, who had arrived in Gokul assuming the form of a bird; whereas in the Brahmavaivarta Purana *(Shri Krishna Janma Khanda, Chapter–10)*, Putana is depicted as Kansa's sister.

Comment: Essentially, one needs to bear in mind that there are as many stories as there are scriptures. Therefore, one can conclude that the stories that are in sync with Krishna's psychology as well as the laws of Nature are true, while the rest are purely fictional. These are the only criteria that can be applied to fathom Krishna's true personality. Otherwise, instead of an intelligent person who was dedicated to diligent action, we will be left with merely a fictional Krishna who performs miracles.

16. Did the kings of that era humiliate Krishna?

This question has a simple answer—yes. On several occasions, many kings humiliated Krishna openly in packed assemblies in royal courts, or they tried to create circumstances whereby they could force him to leave the court or assembly. Here are a few such instances:

i) Rukmini's *Swayamvar*: Kansa's father-in-law, Jarasandha had three to four loyal aides—Shishupala, Rukmi, Dantavakra, Shalva and others. Rukmini's father, King Bhishmak was also a supporter of Jarasandha. And as Jarasandha's son-in-law, Kansa was killed by Krishna, Bhishmak did not invite Mathura to his daughter's *swayamvar.* This was an insult meted out at the political level. Therefore, to protest against this insult, Krishna reached Vidarbha without being invited; and upon meeting Bhishmak, Krishna rebuked him:

ममागमनमेवेह प्रायेन न हितं तव।
अतो न कृतमातिथ्यमपात्राय नरेश्वर।।

Krishna said: "O King! You probably assumed that my arrival here is not in your interest. Perhaps that is why you did not extend any hospitality to me, considering me undeserving of it."

(Harivansha Purana, Vishnu Parva, Chapter–51, Shloka–13)

Although King Bhishmak humiliated him, he did so in a civilised manner; but his son Rukmi and his companions crossed all limits of decency while humiliating Krishna:

अहो कालकृतं कर्म दैवं च केन वार्यते।
किंवाऽहं कथयिष्यामि देवेन्द्राणां च संसदि।।
ग्रहीतुं रुक्मिणीं कन्यां देवयोग्यां मनोहराम्।
आयाति देवैर्मुनिभिर्नन्दस्य पशुरक्षकः।।
साक्षाज्जारश्च गोपीनां गोपोच्छिष्टान्नभोजनः।
जातेश्च निर्मयो नास्ति भक्ष्यमैथुनयोस्तथा।।
किं नु राजेन्द्रपुत्रश्च किं नु वा मुनिपुत्रकः।
वसुदेवः क्षत्रियश्च भक्षणं वैश्यमन्दिरे।।
शिशुकाले च स्त्रीहत्या कृताऽनेन दुरात्मना।

कुब्जा मृता च संभोगाद्वासरसा रजको मृतः॥
राजेन्द्रस्य वधे दुष्टो ब्रह्महत्यां लभेद्ध्रुवम्।
मथुरायां च धर्मिष्ठः सद्यः कंसो निपातितः॥

Rukmi said: "Who can erase time-conditioned deeds and destiny? What shall I say in this assembly of kings, because the caretaker of Nanda's cattle has come to marry a supreme beauty like Rukmini! The paramour of the already married milkmaids, the one who consumes things left over by cowherds, the one whose caste and staple food is unknown, the one who is of a dubious birth—it is not even clear whether he is a prince or the son of a sage—whose father Vasudeva is a Kshatriya, but who has been raised by a Vaishya; the evil soul who had killed a woman in his childhood, who had killed Rajak and had intimate relations with Kubja, a woman of a low caste; the one who killed the great soul, King Kansa of Mathura, thus committing the appalling sin of killing a Brahmin, has arrived here!"

(Brahmavaivarta Purana, Shri Krishna Janma Khanda, Chapter–106, Shloka–18-23)

It is clear from the shlokas quoted above that Rukmi had crossed all limits of royal decorum while humiliating Krishna, who was a guest in his father's court.

ii) Yudhishthira's Rajasuya Yajna[3]: Krishna's cousin Shishupala was enraged when Sahadeva honoured Krishna as the chief guest on the occasion of Yudhishthira's Rajasuya Yajna. Consequently, Shishupala hurled a string of abuses at Krishna in an assembly packed with kings hailing from various regions. He called Krishna a woman-killer, a slayer of cattle, the man who abducted a woman who was already promised to another man, a deserter, a cowherd, a herder, the unscrupulous one and so on. And because of all this, swords were drawn in that assembly, and finally, Krishna killed Shishupala. This entire episode is described in the Mahabharata *(Sabha Parva, Chapter 38–42)*, and this book also mentions it at appropriate points in response to other questions.

iii) Avanti's Princess Mitravinda's *Swayamvar*: Krishna's youngest aunt, Rajadhidevi, was married to the king of Avanti. They had three children—sons Vinda and Anuvinda and daughter Mitravinda. Vinda and Anuvinda were part of Duryodhana's camp and were quite hostile

3. In Hinduism, yajna refers to any ritual performed in front of a sacred fire, often with the chanting of mantras

towards Krishna. At Mitravinda's *swayamvar*, Krishna was present too, and coincidentally, Mitravinda liked none other than Krishna. Seeing this, Vinda and Anuvinda humiliated Krishna and also stopped their sister from marrying him:

विन्ध्यानुविन्ध्यावावन्त्यौ दुर्योधनवशानुगौ।
स्वयंवरे स्वभगिनीं कृष्णे सक्तां न्यषेधताम्।।

Shukdeva said: "Vinda and Anuvinda were the kings of Avanti. They were Duryodhana's minions and were well under his influence. Their sister Mitravinda wished to marry Krishna at her *swayamvar*, but Vinda and Anuvinda prevented her from doing so."

(Bhagavat Purana, Skandha–10, Chapter–58, Shloka–30)

iv) Duryodhana's Diatribe: Throughout their lives, Krishna and Duryodhana remained at odds with each other regarding the Pandavas; and even when Duryodhana was breathing his last, he did not desist from abusing Krishna:

कंसदासस्य दायाद न ते लज्जास्त्यनेन वै।
अधर्मेण गदायुद्धे यदहं विनिपातितः।।

Duryodhana said: "O son of Kansa's servant! I have been killed by unfair means in the mace-fight; aren't you ashamed of committing this malicious deed?"

(Mahabharata, Shalya Parva, Chapter–61, Shloka–27)

Krishna was humiliated in several other assemblies too, in a similar manner.

17. Did Krishna bring Devaki's dead children back to life?

The Mahabharata does not mention any such incident. There is no mention of this incident in the Harivansha Purana and Vishnu Purana either. It is found only in the Bhagavat Purana *(Skandha–10, Chapter–85, Shloka–34-59).*

Comment: Once again, the same pattern can be observed here; the newer the scriptures, the more imaginative the stories. But an individual's real personality can be understood only on the basis of the older scriptures, not the new ones. Newer texts are wont to embellish stories with miracles and 'market' the hero.

18. Did Krishna marry all 16,100 women at the same time?

This episode is mentioned only in the Bhagavat Purana *(Skandha– 10, Chapter–59, Shloka–42)*, which states that Krishna married 16,100 women in different palaces. There is no mention of it in any other scripture.

Comment: As I have been saying over and over again, the newer scriptures have needlessly turned Krishna—a man of action—into a miracle-performing being. But this has only proved to be detrimental, not beneficial.

19. Was Krishna mischievous right from his childhood days?

Many narratives have been written about Krishna's childhood activities in the Puranas, wherein his mischievous antics have been presented in great literary style. The scenario in all of them is the same. Whether it is Harivansha Purana, Bhagavat Purana, Vishnu Purana, Brahmavaivarta or other Puranas or even the Garga Samhita, the literary expression may be different in them, but the story remains the same. It is worth noting that in these texts, Krishna's childlike mischief is described as his divine play and his grace in order to entertain his devotees. But the Mahabharata does not mention anything about Krishna's childhood. The popular version of the Mahabharata in north India, with commentary by Neelkantha, does not contain even a single shloka about Krishna's childhood; but even the popular south Indian version of the Mahabharata does not mention any other childhood activity of Krishna apart from his acts of overturning the pot hanging in the house, killing of Putana, lying in the mud, being tied to the mortar, getting caught red-handed while enjoying dollops of butter, herding the cows grazing in the forests, and driving away the serpent Kaaliya from the Yamuna River.

(South Indian Mahabharata, Sabha Parva, Chapter–52, 53)

And this is despite the fact that this version of the Mahabharata has been unnecessarily expanded into 150,000 shlokas. Therefore, it can be inferred that as per the Puranic accounts, Krishna was certainly mischievous, but according to the narratives given in the Mahabharata, it is difficult to infer anything about his mischief.

20. Did Krishna really confront the serpent Kaaliya, which was present in the Yamuna River?

This incident is not mentioned in the Mahabharata, but it is described in detail in the following Puranas:

Bhagavat Purana, Skandha–10, Chapter–16-17
Vishnu Purana, Part–5, Chapter–7
Brahmavaivarta Purana, Shri Krishna Janma Khanda, Chapter–19
Garga Samhita, Goloka Khanda, Chapter–12

In all the Puranas mentioned above, the story of Krishna confronting the serpent Kaaliya is found in detail.

21. What kind of attire was Krishna fond of?

As far as Krishna's interest in attire is concerned, it is mentioned in only one place, and that too ambiguously. It is only in the popular South Indian version of the Mahabharata that a shloka is found in this regard:

नीलपीताम्बर धरौ पीतेशेतानुलेपनौ।
बभूवतुर्वत्सपालौ काकपक्षधरावुभौ।।

Grandsire Bhishma says: "Balarama wore blue-coloured clothes and Krishna wore yellow-coloured clothes. Yellow sandalwood was applied to Balarama's body and bright-coloured sandalwood to Krishna's body. The two brothers grazed the calves wearing *kakapaksha*.[4]"

(Mahabharata, Sabha Parva, Chapter–52, Shloka–30)

Later on, one of the names given to Krishna was '*Pitambardhari*' and the medieval poets composed thousands of shlokas and prose based on this name in Sanskrit and Hindi. Additionally, some Puranas were doctored on this basis. Otherwise, there is nothing available in the older scriptures regarding Krishna's clothes or grooming.

22. Did Gandhari curse Krishna that his clan would be destroyed?

The Mahabharata mentions this in the following manner:

पाण्डवाः धार्तराष्ट्राश्च क्रुद्धाः ...x... परिपतिष्यन्ति यथैता भरतस्त्रियः।।

Gandhari said: "Krishna! Fighting among themselves, the sons of Dhritarashtra and Pandu were annihilated right before your eyes. How could you ignore this? You were powerful and capable of convincing both sides to heed your advice; you were wise too, but you wilfully

4. The word '*Kakapaksha*' means long hair tied in a bun at the back of the head

gnored the annihilation of the Kuru clan. You have committed a grave crime, and therefore, I am cursing you. You have deliberately turned a blind eye to the Kauravas and Pandavas slaying each other. Therefore, you will destroy your kith and kin too. Thirty-six years from now, all your relatives, ministers and sons will fight each other and die in front of you. You too will die a miserable, lowly death. The women of your clan will mourn over corpses, just like the women of this clan of Bharata!"

(Mahabharata, Stree Parva,
Chapter–25, Shloka–39-46)

Comment: In the shlokas mentioned above, the words 'thirty-six years from now' reveal the truth to a considerable extent. Actually, these shlokas have been added later in the Mahabharata to make it appear that the incident of Yadavasthali was the outcome of a curse. For, as far as a curse is concerned, the one who curses never says when exactly the curse will bear fruit; no such incident has been mentioned in any of the Puranas either. Therefore, in my view, on the basis of my psychological knowledge, I can say that this entire episode is an embellishment.

23. What was the financial condition of Nanda and Yashoda?

According to the Puranas, Nanda was a cowherd and his occupation was animal husbandry and trading in milk and milk products. As cattle was the primary source of income for the cowherds, they lived in and around forests to ensure the availability of sufficient fodder for their animals. They were far removed from the urban civilisation of cities such as Mathura. They were guileless people who lived contentedly in their hamlets. In this regard, Krishna himself says at one point:

न नः पुरोजनपदा न ग्रामा न गृहा वयम्।
नित्यं वनौकस्तात वनशैल निवासिनः॥

Krishna said to Nanda: "Father, neither are we kings of any kingdom, nor do we rule over any city; we do not even have a village or a house. We have always been forest dwellers; forests and hills are our home."

(Bhagavat Purana, Skandha–10, Chapter–24, Shloka–24)

One finds such lines in the Harivansha Purana too:

वयं वनचरा गोपाः सदा गोधनजीविनः।
गावोऽस्मदैवतं विद्धि गिरयश्च वनानि च॥

Addressing the elderly cowherds of Vrindavan, Krishna said: "O Aryas! We are *gopas*[5] living in the forest and we have always been earning our livelihood from cow products. Therefore, you should realise that cows, hills and forests are our gods."

(Harivansha Purana, Vishnu Parva, Chapter–16, Shloka–2)

It is clear from the shlokas mentioned above that Nanda and Yashoda were forest dwellers and their hamlets used to be located far from cities and towns. Besides, according to some shlokas in the Puranas, Nanda was the chief of his hamlet. It can be easily inferred from this evidence that his house must have had more amenities compared to the houses of the other cowherds of the hamlet. He used to maintain the accounts of the royal tax that was levied on his hamlet, and was also responsible for taking care of security and other matters of the hamlet. Here is a shloka related to this in the Bhagavat Purana:

गोपान् गोकुलरक्षायां निरूप्य मथुरां गतः।
नंदः कंसस्य वार्षिक्यं करं दातुं कुरुद्वह।।

Shukdeva said: "O Parikshit! In order to leave for Mathura to pay the annual tax to Kansa, Nanda handed over the responsibility of protecting Gokul to the other cowherds."

(Bhagavat Purana, Skandha–10, Chapter–5, Shloka–19)

Comment: All things considered, Krishna's childhood was mired in struggles and poverty. He had a difficult childhood indeed.

24. What were the names of Krishna's queens?

The Harivansha Purana describes Krishna's wives as:

रुक्मिण्याः केशवः पाणिं जग्राह विधिवत्प्रभुः।।

XXX XXX XXX

कालिन्दीं मित्रविन्दां च सत्यां नाग्नजिनीमपि।
सुतां जाम्बवतश्चापि रोहिणीं कामरूपिणीम्।।
मद्रराजसुतां चापि सुशीलां शुभलोचनाम्।
सात्राजितीं सत्यभामां लक्ष्मणां चारुहासिनीम्।।
शैब्यस्य च सुतां तन्वीं रूपेणाप्सरसोपमाम्।
स्त्रीसहस्राणि चान्यानि षोडशातुलविक्रमः।।

5. Cowherds

"Then Keshava (Krishna), according to prescribed rituals, married:
(1) Rukmini
(2) Kalindi (also known as Yamuna)
(3) Mitravinda (daughter of Krishna's aunt Rajadhidevi, who was married to the king of Avanti)
(4) Satya (also known as Nagnajiti and daughter of Nagnajita, the king of Ayodhya)
(5) Jambavati (daughter of Jambavan)
(6) Rohini (also known as Bhadra and Kaikeyi and daughter of Krishna's aunt Shrutakirti, who was married to king of Kaikaya)
(7) Lakshmana (daughter of Madraraj)
(8) Satyabhama (Satrajit's daughter) and
(9) Gandhari (daughter of King Shaivya)
Apart from these, there were 16,000 women."

(Harivansha Purana, Vishnu Parva, Chapter–60, Shloka–34; 41-43)

It is clear from the details given above that apart from 16,000 other women, the Harivansha Purana mentions the names of nine main queens of Krishna, whereas the more popular belief is that he had eight queens.

According to the marriages of Krishna described in the Bhagavat Purana *(Skandha–10, Chapter–58)*, these queens were:

1) Rukmini	2) Kalindi (Yamuna)	3) Mitravinda
4) Satya	5) Bhadra	6) Lakshmana
7) Satyabhama	8) Jambavati and 16,000 women	

According to the Garga Samhita *(Goloka Khanda, Chapter–16)*, Krishna was married to Radha as a child, and based on this, some people also consider Radha as his wife. According to the Brahmavaivarta Purana *(Shri Krishna Janma Khanda, Chapters 105 and 112)*, these wives of Krishna were:

1) Rukmini	2) Kalindi	3) Satyabhama
4) Satya	5) Sati (Bhadra)	6) Nagnajiti
7) Jambavati	8) Lakshmana and 16,000 women	

In the Mahabharata, there are only sporadic references of Rukmini and Satyabhama, but there is no mention of the total number of Krishna's marriages.

Comment: All things considered, Krishna is said to have had eight marriages, according to all the scriptures.

25. How many children did Krishna have and what were their names?

According to the Bhagavat Purana, each queen of Krishna had ten sons:

तासां या दशपुत्राणां... x...भद्राया वाम आयुश्च सत्यकः॥

Names of Queens	Their Children
Rukmini	Pradyumna, Charudeshna, Sudeshna, Charudeha, Sucharu, Charugupta, Bhadracharu, Charuchandra, Vicharu and Charu
Satyabhama	Bhanu, Subhanu, Swarbhanu, Prabhanu, Bhanuman, Chandrabhanu, Brahabdhanu, Atibhanu, Shribhanu and Pratibhanu
Jambavati	Saamba, Sumitra, Purujit, Shatjita, Sahastrajit, Vijay, Chitraketu, Vasumaan, Dravid and Kritu
Satya	Veer, Chandra, Ashvasen, Chitragu, Vegvaan, Vrusha, Aam, Shanku, Vasu and Kunti
Kalindi	Shruta, Kavi, Vrash, Veer, Subahu, Bhadra, Shanti, Darsha, Purnamas and Somak
Lakshmana	Praghosh, Gatravaan, Simha, Bal, Prabal, Udhvarga, Mahashakti, Saha, Oj and Aparajit
Mitravinda	Vruk, Harsh, Anil, Gadhra, Vardhan, Annaash, Mahaash, Paawan, Vanhi and Kshudhi
Bhadra	Sangramajit, Brahatsen, Shoora, Praharan, Arijit, Jaya, Subhadra, Vaam, Aayu and Satyak

(Bhagavat Purana, Skandha–10, Chapter–61, Shloka–7-17)

The evidence found in Harivansha Purana has the names of Krishna's 14 wives and their respective children:

प्रद्युम्नः प्रथमं जज्ञे...x...समाख्याता वासुदेवस्य ते सुताः॥

Sr. No.	Names of Queens	Sons	Daughters
1.	Rukmini	Pradyumna, Charudeshna, Charubhadra, Charugarbha, Sudeshna, Druma, Sukhena, Charugupta, Charuvinda and Charubahu (10)	Charumati
2.	Satyabhama	Bhanu, Bheemrath, Kshup, Rohit, Deeptiman, Tamrajaksha and Jalantaka (7)	Bhanu, Bheemlika, Taamraparni and Jalandhama (4)
3.	Jambavati	Saamb, Mitravaan, Mitravinda, Mitrabahu and Sunith (5)	Mitravati (1)
4.	Satya (Nagnajiti)	Bhadrakar and Bhadravinda (2)	Bhadravati (1)
5.	Sudatta	Sangramajit, Satyajit, Senajit and Saptnajit (4)	
6.	Subheema	Vrukaashva, Vraknivriti and Vrakdipti (3)	
7.	Lakshmana	Gaatravaan, Gaatragupta and Gaatravrinda (3)	Gaatravati (1)
8.	Kalindi	Ashruta and Shrutsammita (2); Krishna had given Ashruta to his childless wife Shrutasena, who adopted him as her son.	
9.	Brihati	Gada (1)	
10.	Shaivya	Angad, Kumuda and Shwet (3)	Shweta (1)
11.	Sudeva	Agaavaha, Sumitra, Shuchi, Chitrarath and Chitrasen (5)	Chitra and Chitravati (2)

12.	Kaushiki	Vanastamba, Stambavan, Nivaasan and Avanastamba (4)	Stambavati (1)
13.	Sutasoma	Upasanna, Shanku, Vajranshu and Kshipra (4)	
14.	Yaudhishthari	Yudhishthir, Kapaali and Garud (3)	

(Harivansha Purana, Vishnu Parva, Chapter–103, Shloka–5-21)

Comment: According to the list given above, Krishna had a total of 56 sons and 12 daughters from these queens.

According to the Brahmavaivarta Purana, Krishna had ten sons and one daughter each from his wives:

एकस्यां दशपुत्राश्च कन्यकैका क्रमेण च।
हरेरेतान्यपत्यानि बभूवुश्च पृथक्पृथक्।।

(Brahmavaivarta Purana, Shri Krishna Janma Khanda, Chapter– 112, Shloka–39)

In other Puranas, it is said that each of Krishna's wives had only ten sons. In the Mahabharata, Krishna's sons Pradyumna or Saamb have been mentioned occasionally, but even in such a lengthy epic, there is no detailed account of Krishna's offspring. However, it can certainly be said that Krishna had more than 50 children.

26. What was the relationship between Sage Durvasa and Krishna?

The relationship between Krishna and Sage Durvasa is mentioned only in the Brahmavaivarta Purana. There is no mention of it in any other Purana, as well as the Mahabharata. In this Purana, two stories have been woven into a single tale. First, when the infants of Devaki and Yashoda were secretly exchanged after Krishna's birth, Kansa was led to believe that Devaki's eighth child was a girl. This sowed the seed of doubt in his mind, because it was contrary to the divine prophecy. Taking advantage of this, Devaki and Vasudeva prayed to Kansa that after having killed seven infants, he should have mercy on the girl at least; for, how could a girl kill a powerful king like him? To their relief, Kansa yielded to their pleas, spared the newborn girl's life, and returned her to them. Devaki and Vasudeva then began to raise the girl, who was named Ekanansha:

वसुदेवो देवकी च तामादाय मुदान्वितौ।
जग्मतुः स्वगृहं तौ च कन्यां कृत्वा स्ववक्षसि॥
मृतामिव पुनः प्राप्य ब्राह्मणेभ्यो ददौ धनम्।
सा परा भगिनी विप्र कृष्णस्य परमात्मनः॥
एकानंशेति विख्याता पार्वत्यंशसमुद्भवा।
वसुस्तां द्वारकायां तु रुक्मिण्युद्वाहकर्मणि॥

(Brahmavaivarta Purana, Shri Krishna Janma Khanda, Chapter–7, Shloka–129-131)

After Krishna and Rukmini's marriage, Sage Durvasa suddenly arrived in Dwarka, and in the course of welcoming and honouring him, Vasudeva married his daughter Ekanansha to the sage:

ददौ दुर्वाससे भक्त्वाया शंकरांशाय भक्तितः।
एवं निगदितं सर्वं कृष्णजन्मानुकीर्तनम्॥

xxx xxx xxx

एकदा द्वारकां रम्यां दुर्वासा मुनिपुंगवः।
शिष्यैस्त्रिकोटिभिः सार्धमाजगामावलीलया॥
राजा महोग्रसेनश्च सपुत्रः सपुरोहितः।
वसुदेवो वासुदेवोऽप्यक्रूरश्चोद्धवस्तथा॥
नीत्वा षोडशोपचारं प्रणेमुर्मुनिपुंगवम्।
शुभाशिषं च प्रददौ तेभ्यो ब्रह्मन्पृथक्पृथक्॥
एकानंशां च कन्यां तां ददौ तस्मै शुभक्षणे।
मुक्तामाणिक्यहीरांश्च रत्नं च यौतकं ददौ॥

(Brahmavaivarta Purana, Shri Krishna Janma Khanda, Chapter–7, Shloka–132; Chapter–112, Shloka–40-43)

There are hundreds of proofs in Hindu scriptures which show that in ancient times, kings used to marry off their daughters to sages. Therefore, the marriage of Ekanansha with Sage Durvasa cannot be called unnatural either. Of course, one does wonder why this marriage has not been discussed in the Mahabharata or other Puranas.

27. Several scriptures in the name of Gita are available today. Are they copies of the Bhagavad Gita?

Gita means 'music'. When supreme knowledge is presented in exquisite language, it is called the Gita. Many scholars have stated spiritual truths of a high calibre in the Hindu scriptures, which are still available in various texts, and have been compiled into various books, published with different names. Some of these prominent Gitas are:

- **Ashtavakra Gita:** This Gita contains a dialogue between King Janaka of Mithila and his guru, Sage Ashtavakra. It is an independent book, meaning, it is not part of any major Hindu scripture, and its author is unknown. It was probably composed around 400–200 BC. This treatise provides a detailed discussion on renunciation, wisdom and liberation.
- **Pandava Gita:** The name of its author is unknown and scholars have differing opinions about the date of its composition. Actually, it is not an independent composition but a compilation of 76 shlokas, and all these shlokas are selected from the Mahabharata and other texts. Its main subject is the invocation of Vishnu and Krishna for the attainment of liberation.
- **Anu Gita:** The text from Chapter 16–51 of the Ashwamedhika Parva of the Mahabharata has been compiled and termed the Anu Gita. Its 36 chapters contain a detailed discussion on religion and morality.
- **Vyadh Gita**: The text from Chapter 206–208 of the Vana Parva of the Mahabharata has been compiled and published as Vyadh Gita. In this text, Sage Markandeya narrates to Yudhishthira the story of a butcher and a Kaushika Brahmin of Mithila to illustrate that no *karma* is inferior. Through this story, the sage explains that what matters is the sentiment and the manner of performing *karma;* if they are pure, then the *karma* becomes pure too; but if the sentiment is impure, then the *karma* will be impure too, no matter how noble it is. This brief Gita is extremely relevant in modern times, which is why Swami Vivekananda placed a lot of emphasis on it.
- **Guru Gita:** This Gita has been published by compiling some portions from the Maheshwar Khanda of the Skanda Purana. This Gita attempts to shed light on the three-dimensional relationship between the guru, disciple and God.
- **Avadhuta Gita:** This Gita is an independent work composed during 900–1000 CE by the Nath order of yogis, which comprises 289 shlokas across eight chapters.

• **Rama Gita:** This Gita has been published by compiling all the 62 shlokas of Chapter 15 of the Uttara Kanda of the Adhyatma Ramayana. It is a dialogue between Rama and Lakshmana.

• **Bhagavad Gita:** This Gita has been published by compiling the text of the Bhishma Parva of the Mahabharata from Chapters 23–40. It contains 700 shlokas and is mainly a dialogue between Krishna and Arjuna.

It should now be clear to everyone that almost all the Gitas are a part of some major scripture, with the exception of a few which have been composed independently. It is also true that it was only after the phenomenal popularity of the Bhagavad Gita that others composed their Gitas independently or compiled them from other texts.

28. Is it true that Krishna's first child was abducted?

There is no mention of this incident in the Mahabharata. However, this episode is described in detail in Chapter 104 of the Vishnu Parva of the Harivansha Purana, which is considered to be a supplementary text of the Mahabharata. On the seventh day of Pradyumna's birth, a childless *Asura* named Shambara abducted him from the delivery room. He then took Pradyumna to his city and handed him over to his wife, Mayawati. This story is also narrated in *Chapter–55, Skandha–10* of the Bhagavat Purana, but this version is slightly different. According to this Purana, Shambara disguised himself and entered Rukmini's delivery room, and then, observing extreme caution, he abducted the child. This Purana states that Shambara threw Pradyumna into the sea, where a fish swallowed him, but Pradyumna remained safe in its belly. A few days later, a fisherman caught this fish in his net. On cutting open the fish, when he found a child in its belly, the fisherman handed the child over to his chief, Shambara. Then, Shambara handed the child over to a maid named Mayawati, asking her to raise him. The story mentioned in the Bhagavat Purana is also narrated in the Garga Samhita *(Dwarka Khanda, Chapter–8, Shloka–23-26).*

29. What food items constituted Krishna's *'Chhappan Bhog'*?

The Indus Valley and the Indian civilisation are among the most ancient and developed human civilisations in the world. And even in that ancient period in India, people enjoyed more than one delicacy. The Rigveda, the world's oldest written text, lists food items such as paddy (rice), urad (split black gram), moong (split green gram), masoor (red lentil), vegetables such as lotus stem, akka, avaka and andika (aquatic plants), and fruits such as mangoes, grapes and so on. Apart from this, black pepper, cardamom, cloves, mustard leaves and seeds were also used at that time. Consumption of cooling energy drinks and honey was a trend in royal households. Somaras, an intoxicating drink, was most popular among these drinks. Along with vegetarian food, consumption of non-vegetarian food was also prevalent in Vedic culture. According to experts, the tradition of consuming chicken developed in India. However, consumption of bird's eggs was strictly forbidden in those days. Additionally, foods with sweet, sour, salty, pungent and astringent tastes were considered essential in royal meals, which is confirmed by Sushruta, the author of Sushruta Samhita, a treatise on Ayurveda. According to him, the royal meal began with a serving of appetising fruits. The king and his family used to partake of only one food item at a time. Usually, dessert was the fourth course, and the practice of consuming kheer (rice boiled in sweet milk) was especially prevalent everywhere from the north to the south of India. The final course comprised yogurt and dried papad. According to these masters of Ayurveda, consumption of yogurt was forbidden at night. Even in those days, betel leaf, areca nuts, cardamom, cloves, fennel seeds, and other such mouth-freshening spices were served after meals. This was the general and royal food consumed in those times. Now, as far as the *'Chhappan Bhog'* is concerned, there was a math behind it, based on which it gained traction in the public consciousness.

The Math behind *'Chhappan Bhog'*

A *'Chhappan Bhog'* meal comprises six types of tastes:

1. Pungent	2. Bitter	3. Astringent
4. Sour	5. Salty	6. Sweet

A total of 63 groups of foods are formed by combining these six tastes. Out of these, six are solitary tastes from which no dish is made;

moreover, these six tastes cannot be included in a single dish either. This excludes seven groups of foods out of 63, leaving a total of 56 foods. After the Vedic period, the *'Chhappan Bhog'* platter was propagated even during the Puranic period based on this mathematics; and the tradition of Krishna's *'Chhappan Bhog'* evolved from this.

Food Items Constituting the Famed *'Chhappan Bhog'* of Krishna

The meal began with fruits	
1. Tubers	2. Lotus roots
3. Mango	4. Grapes
5. Banana	6. Wood Apple
7. Sugar Palm Fruit	8. Guava
9. Papaya	
Drinks	
10. Indian Gooseberry Juice (Sweetened)	11. Rabri (Condensed Milk-based Dish)
12. Sweet Buttermilk	13. Beetroot Broth
14. Cream of Milk	15. Somaras
16. Dudhiroopa	17. Lassi (Drink made from yogurt)
18. Soobat	19. Honey
20. Khurma	21. Paarikha
Main Food Items	
22. Poori (Unleavened bread)	23. Mesu (Unleavened bread in clarified butter)
24. Seera (pudding)	25. Rice
26. Mohan Thaal (sweet prepared from gram flour)	27. Mohanbhog
28. Lentil soup	29. Sikharini (milk product)
30. Shaak (vegetable)	31. Vada (Gram flour ball)
32. Mathree (Deep fried flaky biscuit)	33. Kheer (Rice pudding)

34. Clarified Butter	35. Madhupark (prepared from meat & four other ingredients)
(Rigveda, Mandala–10, Sukta–72, 86, 91 and others)	
Chutneys	
36. Chutney	37. Khajra (Shatapatra)
38. Vati (Balaka – mixture of treacle and milk)	39. Pickle
40. Curry	41. Spinach or Mustard leaves curry
42. Laungpoori	
Sweets	
43. Modak (sweet flour dumpling)	44. Laddoo (sphere-shaped sweet)
45. Murabba (marmalade)	46. Shakkarpara (a sweet, crunchy snack)
47. Ghevar (disc-shaped sweet cake)	48. Butter
49. Milk Cream	50. Chila (sweet pancake)
Final Course	
51. Yogurt	52. Papad (thin, crisp, disc-shaped food item)
After Meal	
53. Betel Leaf	54. Areca Nut
55. Fennel Seeds and	56. Cardamom

In Dwarka, the food of people from all walks of life, whether they were commoners or the elite, comprised a variety of dishes, alcohol, meat and so on:

ततो भोज्यं च भक्ष्यं च पेयं चान्धकवृष्णयः।
बहु नानाविधं चक्रुर्मद्यं मांसमनेकशः॥

"Then, the Andhaks and the Vrishnis had a variety of foods prepared that could be swallowed and chewed along with drinks, including alcohol, and various kinds of meat."

(Mahabharata, Mausala Parva, Chapter–3, Shloka–8)

30. Is it true that during Krishna's birth, the doors of the prison opened automatically?

There is no mention of this incident in the Mahabharata. The popular north Indian version of the Mahabharata, with a commentary by Neelkantha, does not even mention Krishna's birth. However, the popular south Indian version has only one shloka mentioning the birth of Krishna:

वासुदेवस्ततो जातं बालमादित्यसंनिभम्।
नंदगोपकुले राजन् भयात् प्राच्छादयद्धरिम्।।

Grandsire Bhishma said: "O King Yudhishthira, then Vasudeva, fearing Kansa, took his newborn child, who was radiant like the sun, to the cowherd Nanda's house and hid him there."

(South Indian Mahabharata, Sabha Parva, Chapter–38)
(As an interpolation in the Gita Press Edition)

Even the Harivansha Purana, which is called the supplementary of the Mahabharata, contains a single shloka that mentions Krishna being transported to Gokul:

वसुदेवस्तु संगृह्य दारकं क्षिप्रमेव च।
यशोदायां गृहं रात्रौ विवेश सुतवत्सलः।।

Vaishampayan said: "Then Vasudeva, the loving father, quickly entered Yashoda's house at night with that child in his arms."

(Harivansha Purana, Vishnu Parva, Chapter–4, Shloka–25)

Evidently, the early scriptures do not mention Krishna's miracles at all. But apart from these two texts, several other Puranas revolving around Krishna such as the Vishnu Purana, Bhagavat Purana, Brahmavaivarta Purana, Garga Samhita and so on contain lavish descriptions of miracles that occurred during Krishna's birth. But to what extent can the newer texts be trusted? Well, once again, it depends on the discernment of the readers.

31. Did Krishna really steal butter?

The Mahabharata, Vishnu Purana and Harivansha Purana contain not even a hint or suggestion about Krishna consuming and stealing butter. It is described only in the later Puranas and their supplementary texts, which give a detailed account of how Krishna consumed, spilled and wasted butter even when he did not need it, thus, causing financial loss to his community, by feeding the butter to animals and birds. According to these texts, he also smashed the pots of the milkmaids who would step out to sell milk, yogurt and clarified butter.

32. Which scriptures provide the most authentic information about Krishna and his life?

The entire body of information about Krishna cannot be obtained from merely a single scripture. Among all the Hindu religious texts, the Rigveda, composed between 3000 and 1500 BCE, is the oldest. And one Sukta in this Veda describes Krishna as an enemy of Indra. In the Aitareya Brahmana, a Brahmin scripture of this very Rigveda, Krishna himself is not described, but his friend Arjuna's great-grandson Janamejaya and his snake-sacrifice are described in detail. *(Aitareya Brahmana, Panchika–8, Khanda–21)* Thereafter, in Shukla Yajurveda's Brahmin treatise Shatapatha Brahmana (900–800 BC), there is a description of Janamejaya performing the Ashwamedha sacrifice to atone for the sin of killing a Brahmin. In this text, Krishna is described as a warrior of the Vrishni clan. In the Chandogya Upanishad, composed between 800–600 BC, there is a shloka - **तद्धैतद्घोर आंगिरसः कृष्णाय देवकीपुत्राय** *(Chapter–3, Khanda–17, Sutra–6)*, which describes Krishna, the son of Devaki, learning the technique of self-sacrifice from the formidable sage Angiras. There is no other information in this Upanishad about the life of Krishna.

After this, the term Syamantaka Mani (gem) is used in Nirukta, composed by Sage Yaska in 6th Century BC. The Syamantaka gem and the incident related to it is an important part of Krishna's life, and this also provides evidence that Krishna is a historical personality. Panini's grammar treatise Ashtadhyayi (6th Century BC) also defines and grammatically analyses several words related to Krishna and his life. From these sporadic descriptions provided in the ancient texts, it can certainly be proved that Krishna was not a fictitious personality.

Indeed, he was a legendary and significant personality, who during his lifetime, altered the course of Indian politics and public life, giving it a new direction. This sporadic evidence also proves that a complete biography of Krishna was not available at that time. At the time, stories related to Krishna were prevalent in the Indian subcontinent only in the form of legends, folklore, fables and so on. And it was on the basis of this that later on, writers endeavoured to piece together the entire life of Krishna and write about it. At this point, it is necessary to mention the Mahabharata, because it is the only ancient text that provides authentic documentation of most of the incidents related to Krishna. The author of Mahabharata, Veda Vyasa himself is an important attestor of this work. However, the voluminous version of Mahabharata, which is available to people today, has not been composed entirely by Veda Vyasa. The first Parva of the Mahabharata is the Adi Parva, and its first three chapters comprise what is termed as the Anukramanika Parva. This Parva is an index that lists the chapters in the entire epic, the events that will be covered in each of them, and the circumstances under which this scripture has been composed. In shloka 81 of the first chapter, Veda Vyasa clearly writes that he has composed only 8,800 shlokas:

अष्टौ श्लोकसहस्राणि अष्टौ श्लोकशतानि च।
अहम् वेद्मि शुको वेत्ति संजयो वेत्ति वा न वा।।

(Mahabharata, Adi Parva, Chapter–1, Shloka–81)

Later, one of his disciples, Vaishampayan composed 24,000 additional shlokas and added them to the original text, and narrated 32,800 shlokas to Janamejaya during his snake-sacrifice. Thereafter, Ugrashrava Sauti, a disciple of Vaishampayan, composed shlokas that were several times greater in number compared to those composed by Veda Vyasa and Vaishampayan, and added them to the epic. He then narrated as many as 84,000 shlokas to a large group of sages present in Naimisharanya (a forest in northern India). When it was felt that even these 84,000 shlokas lacked the complete life story of Krishna, the Harivansha Purana was composed as a supplement, containing 16,000 shlokas. In this manner, one can find that the present, popular version of the Mahabharata contains around 100,000 shlokas. This is only about the north Indian version. Simultaneously, another version of the Mahabharata was being composed in the south of India, which at present has about 150,000 shlokas. So, naturally, as one can expect, this version has all the stories prevalent in India, along with the accounts of all the sages and discussions on all the branches of knowledge that existed till the final phase of the creation of the Mahabharata. And the text itself provides evidence of this:

धर्मे चार्थे च कामे च मोक्षे च भरतर्षभे।
यदिहास्ति तदन्यत्र यन्नेहास्ति न तत्क्वचित्॥

"Among all the propositions related to Dharma (right conduct, duty, moral values), Artha (economic values), Kama (pleasure, love, psychological values) and Moksha (liberation, spiritual values) prevalent all over India, those that are found in this book will be found in other texts too, but what is not found here will not be found anywhere else."

(Mahabharata, Adi Parva, Chapter–62, Shloka–53)

So, this was what the Mahabharata was subjected to. Even a great text such as this, written by Veda Vyasa, was extended into a voluminous tome later. Therefore, most of the shlokas of the Mahabharata cannot be trusted blindly. And as for the Puranas, they were composed several years after the Mahabharata. So, when it came to the composition of the Puranas, in order to propagate the concept of the 'avatar', all the boundaries of anthropology, natural science and physics were violated, giving way to absurd ravings about Krishna. The Brahma Purana, Padma Purana, Vishnu Purana, Bhagavat Purana, Brahmavaivarta Purana, Kurma Purana, Garga Samhita and several big and small texts were filled with fanciful stories about Krishna. Furthermore, there is so much contradiction amongst them that it is difficult to grasp even a single notion. Therefore, if a person really wants to obtain genuine, authentic information about Krishna, he should consider only the Mahabharata and the Harivansha Purana as proofs, and that too, with utmost caution. For, the truth is, Krishna has shed light on his own personality in the Gita. Krishna's entire life and his mind can be fathomed just by extending his psychology that he himself has explained. And that is precisely what I have endeavoured to do through his biography 'I am Krishna', which is a comprehensive set spanning six volumes. It not only focuses on his life but greatly emphasises on his psychology too. Indeed, this makes it easy for readers to comprehend Krishna's real life and optimally utilise this understanding to improve their own life.

33. Did Krishna marry Radha?

Krishna's marriage to Radha is not mentioned in any text except the Brahmavaivarta Purana and the Garga Samhita. According to both these texts, Brahma got Radha and Krishna married in the Bhandir forest near Vrindavan.

(Brahmavaivarta Purana, Sri Krishna Janma Khanda, Chapter–15, Shloka–120-131); (Garga Samhita, Goloka Khanda, Chapter–16, Shloka–30-34)

34. Did Krishna demand the Syamantaka gem from Satrajit to improve Mathura's financial condition?

In this regard, the Garga Samhita states:

सत्राजिताय सूर्येण दत्तः साक्षात्स्यमंतकः।
उग्रसेनाय स मणिः श्रीकृष्णेनाभियाचितः॥
सत्राजितस्तं न ददौ द्रव्यलोभेन मैथिल।
दिनेदिने स्वर्णभारानष्टौ यः सृजति स्वतः॥

Narada said to King Bahulashva: "O Maithil! A reputed Yadava named Satrajit from amongst Mathura's elite was given the Syamantaka gem by the Sun himself. Krishna had asked him for that gem for Mathura's King Ugrasen, but Satrajit refused to give it to him due to his greed for wealth, as that gem produced eight Bhara (one Bhara* = 8,000 tola = 1 quintal) of gold per day."

(Garga Samhita, Dwarka Khanda, Chapter–8, Shloka–2-3)
*(*Rasaratna Samuchhaya; Translation – Dharmanand Sharma, 2nd Edition – 1962, Motilal Banarasidas Press, page-159)*

According to the Bhagavat Purana, when Satrajit, due to embarrassment, married off his daughter Satyabhama to Krishna, he wished to gift the Syamantaka gem in dowry, but Krishna refused him saying:

भगवानाह न मणिं प्रतीच्छामो वयं नृप।
तवास्तां देवभक्तस्य वयं च फलभागिनः॥

Krishna said to Satrajit: "We will not accept the Syamantaka gem. You are a devotee of the Sun, so let the gem remain with you. We are only entitled to its fruit, that is, the gold emanating from it; give that to us."

(Bhagavat Purana, Skandha–10, Chapter–56, Shloka–45)

Comment: Krishna did not accept the Syamantaka gem in the dowry, but he definitely accepted the gold produced from it.

35. Is it true that Krishna did not kill Jarasandha despite getting the opportunity to do so?

It is written in almost every Purana as well as the Mahabharata, that Krishna, on many occasions, had condoned Jarasandha despite having the king within his grasp. The South Indian Mahabharata mentions that Krishna defeated Jarasandha:

ततः पार्थिवमायान्तं सहितं सर्वराजभिः।
सरस्वत्यां जरासन्धमजयत् पुरुषोत्तमः।।

Grandsire Bhishma said: "Thereafter, Krishna defeated Jarasandha who had attacked him along with all the kings, on the banks of the Yamuna adorned by lakes and reservoirs."

(South Indian Mahabharata, Sabha Parva, Chapter–54, Shloka–33)

This incident is described in the Bhagavat Purana in this manner:

जग्राह विरथं रामो जरासन्धं महाबलम्।
हतानीकावशिष्टासु सिंहः सिंहमिवौजसा।।
बध्यमानं हतारातिं पाशैर्वारुणमानुषैः।
वारयामास गोविन्दस्तेन कार्यचिकीर्षया।।

Shukdeva said: "In this manner, Jarasandha's army was eliminated, while Jarasandha himself was grievously wounded too. Then, Balarama tied up Jarasandha, who had killed several kings, but Krishna thought that if Jarasandha survived, he would garner more troops and return to fight. And if this happened, then Krishna and the others would get yet another opportunity to ease the earth's burden to a greater extent. That is why Krishna freed Jarasandha from Balarama's clutches."

(Bhagavat Purana, Skandha–10, Chapter–50, Shloka–30-32)

The Harivansha Purana says:

विदितोऽस्य मया मृत्युस्तस्मात्साधु व्युपारम।
अचिरेणैव कालेन प्राणांस्त्यक्ष्यति मागधः।।

जरासंधस्तु तच्छ्रुत्वा विमनाः समपद्यत।
न प्रजह्रे ततस्तस्मै पुनरेव हलायुधः॥

The divine prophecy said: "O Balarama, the one who respects others! Jarasandha will not be killed by you, so there is no need to regret it. The cause of his death is now clear; do not be distressed over it. This king of Magadha will die soon." On hearing this prophecy, Balarama did not attack him again.

(Harivansha Purana, Vishnu Parva,
Chapter–36, Shloka–29-30)

The Vishnu Purana describes it in the following manner:

ततो युद्धे पराजित्य ससैन्यं मगधाधिपम्।
पुरीं विविशतुर्वीरावुभौ राम जनार्दनौ॥
जिते तस्मिन्सुदुर्वृत्ते जरासन्धे महामुने।
जीवमाने गते कृष्णस्तं नामन्यत निर्ज्जितम्॥

Parashara said: "O Maitreya! Both the valiant warriors, Balarama and Krishna, returned to Mathura along with their army after defeating the king of Magadha. O Sage! Even after defeating the vicious Jarasandha, Krishna did not consider himself to be undefeated, and that was because Jarasandha had retreated alive."

(Vishnu Purana, Part–5, Chapter–22, Shloka–8-9)

The Garga Samhita says:

जग्राह मुसलं घोरं क्रोधपूरितविग्रहः।
परिपूर्णतमेनाथ श्रीकृष्णेन महात्मना॥
निवारितस्तदैवाशु तं मुमोच यदूत्तमः।
तपसे कृतसंकल्पो व्रीडितोपि जरासुतः॥

Narada said: "When Balarama knocked Jarasandha down and was about to strike him with the pestle, as he sat on his chest, Krishna stopped him. Thereafter, Balarama spared his life. Jarasandha, who was embarrassed by this, set off to perform penance."

(Garga Samhita, Dwarka Khanda, Chapter–1, Shloka–46-47)

There is no mention of this incident in the Brahmavaivarta Purana, but considering all the Puranic references given here, one aspect becomes quite clear that Krishna never killed anyone unnecessarily. He was far above ignoble qualities such as selfishness, self-assertiveness or the greed for a larger empire.

36. Who became the king of Dwarka after Krishna's death?

A few days after Krishna's death, Dwarka was submerged in the sea, and that was the end of the kingdom. In Chapter–31, Skandha–11 of the Bhagavat Purana, it is said that after the Yadavasthali incident, there were a few men left in Dwarka, so Arjuna performed the last rites of all those who died. Thereafter, the entire kingdom was submerged in the sea. Following Krishna's instructions, which were conveyed to him through Daruka, Arjuna then took all the men and women who had survived in Dwarka to his own kingdom, Hastinapur, and there, he made Krishna's great-grandson, Vajra, the king of another region.

In Chapter 4–7 of the Mausala Parva of the Mahabharata, it is said that after the Yadavasthali incident, Krishna himself came to Dwarka, and gathering the women and the surviving men such as Vasudeva, he gave them some instructions. He told them that Arjuna would soon arrive in Dwarka, and henceforth, all of them had to follow his orders. At the same time, Krishna said that everyone should leave for Hastinapur with Arjuna. Krishna also told them that hereafter, he would never be able to return to Dwarka. According to Krishna's instructions, after performing the last rites of those who died in the Yadavasthali incident, Arjuna left for Hastinapur with the surviving inhabitants of Dwarka. But en route to Hastinapur, a horde of bandits abducted several women from the caravan and stole valuables being carried by the group. Arjuna took the survivors to Hastinapur, and as per Krishna's wish, he made Krishna's great-grandson Vajra the king of the very Indraprastha that was once built with the help of Krishna.

The Vishnu Purana also states that Arjuna made Vajra the king of Indraprastha:

इत्थं वदन्ययौ जिष्णुरिन्द्रप्रस्थं पुरोत्तमम्।
चकार तत्र राजानं वज्रं यादवनन्दनम्॥

"With these words, Arjuna arrived in his capital, Indraprastha, and performed the coronation of Vajra, the son of the Yadavas."

(Vishnu Purana, Part–5,
Chapter–38, Shloka–34)

There is no mention of Vajra's coronation in the Garga Samhita. Even the Brahmavaivarta Purana contains an incomplete description of

Krishna's demise in Chapter 128 of the Shri Krishna Janma Khanda, and does not say anything about the coronation of Vajra either.

37. Is there no mention of Krishna's life in the Vedas?

In the Rigveda, there is an extremely vague description of a battle between Krishna and Indra, which mentions that Indra destroyed Krishna's army.

अव द्रप्सो अंशुमतीमतिष्ठदियानः कृष्णो दशभिः सहस्रैः।
आवत्तमिन्द्रः शच्या धमन्तमप स्नेहितीर्नृमणा अधत्त॥

"On the banks of the river Anshumati (Yamuna), there lived an Asura called Krishna who launched an attack with 10,000 troops. Indra cleverly overwhelmed the Asura who created such a ruckus. Thereafter, Indra destroyed the violent army of Krishnasura for the benefit of humans."

द्रप्समपश्यं विषुणे चरन्तमुपह्वरे नद्यो अंशुमत्याः।
नभो न कृष्णमवतस्थिवांसमिष्यामि वो वृषणो युध्यताजौ॥

Indra said: "I have seen the nimble-footed Krishna. He wanders in a vast, mysterious location on the banks of the river Anshumati, and sojourns like the sun. O Maruts who grant all wishes! I want you to fight and destroy him in battle."

अध द्रप्सो अंशुमत्या उपस्थेऽधारयत्तन्वं तित्विषाणः।
विशो अदेवीरभ्याचरन्तीर्बृहस्पतिना युजेन्द्रः ससाहे॥

"Near the river Anshumati, the nimble-footed Krishna assumes a physical form, becoming effulgent. With the help of Brihaspati, Indra killed Devashunya and the approaching army along with Krishna."

(Rigveda, Mandala–8, Sukta–85, Mantra–13-15)*
*(*Supplementary Edition, Sukta–96)*

Indra is the god of this sukta of the Rigveda, that is, this mantra is meant to eulogise him, and that is why Krishna is termed as an Asura or a powerful being, and is said to be opposed to Vedic beliefs. The sages of these mantras are the sons of Marutas or Vayu Deva,[6] and these mantras are composed in Trishtupa metre; this means they are to be used by Kshatriyas.[7] Actually, the reason behind the dispute between Indra and Krishna was that animal slaughter was compulsory in the oblations of the Aryans; and Indra, the chief of the Aryans, supported oblations and animal slaughter. Krishna, on the other hand,

6. The God of wind
7. Warriors and kings

was probably the first non-violent cowherd of India; therefore, he was opposed to such oblations. This annoyed Indra and he tried to harass Krishna and the Yadavas. The Krishna who is mentioned at this point in the Rigveda is an opponent of Indra, and is fond of spending his leisure time near the banks of the Yamuna and is an extremely powerful, swift-footed chief of a great army.

The argument that Vedic commentators uphold for terming Krishna as an Asura is that the one who is opposed to oblations would obviously be an Asura for Indra and the Aryans. The Padma Purana distinguishes Deva and Asura using the following yardstick:

द्वौ भूतसर्गौ लोकेऽस्मिन् दैव आसुर एव च।
विष्णुभक्तः स्मृतो दैव आसुरस्तद्विपर्ययः।।

There are two types of people who live on this earth—the gods and the demons. Those who believe in Vishnu, the oblations and the practices established by the Vedas are the gods, and the rest are all Asuras.

(Vaidik Sanskruti: Aasuri Prabhav, Page–197)

In this regard, the second president of India, Dr. S. Radhakrishnan's statement is also quite significant. In his book 'Indian Philosophy', he has described this Vedic event in these words: "During the period of the Rigveda, another arch-enemy of Indra was Krishna, who was the God-like, valorous chieftain of the forest tribes (also) called Krishna. The shloka is as follows: 'The agile Krishna lived on the banks of the river Anshumati (Yamuna) with his 10,000 troops. Indra used his intelligence to track down this chieftain who used to scream in a harsh and raucous manner. For our benefit, he destroyed this enemy who plundered and attacked us.' This is the explanation as presented by Sayanacharya, and this story holds some significance in relation to the Krishna Sect."

(Indian Philosophy,
Part–1, 1969 Edition, Page–79)

In addition to the Rigveda, the Chandogya Upanishad also mentions Krishna at one point. In Khanda 17 of Chapter 3 in this Upanishad, Ghor Angiras has delivered a discourse on self-knowledge to Devaki's son, Krishna, in the name of oblations:

"तद्धैतद्घोर आङ्गिरसः कृष्णाय
देवकीपुत्रायोक्त्वोवाचापिपास एव स बभूव

सोऽन्तवेलायामेतत्त्रयं प्रतिपद्येताक्षितमस्यच्युतमसि
प्राणसँशितमसीति तत्रैते द्वे ऋचौ भवतः॥"

(Chandogya Upanishad, Chapter–3, Khanda–17, Sutra–6)

"Ghor Angiras said that this life itself is an oblation. By describing life as an oblation, he dissuaded Krishna from external oblations. He explained to Krishna that when a person spends his life practising austerities, charity, simplicity and truth, his entire life becomes an offering in itself. When Ghor Angiras explained this secret of turning life into an oblation to Krishna, the son of Devaki, his thirst for knowledge was quenched."

Apart from the references mentioned above, there is hardly any information about Krishna in the Vedas and other Vedic texts.

38. Were Krishna and Duryodhana related?

According to the descriptions given in the Puranas, Krishna and Duryodhana were close relatives. Krishna's son Saamb was married to Duryodhana's daughter Lakshmana, long before the Mahabharata war.

(Vishnu Purana, Part–5, Chapter–35)

(Bhagavat Purana, Skandha–10, Chapter–68)

(Harivansha Purana, Vishnu Parva, Chapter–62, Shloka–8-15)

(Garga Samhita, Balabhadra Khanda, Chapter–8, Shloka–6)

All the above texts mention the relationship between Krishna and Duryodhana.

39. Was Balarama's daughter Vatsala married to Abhimanyu?

Evidence of this is not available in the Mahabharata nor is it mentioned in any of the Puranas. Actually, it is Telugu folklore and according to this tale, Balarama's daughter Vatsala was engaged to Subhadra and Arjuna's son Abhimanyu; but after the Pandavas lost their kingdom in gambling and went into exile, Balarama's wife Revati changed her mind. She posed a question to her husband Balarama as to how their daughter could be happy in a family that did not possess a kingdom. Balarama saw merit in her argument, so he immediately announced that he was breaking off the engagement. Balarama then decided to get his daughter engaged to Duryodhana's son Laxman Kumar.

When Abhimanyu learned about this, he went to his beloved maternal uncle Krishna for help, but Krishna chose to not oppose his brother Balarama's decision, and instead suggested a solution. He advised Abhimanyu to seek help from Ghatotkachha. Abhimanyu then rushed to his cousin Ghatotkachha and apprised him of the entire issue, hearing which the latter was enraged. He was already annoyed with Balarama, because Balarama maintained as much distance from the Pandavas as he maintained his closeness to the Kauravas. Therefore, Ghatotkachha assured Abhimanyu, offering him complete support, and after asking him to stay put in Varnavat, Ghatotkachha began lingering around Dwarka, biding his time. And finally, on the very day that Duryodhana reached Dwarka with his son Laxman Kumar's wedding procession, Ghatotkachha abducted Vatsala and left for Varnavat. Upon reaching there, he arranged for Vatsala to be married to Abhimanyu. When Laxman Kumar learned about this, he vowed that he would remain a bachelor all his life. This is the only folklore in which their marriage is mentioned.

40. What is the truth about Krishna and Sudama's friendship?

Of all the ancient texts available today, the Mahabharata is the only one which is considered reliable among scholars, if one wishes to learn about incidents related to Krishna's life. But the Mahabharata does not even mention Sudama's name! He is not mentioned in the Harivansha Purana and Vishnu Purana either. It is only in the Bhagavat Purana that one finds a mention of Sudama. Even the Bhagavat Purana *(Chapter 45 of Skandha 10)*, which dwells on Krishna's education in Sage Sandipani's ashram, does not mention a Brahmin named Sudama, and nor does it mention anything about chunks of wood being collected from the forest, or about Sudama hiding the rice from Krishna and eating it. However, Chapter 80 of Skandha 10 of the same Bhagavat Purana describes Sudama's visit to Dwarka. It also narrates the story of how Krishna and Sudama collected wood from the forest.

The Garga Samhita also does not mention Sudama's presence in the ashram of Sage Sandipani *(Mathura Khanda, Chapter–9)*. However, Chapter 22 of the Dwarka Khanda narrates the story of a Brahmin named Sudama and also describes the incident that took place in the forest.

Chapter 102 of the Shri Krishna Janma Khanda in the Brahmavaivarta Purana mentions Krishna's education in the ashram of Sage Sandipani, but even this Purana does not mention Sudama's presence in the ashram. Even in the latter part of this Purana, there is no mention of the friendship between Krishna and Sudama. So, the Bhagavat Purana and Garga Samhita are the only two scriptures in which Krishna and Sudama are mentioned. Nevertheless, it is certain that there is not a single scripture that describes Krishna and Sudama's friendship in the manner in which it is depicted in the TV serials today.

41. Was Draupadi really disrobed and did Krishna really lengthen her saree to save her from disgrace?

Chapters 58–63 of the Sabha Parva of the Mahabharata provide a detailed account of the gambling episode, in which Krishna is not present. This also raises another question—was Draupadi the only person who was dear to Krishna? Were the Pandavas despised by Krishna that he did not save them from losing their kingdom but chose only to save Draupadi? Actually, according to the Mahabharata, Draupadi was menstruating at the time, and as is the custom prevalent in some societies of India till today, women wear only a single garment while they are menstruating; so, Draupadi too was dressed in a single garment and was resting in her chamber, when Dushasana caught hold of her and dragged her to the royal court. Draupadi must have obviously been stripped due to the use of such brute force. As for Krishna, he was not present on this occasion, and the solid proof of this is that when Krishna meets the Pandavas and Draupadi in the forest, he says that had he been present there, the game of dice would not have taken place, and nor would Draupadi's dignity be put at stake *(Mahabharata, Vana Parva, Chapter–13, Shloka–1-2)*. He says that had he been present even in or around Hastinapur, he would have reached there, even without being invited by Duryodhana or Dhritarashtra, and would not have allowed the gambling to take place. So, the gist of this answer is, the entire story of Krishna extending the length of Draupadi's saree is fictional and facts about the incident have been exaggerated. And Kunti says to Krishna in the Udyoga Parva of the Mahabharata:

न राज्यहरणं दुःखं द्यूते चापि पराजयः।
प्रव्राजनं सुतानां वा न मे तद्दुःखकारणम्॥
यत्र सा बृहती श्यामा सभायां रुदती तदा।
अश्रौषीत्परुषा वाचस्तन्मे दुःखतरं महत्॥
स्त्रीधर्मिणी वरारोहा क्षत्रधर्मरता सदा।
नाध्यगच्छत्तदानाथं कृष्णा नाथवती सती॥

"O Krishna! Losing the kingdom has not caused me much anguish. I am not so distressed even by the fact that my sons lost the game of dice and were exiled; but the barbs that my beautiful and young daughter-in-law Draupadi had to hear from Duryodhana as she stood weeping, have caused me immense anguish. My enchantingly beautiful, pious and saintly daughter-in-law Krishnaa (Draupadi), who is always eager to perform her duties as a Kshatriya woman, was menstruating during those days. She had several father figures around her, and yet, she could not find a single protector in the assembly of the Kauravas that day."

(Mahabharata, Udyoga Parva, Chapter–137, Gita Press–138, Shloka–17-19)

This is sufficient evidence to prove that Krishna was not present on that occasion, and neither did he supply any saree to Draupadi. In fact, there is one more proof that Krishna was not present during this incident:

ऋणमेतद्प्रवृद्धं मे हृदयान्नापसर्पति।
यद् गोविन्देति चुक्रोश कृष्णा मां दूरवासिनम्॥

Krishna tells Sanjaya to go and tell the Kauravas: "When Draupadi's clothes were being pulled in the assembly of the Kauravas, I was far away from Hastinapur. At that time, a frightened Krishnaa (Draupadi) had called out to me, using my name 'Govind'. For this, I am deeply indebted to her, and this debt is mounting ever so much. My heart cannot be freed from the burden of this debt until the Kauravas are killed."

(Mahabharata, Udyoga Parva, Chapter–59, Shloka–22)

From the shlokas above, it is absolutely clear that neither was there a deliberate attempt to disrobe Draupadi, nor did Krishna miraculously extend the length of her saree. Kunti states unambiguously that Draupadi did not find any protector in the royal assembly on that day.

She was forcefully dragged from her chamber, while lewd gestures were made at her, and harsh words were used against her. And there is plenty of evidence of all these acts of brutality and inhumanity that she was subjected to. So, it is only through the newer Puranas that such exaggerated stories have been circulated. Such being the case, it is a person's own prudence that can determine whether to trust the reliable ancient scriptures or the newer texts embellished with miracles.

42. Was Draupadi pithy and eloquent?

Draupadi's eloquence was unmatched, and this can be gauged from the incident wherein Yudhishthira lost his kingdom as well as Draupadi, along with his five brothers, to Shakuni in the game of dice held at the royal court of Hastinapur. Dushasana had dragged Draupadi, who was resting in her chamber, to the royal court. Draupadi was menstruating at that time, so according to the prevalent custom, she was wearing only a single saree. In such a situation, she obviously felt extremely humiliated. She was also unable to save her dignity in the royal court teeming with a host of men, including her father-in-law, grandfathers-in-law, brothers-in-law, her five husbands, ministers, servants, other kings and sages who had come from far and wide. Naturally, she was aghast and livid with rage.

While she was still present in her chamber and apprised of the situation at the court, Draupadi, being the intelligent woman that she was, posed an extremely sombre and earnest question to her husband Yudhishthira:

कस्येशो नः पराजैषीरिति त्वामाह द्रौपदी।
किं नु पूर्वं पराजैषीरात्मानमथवापि माम्।।

Draupadi ordered Pratikami (the servant at the royal court) to go and ask King Yudhishthira what all he owned before losing her (Draupadi) in the game of dice. She also asked, whom did he lose first—himself or her?

(Mahabharata, Sabha Parva, Chapter–67, Shloka–10)

The servant went back to the court with Draupadi's question, and when Duryodhana saw him return without Draupadi, he asked him why he had come empty-handed. The servant conveyed Draupadi's message, to which Duryodhana said, "Go at once and bring her here, for, the answers to her questions will be given only in the court." The servant went back to bring Draupadi with him, but once again, she refused to go with him. Then, Duryodhana sent Dushasana, who dragged Draupadi by her hair and brought her to the royal court. Draupadi had repeated her question in the royal court too:

इमं प्रश्नमिमे ब्रुत सर्व एव सभासदः ।
जितांवाप्यजितां वा मां मान्यध्वे सर्वभूमियाः ॥

Draupadi said: "All the members of this assembly must answer this question of mine. O Kings! Ethically speaking, do you think that I have been won? Meaning, you all must tell me the truth, did King Yudhishthira lose himself first, or was it me that he lost first?"

(Mahabharata, Sabha Parva, Chapter–68, Shloka–41, Gita Press)

Then, Grandsire Bhishma who was present in the royal court stood up and addressed Draupadi:

न धर्मसौक्ष्म्यात् सुभगे विवेक्तुं
शक्नोमि ते प्रश्नमिमं यथावत्।
अस्वाम्यशक्तः पणितुं परस्वं
स्त्रियाश्च भर्तुर्वशतां समीक्ष्य॥

Grandsire Bhishma said: "O blessed daughter-in-law! Due to the very subtle nature of ethics, I am unable to decide how to answer your question. No person can sell or wager anything that he does not own; that is correct. But it is also true that according to social customs, a woman is always seen as her master's subordinate. Therefore, considering all these things, I am unable to arrive at any decision."

(Mahabharata, Sabha Parva, Chapter–68, Shloka–47)

Now, the truth was crystal clear and all the people present there also knew that Yudhishthira had lost himself first, so how could a slave wager someone else? Thus, there was no one in the royal court who could answer this question, or no one wished to say anything in this regard. However, one of Duryodhana's brothers, Vikarna, did support Draupadi's argument and began reprimanding his brothers, but Karna scolded and silenced him. From this entire episode, it is worth learning that when a person himself faces adversity, he cries that no one is speaking the truth, but when it comes to speaking the truth for someone else, this same person evades the situation. It is only a rare and exceptional person who dares to speak the truth for everyone, including himself.

43. How did Krishna meet his death?

According to the Mahabharata and the Puranas, a hunter named Jara in the Prabhasa region shot an arrow at Krishna, mistaking him for a deer, and this arrow pierced Krishna's foot and became the cause of his death.

(Mahabharata, Mausala Parva, Chapter–4, Shloka–22-23)
(Vishnu Purana, Part–5, Chapter–37, Shloka–68-71)
(Bhagavat Purana, Skandha–11, Chapter–30, Shloka–33)

However, there is no description of Krishna's death in the Harivansha Purana and the Brahmavaivarta Purana.

44. Was Sanjaya giving Dhritarashtra a real-time account of the activities occurring in the battlefield of Kurukshetra from Hastinapur's royal palace itself?

The Mahabharata *(Bhishma Parva, Chapter–2, Shloka–6)* states that Veda Vyasa wanted to bless Dhritarashtra with divine vision so that he could sit in the royal palace and witness the action on the battlefield, but Dhritarashtra refused to witness the horrors of the battlefield. However, he said that he certainly wished to hear about every incident on the battlefield. Then, Veda Vyasa said:

एष ते संजयो राजन् युद्धमेतद् वदिष्यति।
एतस्य सर्वसंग्रामे न परोक्षं भविष्यति।।

Veda Vyasa said: "O King! Sanjaya here will give you an account of everything that occurs on the battlefield. Nothing on the battlefield will remain hidden from him."

(Mahabharata, Bhishma Parva, Chapter–2, Shloka–9)

Meaning, Sanjaya will go to the battlefield and return from time to time to tell you about the latest developments occurring in the battlefield. Even the thoughts of the people from both sides of the battlefield will not be hidden from Sanjaya.

नैनं शस्त्राणि छेत्स्यन्ति नैनं बाधिष्यते श्रमः।
गावल्गणिरयं जीवन् युद्धादस्माद् विमोक्ष्यते॥

"No weapon can cut him. He will not be hindered by exertion or fatigue. Sanjaya, the son of Gavalgana, will survive this war."

(Mahabharata, Bhishma Parva, Chapter–2, Shloka–12)

From the shlokas above, it is crystal clear that Sanjaya used to visit the battlefield. Now, the question is, if he used to visit the battlefield in Kurukshetra, how did he give Dhritarashtra a real-time account of the war in Hastinapur? That is the problem with the ancient scriptures; there are contradictions galore. Therefore, while trying to comprehend the scriptures, it is necessary for a person to exercise his prudence at all times. In Chapter 13 of the same Bhishma Parva, it is mentioned that Sanjaya returned from the battlefield and gave Dhritarashtra an account of the past ten days of battle, including that of the fall of Grandsire Bhishma on the bed of arrows:

वैशम्पायन उवाच
अथ गावल्गणिर्विद्वान् संयुगादेत्य भारत।
प्रत्यक्षदर्शी सर्वस्य भूतभव्यभविष्यवित्॥
ध्यायते धृतराष्ट्राय सहसोत्पत्य दुःखितः।
आचष्ट निहतं भीष्मं भरतानां पितामहम्॥
संजय उवाच
संजयोऽहं महाराज नमस्ते भरतर्षभः।
हतो भीष्मः शान्तनवो भरतानां पितामहः॥

Vaishampayan said: "O Janamejaya, scion of the Bharatas! After that, the knower of the past, present and future, the one who witnessed all the events with his own eyes, Sanjaya, the knowledgeable son of Gavalgana, returned from the battlefield, went to Dhritarashtra, and mournfully conveyed to him the news of the death of Bhishma, the Grandsire of the Bharata clan, in the battlefield. Sanjaya said, 'O King, the supreme one among the Bharatas! I pay my obeisance to you. I, Sanjaya, present myself at your service. Bhishma, the Grandsire of the Bharata clan and son of King Shantanu, was killed in the war today.'"

(Mahabharata, Bhishma Parva, Chapter–13, Shloka–1-3)

Not only that, while giving an account of the first day's battle, Sanjaya clearly states that the army of the Pandavas attacked us (Duryodhana's army) in a vicious manner:

क्ष्वेडाः किलकिलाशब्दाः क्रकचा गोविषाणिकाः।
भेरीमृदङ्ग मुरजा हयकुंजरनिःस्वनाः॥
उभयो सेनयोर्ह्यासंस्ततस्तेऽस्मान् समाद्रवन्।
वयं तान् प्रतिनर्दन्तस्तदासीत् तुमुलं महत्॥

"Then, roars, screams and the sounds of musical instruments such as Krakacha, Narsingha[8], Bheri, Mridanga and other drums, as well as the neighing of horses and the trumpeting of elephants began to resonate from both the armies. The Pandava soldiers charged at us and we also attacked them with equal ferocity. In this manner, an extremely fierce battle ensued."

(Mahabharata, Bhishma Parva, Chapter–42,
Gita Press Chapter–44, Shloka–4-5)

Moreover, Sanjaya was also captured by the Pandava army in the battlefield:

धृष्टद्युम्नस्तु मां दृष्ट्वा हसन्सात्यकिमब्रवीत्।
किमनेन गृहीतेन नानेनार्थोऽस्ति जीवता॥
धृष्टद्युम्नवचः श्रुत्वा शिनेर्नप्ता महारथः।
उद्यम्य निशितं खड्गं हन्तुं मामुद्यतस्तदा॥
तमागम्य महाप्राज्ञः कृष्णद्वैपायनोऽब्रवीत्।
मुच्यतां संजयो जीवन्न हन्तव्यः कथंचन॥
द्वैपायनवचः श्रुत्वा शिनेर्नप्ता कृतांजलिः।
ततो मामब्रवीन्मुक्त्वा स्वस्ति संजय साधय॥

Sanjaya said: "On seeing me in captivity, Dhrishtadyumna laughed and said to Satyaki, 'What is the point in keeping him in captivity? His survival will not benefit us in any way.' On hearing these words from Dhrishtadyumna, the intrepid warrior Satyaki, the grandson of Shini, picked up a sharp sword and was ready to kill me that very instant. But just then, the great wise sage Krishnadvaipayan Vyasa arrived and said, 'Leave Sanjaya alone. There is no reason to kill him.' Then, with folded hands, Satyaki, the grandson of Shini, paying heed to Vyasa's words, freed me and said, 'Sanjaya, may you be well. Go, do what you wish to.'"

(Mahabharata, Shalya Parva, Chapter–29, Shloka–18-21;
Gita Press Edition, Shloka–37-40)

8. Brass fog horn

Therefore, it is proved in all respects that Sanjaya used to go to the battlefield every day, while Dhritarashtra did not go to the battlefield at all. So, how could Sanjaya sit beside Dhritarashtra and give him a live, real-time account of the developments occurring in the Mahabharata war? Hence, it can be inferred that it was Sanjaya who used to pay a visit to Dhritarashtra and apprise him of the situation in the war.

45. Did Eklavya participate in the Mahabharata war?

It is often said that Eklavya fought on behalf of the Pandavas in the Mahabharata war in order to wreak vengeance on Dronacharya; but this is not true. Eklavya did wish to participate in the Mahabharata war and had certainly arrived in Kurukshetra. However, he wanted to fight only from Duryodhana's side, so the story that he wanted to wreak vengeance on Dronacharya becomes baseless. Moreover, Eklavya was reputed not only for being a pre-eminent archer of his time but also for being an ardent devotee of his master. So, he could not have even imagined wreaking vengeance on his guru. Besides, had Krishna received even the slightest indication that Eklavya wished to fight on behalf of the Pandavas, he would not have killed him before the commencement of the war.

एकलव्यं हि साङ्गुष्ठमशक्ता देवदानवाः।
सराक्षसोरगाः पार्थ विजेतुं युधि कर्हिचित्।।
किमु मानुषमात्रेण शक्यःस्यात् प्रतिविक्षितुम्।
दृढमुष्टिः कृती नित्यमस्यमानो दिवानिशम्।।
त्वद्धितार्थं तु स मया हतः संग्राममूर्धनि।
चेदिराजश्च विक्रांतः प्रत्यक्षं निहतस्तव।।

Krishna says: "O Son of Kunti! Had Eklavya's thumb been intact, he would have been invincible in battle even for the gods, the Danavas, the demons and the Nagas put together. Then, how could a mere human even dare to look at him? He had a strong fist. He was an adept at archery and practised it day and night. For your benefit, I killed him just before the commencement of this war. As for Shishupala, the mighty king of Chedi, he was killed right before your eyes."

(Mahabharata, Drona Parva,
Chapter–181, Shloka–19-21)

Hopefully, the evidence provided above from the Mahabharata clears everyone's confusion.

46. Why had Jarasandha become Krishna's enemy?

In those days, Jarasandha was a powerful king of Aryavarta, who abided by policies and regulations rigorously, but was also extremely ambitious. His political and administrative skills were acknowledged and appreciated by all. The beauty of his kingdom, Magadha, and its capital Girivraj, and the prosperity of its citizens had been praised by Krishna himself when he had visited Rajgriha along with Bhima and Arjuna:

एष पार्थ महान् भाति पशुमान् नित्यमम्बुमान्।
निरामयः सुवेश्माढ्यो निवेशो मागधः शुभः॥

Krishna said: "O Arjuna! Look at the grandeur of this vast and beautiful capital of Magadha! There are plenty of animals here. There seems to be an uninterrupted supply of water too. Even the citizens look healthy. Bedecked with beautiful mansions and palaces, this city looks enchanting."

(Mahabharata, Sabha Parva, Chapter–21, Shloka–1)

A powerful and efficient king like Jarasandha had married his two daughters to Kansa, the crown prince of Mathura. Later, when Kansa imprisoned his father Ugrasen and became king himself, the elite Yadavas of Mathura did not oppose him explicitly out of fear of Jarasandha, but they surely began to distance themselves from Kansa. With no one to restrain him, Kansa went berserk and began tormenting his subjects in various ways. As a consequence, he was ultimately killed by his own nephew, Krishna.

This was a double assault on Jarasandha; the first being, his two daughters were widowed in a single stroke. The second assault hurt him on a deeper level – his supremacy, power and reign of terror were now being openly challenged. Till Kansa's death, no one could muster the courage to invite Jarasandha's wrath upon themselves by provoking his son-in-law. But these two cowherds, who neither had a crown on their heads nor any connections in high places, had inadvertently provoked him, thereby inviting his hostility. Thereafter, Jarasandha made a series of attempts to wreak vengeance on them, which never seemed to end. However, pitted against a great personage like Krishna, he was either checkmated or had to face disappointment. The countereffect of Jarasandha's attempt to wreak vengeance was that every attack of his accorded Krishna an opportunity to raise his political stature a notch higher, quite fortuitously. People who know and fathom Krishna's life are aware of this.

47. What was the relationship between Krishna and Uddhava?

Krishna was Uddhava's cousin. King Shursen had ten sons, out of which Vasudeva was the eldest, and younger to him was Devabhaga. Uddhava was Devabhaga's son.

(Harivansha Purana, Harivansha Parva, Chapter–34, Shloka–31)

Satyaki was also a cousin of Krishna and his real name was Yuyudhaan. But as he was the son of Satyak, he became known in the Sanskrit texts as Satyaki *(Harivansha Purana, Harivansha Parva, Chapter–34, Shloka–30)*. Uddhava is not mentioned in any of the texts in the episodes related to Gokul or Vrindavan. It is only after Krishna arrived in Mathura that he received the support of Uddhava, which continued throughout his life. When Kansa was discussing sending an envoy to Vrindavan to summon Krishna to Mathura, a minister named Satyak advised him to send Akrura, Uddhava or Vasudeva as a messenger:

अक्रूरमुद्धवं वाऽपि वसुदेवमथापि वा।
प्रस्थापय महाभाग नन्दव्रजमभीप्सितम्॥

Satyak said: "O King! Send Akrura, Uddhava or Vasudeva to the desired location in Nandvraj."

(Brahmavaivarta Purana, Shri Krishna Janma Khanda, Chapter–64, Shloka–31)

The above-mentioned shloka shows that Uddhava frequently visited Mathura's royal court, long before Krishna's arrival in Mathura. After Kansa's death, when Krishna sent Uddhava to Vrindavan to meet the milkmaids and speak to them, none of them recognised him:

सुविस्मिताः कोऽयमपीव्यदर्शनः कुतश्च कस्याच्युतवेषभूषणः।
इति स्म सर्वाः परिवव्रुरुत्सुकास्तमुत्तमःश्लोकपदाम्बुजाश्रयम्॥

तं प्रश्रयेणावनताः सुसत्कृतं सव्रीडहासेक्षणसूनृतादिभिः।
रहस्यपृच्छन्नुपविष्टमासने विज्ञाय सन्देशहरं रमापतेः॥

"The milkmaids with an innocent smile said amongst themselves: 'This man is quite handsome. But who is he? Where has he come from? Whose messenger is he? Why is he dressed like Krishna?' All the milkmaids were eager to get acquainted with him and many of them surrounded Uddhava, the messenger of Krishna."

(Bhagavat Purana, Skandha–10, Chapter–47, Shloka–2-3)

Unlike Krishna, Uddhava had an urban upbringing, in addition to being supremely intelligent. Krishna used to assign work to Uddhava, and rest assured; for, the work would always be completed satisfactorily. In matters of politics and diplomacy, Uddhava was no less astute than Krishna; the only difference being, Krishna was active in public life, whereas Uddhava was active behind the scenes. This proves that he was already well acquainted with the urban culture.

48. Did Krishna really wear a peacock feather?

In ancient times, the people living in and around forests used to adorn themselves with natural objects. And as the people of Gokul and Vrindavan lived in the forests due to their profession of animal husbandry, they too used flowers, leaf buds, feathers of birds and animal horns for the purpose of grooming. Humans had also discovered gold by that time, so people belonging to the affluent class had begun wearing gold ornaments. And as Nanda was affluent to some extent, gold ornaments were used in his house too. Krishna was also adorned in gold ornaments, but on seeing the other cowherds use peacock feather, he used to emulate them and tuck one such feather in his hair too:

फलप्रबालस्तवक सुमनः पिच्छधातुभिः।
काचगुंजामणिस्वर्णन्भूषिता अप्यभूषयन॥

Shukdeva says: "Although the young cowherds wore glass, rosary pea, precious gems and gold ornaments, they still adorned themselves with the red, yellow and green fruits of Vrindavan, and with leaf buds, bunches of flowers and leaves, vibrant flowers, peacock feather and colourful articles like ochre."

(Bhagavat Purana, Skandha–10, Chapter–12, Shloka–4)

बर्हप्रसून नवधातुविचित्रतांग:
प्रोद्दामवेणुदलशृंगरवोत्सवाढ्य:।
वत्सान् गृणन्ननुगगीत पवित्र कीर्ति:
गोपीदृगुत्सवदृशि: प्रविवेश गोष्ठम्।।

Shukdeva says: "Shri Krishna's head was adorned by the enchanting crown of peacock feathers, and beautiful, fragrant flowers were entwined in his curly locks. His dark-complexioned body was painted with new coloured materials. He was lost in a celebration of music as he walked along, loudly playing his flute at times, or producing sounds from mouth organs fashioned out of leaves or animal horns. Behind him, the other cowherds walked, singing his praises. At times, they called their calves with their names and sometimes petted them. Milkmaids stood on both sides of the road, and they became enchanted the moment their eyes met Krishna's. Thus, Shri Krishna entered the hamlet."

(Bhagavat Purana, Skandha–10, Chapter–14, Shloka–47)

The scene that the authors of the Bhagavat Purana have brought alive is of the time when Krishna and all the cowherds are returning to the hamlet with their cattle at dusk. This single shloka quoted above is sufficient to give readers an inkling of the culture and way of life of the inhabitants of Vrindavan. Therefore, it is also quite natural that the peacock feather, which was an integral part of Krishna's personality in childhood, remained so throughout his life. The South Indian version of the Mahabharata describes it as follows:

मयूरांगजकर्णौ तौ पल्लवापीडधारिणौ।
वनमालापरिक्षिप्तौ सालपोताविवोद्गलौ।।

Grandsire Bhishma says: "They used to stick peacock feathers on both ears to make them look like the ears of an elephant; and they used to wear a crown of buds and twigs and a garland of wild flowers. On such occasions, both of them would look as enchanting as the new plants of Sal."

(South Indian Mahabharata, Sabha Parva, Chapter–52, Shloka–32)

49. What are the various names that Krishna has been addressed with in the scriptures?

Every individual born in this world is given a name by his parents, and that becomes his primary social identity throughout his life. Some people need to change their name at some point in their life due to a specific requirement, while some people who are worthy and capable are honoured in their lifetime with a couple of other names based on their qualities and deeds. Even so, all these honorific titles are always based on the person's original name. But apart from this, there have been some legendary people who are addressed today with not just a couple but dozens, hundreds and even thousands of names! And Krishna's name tops this list of great people.

Hundreds of people have created names for Krishna so far, but only two sources have been given prime status. One is the Vishnu Sahastranaam Stotra, which was a part of the sermon given to Yudhishthira by Grandsire Bhishma, as the latter lay on the bed of arrows in the Mahabharata war; and the other is the Vishnu Sahastranaam Stotra in the Uttara Khanda of the Padma Purana. The two lists are almost similar, with barely a few differences. All the recent lists of Krishna's names composed by most people are also based on and inspired by these two lists.

The first list given here contains the names of Krishna as per the Vishnu Sahastranaam Stotra that appears in the Mahabharata *(Anushana Parva, Chapter–149)*; and the number in the parentheses indicates the order in which that name appears in this Stotra:

1. Keshava (23)	2. Pushkaraksha (40)	3. Hrishikesh (47)
4. Krishna (57)	5. Medhavi (77)	6. Aatmavaan (84)
7. Pundarikaksha (111)	8. Janardan (127)	9. Upendra (151)
10. Amogh (154)	11. Ameyaatma(179)	12. Govinda (187)
13. Mahendra (268)	14. Achyuta (318)	15. Samitinjaya (362)
16. Adhokshaja (415)	17. Parameshthi (419)	18. Vatsi (472)
19. Gopati (495)	20. Daashaarha (511)	21. Chakragadadhar (546)
22. Kalaneminiha (642)	23. Shauri (644)	24. Keshiha (649)
25. Kamadeva (651)	26. Kaampaal (652)	27. Kaami (653)

28. Vasudeva (695)	29. Yadushreshta (705)	30. Suyamun (707)
31. Madhav (735)	32. Gadagraj (764)	33. Shubhang (782)
34. Indrakarma (786)	35. Chanurandhra Nishudan (825)	
36. Devakinandan (989)	37. Gadadhar (997)	38. Rathangapani (998)

In this list from the Mahabharata, 1,000 names have been mentioned based on the deeds performed by Vishnu and his avatars and their respective nature at those times. Out of these 1,000, 38 are the names of Krishna, which have been listed above. There are several names in this Vishnu Sahastranaam Stotra of the Mahabharata which have been repeated either inadvertently or deliberately. They are:

Govind (187), (539)	Pushkaraksha (40), (556)	Gopati (495), (592)
Keshava (23), (648)	Vasudeva (695), (709)	

So, this list, which is known as the 'Stotra with a thousand names' actually contains less than 1,000 names. Now, let us take a look at the names of Krishna that have been listed in the Vishnu Sahastranaam Stotra of the Padma Purana that begins from Shloka 120 of Chapter 71 of the Uttara Khanda:

1. Vasudeva (1)	2. Vishwamohan (120)
3. Hrishikesh (130)	4. Hari (158)
5. Pitambar (168)	6. Shakradhyadhishwar (186)
7. Vanamali (198)	8. Chakri (208)
9. Sarangadhanwa (209)	10. Gadadhar (210)
11. Shankhbhut (211)	12. Nandaki (212)
13. Kuberakotilakshmivaan (231)	14. Shakrakotivilasvaan (232)
15. Mukunda (247)	16. Kalanemiha (248)
17. Narakantaka (255)	18. Yogeshwar (261)
19. Adhokshaj (264)	20. Vishvakasen (281)
21. Virat (306);	22. Manjukeshi (332)

23. Krishna (347)	24. Madhusudan (368)
25. Ekveer (410)	26. Upendra (294)
27. Achyuta (500)	28. Jagdish (590)
29. Janardana (619)	30. Varshneya (743)
31. Satvatashreshtha (744)	32. Shauri (745)
33. Yadukuleshwar (746)	34. Putanaghna (751)
35. Keshighna (755)	36. Gavishvara (757)
37. Damodar (758)	38. Gopadeva (759)
39. Yashodanandan (760)	40. Kaliyamardan (761)
41. Lilagovardhanadhar (763)	42. Govind (764)
43. Chanuramardan (769)	44. Kansari (770)
45. Rukminiraman (780)	46. Murari (784)
47. Yamunapati (812)	48. Dwarkeshwar (816)
49. Kamadeva (829)	50. Ratipati (830)
51. Manmath (831)	

This list given in the Padma Purana also mentions 1,000 names, out of which Hari (158), (348); Jagdish (590), (607) and Narakantak (255), (782) have been repeated. On comparing the two lists given above, one aspect becomes clear that the Vishnu Sahastranaam Stotra of the Mahabharata is older than that of the Padma Purana. The basis of this assertion is that several new names of Krishna appear in the Padma Purana. The reason given is that with the passage of time, the list of Krishna's names kept burgeoning in direct proportion to the fictional stories that were written in his name. Well, this is the evidence from two major texts of the BC era. Several more names of Krishna were coined by authors after 800 CE, which are not mentioned here. That is because, our aim is to focus on the fundamental facts related to Krishna's life. But the main point here is that the numerous names given to Krishna are a clear indication of his multi-faceted personality.

50. What happened to Dwarka after Krishna's death?

Dwarka submerged in the sea after Krishna's death. Had it not gone underwater, it would have been a thriving city even today, just like Mathura and Vrindavan. It was shortly after Krishna's death that Dwarka submerged in the sea. Years later (approximately 20–25 years), when the Pandava brothers and Draupadi renounced their kingdom and set out to travel across India, they went to the ghats of Dwarka, and on seeing the surging waves of the sea, they could not control their emotions and burst into tears. Verily, the memories associated with Dwarka and Krishna had shattered them. That is because, the memories were very much alive, but there was no sign of Dwarka.

ततः पुनः समावृत्ताः पश्चिमां दिशमेव ते।
ददृशुर्द्वारकां चापि सागरेण परिप्लुताम्॥

(Mahabharata, Mahaprasthanik Parva, Chapter–1, Shloka–45)

51. Did Arjuna marry anyone apart from Draupadi?

Arjuna had four wives, namely Draupadi, Ulupi, Chitrangada and Subhadra. Arjuna was able to marry Draupadi, the daughter of King Drupad, after fulfilling the daunting condition laid down in her *swayamvar*. Later, as a result of Krishna's mediation, the Pandavas were able to obtain the kingdom of Indraprastha; and after acquiring the kingdom, a rule was laid down that if one of the Pandava brothers was already present in Draupadi's palace, then no other brother would go there. This arrangement was made to avoid conflict among the brothers on account of Draupadi. And if any of the brothers broke this rule, he would have to undergo 12 years of exile:

एकैकस्य गृहे कृष्णा वसेद् वर्षमकल्मषा।
द्रौपद्या नः सहासीनानन्योन्यं योऽभिदर्शयेत्।
स नो द्वादश वर्षाणि ब्रह्मचारी वने वसेत्॥

Vaishampayan said that all the Pandavas unanimously laid down this rule – "Let the sinless Draupadi reside in the house of each one of us for one year. If any one of us espies another brother sitting in private with Draupadi, he would take residence in a forest for twelve years as a renunciant."

(Mahabharata, Adi Parva, Chapter–212, Shloka–21)

Coincidentally, a day after the end of Arjuna's one year with Draupadi, when it was Yudhishthira's turn to live with her, Arjuna could not avoid meeting him, and due to this, he had to break the very rule he had laid down himself; and as punishment for it, he had to leave for the forest for twelve years. During this period of exile, one day, near Gangadwar (Hardwar), Arjuna met Ulupi, the daughter of the chief of the Naga clan, Kauravya, and entered into Gandharva marriage[9] with her.

एवमुक्तस्तु कौन्तेयः पन्नगेश्वरकन्यया।
कृतवांस्तत् तथा सर्वं धर्ममुद्दिश्य कारणम्॥

Vaishampayan said: "Janamejaya! At the behest of Nagraj's daughter Ulupi, Kunti's son Arjuna completed all the proceedings with virtue as his motive."

(Mahabharata, Adi Parva, Chapter–213, Shloka–33)

He then proceeded towards Manipur, where he married Chitrangada, the daughter of King Chitravahana:

मणिपूरेश्वरं राजन्... x...कुन्तीसुतः समाः॥

Vaishampayan said: "O King Janamejaya! On seeing Chitrangada, the daughter of King Chitravahana of Manipur, Arjuna was attracted to her; he then straightaway went to the king and expressed his desire to marry his daughter. The king, impressed by the courage shown by this unfamiliar young man, asked him to introduce himself. When Arjuna introduced himself, the king laid down a condition for the marriage; he said that since he did not have a son, Arjuna's son born to Chitrangada, would not be Arjuna's but his (the king's) heir. Arjuna accepted the condition set by the king, and thus, Chitrangada and Arjuna's marriage took place according to the prescribed rituals. Thereafter, Arjuna lived in Manipur for three years."

(Mahabharata, Adi Parva, Chapter–214, Shloka–15-26)

In the final phase of his exile, Arjuna reached Dwarka, where he received a grand reception. Meanwhile, on the occasion of a festival, all the inhabitants of Dwarka had gathered on the Raivataka Mountain to partake in a fair. When Subhadra arrived there, Arjuna, who was also present at the fair, saw her and instantly felt the stirrings of attraction. When Krishna tried to ferret out his feelings, Arjuna confided in him and said:

9. An ancient marriage tradition based on mutual consent

दुहिता वसुदेवस्य वासुदेवस्य च स्वसा।
रूपेण चैषा सम्पन्ना कमिवैषा न मोहयेत्॥
कृतमेव तु कल्याणं सर्वं मम भवेद् ध्रुवं।
यदि स्यान्मम वार्ष्णेयी महिषीयं स्वसा तव॥

Arjuna said: "This daughter of Vasudeva and your sister is endowed with unmatched beauty, so how can anyone not be enraptured by her? Friend! If this maiden of the Vrishni clan and your sister Subhadra could be my queen, then my heartfelt desire, which is noble in all respects, will certainly be fulfilled."

(Mahabharata, Adi Parva, Chapter–218, Shloka–18-19)

After that, Arjuna abducted Subhadra and took her to Indraprastha. Krishna not only knew about it, but had also given his consent to it, which has been discussed elsewhere in this book. Thus, evidence of Arjuna's four wives including Draupadi, can be found in the Mahabharata. Except his marriage to Draupadi, Arjuna's other marriages took place while he was in exile.

52. Is it true that Krishna could change his form and transform into a woman?

No, this is not true. The Mahabharata does not mention any such instance, and neither is it mentioned in the numerous well-known Puranas written on the life and deeds of Krishna, such as Vishnu Purana, Harivansha Purana, Bhagavat Purana, Brahmavaivarta Purana, Kurma Purana, Garga Samhita and others. The hypocritical storytellers of today who spin yarns have made such nonsensical and absurd statements in their religious discourses, and authors have subsequently written about them in books.

53. Did Krishna really have a dark complexion?

Yes, Krishna had a swarthy complexion, and here is the evidence found in the Puranas. The Bhagavat Purana says:

आसन् वर्णास्त्रयो ह्यस्य गृह्णतोऽनुयुगं तनूः।
शुक्लो रक्तस्तथा पीत इदानीं कृष्णतां गतः॥

"And he, who has a dark complexion, is born in every age. In the previous ages, he had accepted fair, red and yellow complexions respectively, and now he has been born with a dark complexion."

(Bhagavat Purana, Skandha–10, Chapter–8, Shloka–13)

The Harivansha Purana says:

मेघकृष्णस्तु कृष्णोऽभूद् देहान्तरगतो हरिः।
व्यवर्धत गवां मध्ये सागरस्य इवाम्बुदः॥

"Shrihari, who was born in another body, became known by the name Krishna. His complexion was swarthy, akin to the dark clouds. Just as dark clouds keep emanating from the sea, so he began growing among the cows."

(Harivansha Purana, Vishnu Parva, Chapter–6, Shloka–3)

Here, the complexion of the cowherds and the cattle has been compared to the sea, while Krishna has been compared to the clouds. Just as the sea glimmers like silver in the sunlight, most of the cows are also bright-coloured, and just as the clouds emanating from the sea are dark, Kanhaiya too was dark-complexioned, amidst all the fair-complexioned cowherds and cattle. This is the gist of this analogy.

The Vishnu Purana says:

ददृशे च प्रबुद्धा सा यशोदा जातमात्मजम्।
नीलोत्पलदलश्यामं ततोऽत्यर्थं मुदं ययौ॥

"When Yashoda woke up and saw that a boy with a dark complexion, akin to a bunch of blue lotuses, was born to her, she was elated."

(Vishnu Purana, Part–5, Chapter–3, Shloka–22)

The Brahmavaivarta Purana says:

इत्युक्त्वा श्रीहरिस्तत्र बालरूपो बभूव ह।
नग्नं भूमौ शयानं च ददर्श श्यामलं सुतम्॥

Narayana said: "Saying this, Shrihari was soon born as a child over there, and Vasudeva saw his dark-complexioned son sleeping naked on the floor."

(Brahmavaivarta Purana, Shri Krishna Janma Khanda, Chapter–7, Shloka–103)

Thus, Krishna has been depicted as dark-complexioned in not one but all the texts.

54. When and how was Krishna's mother Devaki married?

According to the Mahabharata, a *swayamvar* was held for Devaki. King Ugrasen had invited kings from far and wide to the *swayamvar* of his brother Devak's daughter. But the *swayamvar* ran into a major hindrance. Shursen, Krishna's grandfather, and Shini, Satyaki's grandfather, were cousins. In Devaki's *swayamvar*, Shini took Devaki in his possession for his nephew Vasudeva, to which all the kings present there objected strongly. Somadutt, the son of Grandsire Bhishma's uncle, Baahlik, could not tolerate Shini's audacious act and attacked him. But to his misfortune, he suffered a humiliating defeat at the hands of Shini. In any case, Devaki was eventually married to Vasudeva.

(Mahabharata, Drona Parva, Chapter–144, Shloka–7-14)

It is worth noting here that five sisters of Somadutt, including Rohini, were already married to Vasudeva. Balarama, Krishna's elder brother, was the nephew of Somadutt.

55. How was Devaki's relationship with her brother Kansa?

According to the Puranas, Kansa was extremely fond of his youngest cousin, Devaki. She was his dearest sister.

उग्रसेनसुतः कंसः स्वसुः प्रियचिकीर्षया।
रश्मीन् ह्यानां जग्राह रौक्मै रथशतैर्वृतः॥

Shukdeva said: "Ugrasen's son, Kansa took hold of the chariot's reins to please his cousin Devaki. He himself began riding the chariot, even though hundreds of golden chariots were accompanying him."

(Bhagavat Purana, Skandha–10, Chapter–1, Shloka–30)

The fact that Kansa enthusiastically rode Devaki's chariot himself shows how much he loved her. However, nothing has been mentioned in this regard in the Harivansha Purana and the Mahabharata, but one shloka in the Garga Samhita says:

स्वसुः प्रियं कर्तुमतीव कंसो जग्राह रश्मींश्चलतां ह्यानाम्।
उवाह वाहांश्चतुरंगिणीभिर्वृतः कृपास्नेहपरोऽथ शौरो।

Narada said: "Kansa felt great affection for Vasudeva and was very kind to him. To please his sister, Kansa arrived with all four wings of his army, took the reins of the horses himself and began riding the chariot."

(Garga Samhita, Goloka Khanda, Chapter–9, Shloka–10)

The Brahmavaivarta Purana also mentions something similar:

तां गृहीत्वा रथे कृत्वा प्रस्थान समये तदा।
कंसो हृष्टःसहचरो भगिन्युद्वाहकर्मणि।।
तस्या रथसमीपस्थे कंसे गच्छति तत्क्षणे।

"When Vasudeva was leaving with Devaki in the chariot, Kansa, brimming with joy on the occasion of his sister's marriage, accompanied him. And his chariot instantly came close to Devaki's chariot."

(Brahmavaivarta Purana, Shri Krishna Janma Khanda, Chapter–7, Shloka–14-15)

Based on this Puranic evidence, it can be said that Kansa loved his sisters, especially Devaki.

56. What was Nanda and Yashoda's age when Krishna was born?

In the Bhagavat Purana, Vasudeva, talking about Nanda's age, says:

दिष्ट्या भ्रातः प्रवयस इदानीमप्रजस्य ते।
प्रजाशाया निवृत्तस्य प्रजा यत् समपद्यत।।

Vasudeva said: "Brother! You are advancing in age and you had no children until now. In fact, you had lost all hopes of ever having children. So, it is very fortunate that you have been blessed with a child."

(Bhagavat Purana, Skandha–10, Chapter–5, Shloka–23)

Yashoda's age has not been discussed in this Purana, so the only way to guess her age is in relation to that of Nanda's. None of the scriptures say that Nanda had other wives besides Yashoda. Therefore, it is likely that Nanda and Yashoda may have been of a similar age.

In the Vishnu Purana, Vasudeva says something similar to his friend Nanda:

वसुदेवोऽपि तं प्राह दिष्ट्या दिष्ट्येति सादरम्।
वार्द्धकेऽपि समुत्पन्नस्तनयोऽयं तवाधुना।।

Vasudeva says: "Now, despite your old age, you have seen the face of your (newborn) son, so it is, indeed, a matter of great fortune."

(Vishnu Purana, Part–5, Chapter–5, Shloka–2)

Comment: It is clear from the facts mentioned above that Nanda was an elderly man. And yet, all the TV series based on Krishna depict Nanda and Yashoda as a young couple. But such travesty of Krishna's real life must be stopped now. In their bid to create preposterous stories about

Krishna, authors should remember that everyone has the right to know and learn about the true character of their hero.

57. Why did Krishna and his sons mostly marry their first cousins?

This was a very common custom in Hinduism, and not a taboo as it is today. To save Yashoda's daughter—who had replaced Krishna in the prison—from Kansa's wrath, Devaki prayed to Kansa that she was like his daughter-in-law, and therefore, he should at least spare her:

तं आह भ्रातरं देवी कृपणा करुणं सती।
स्नुषेयं तव कल्याण स्त्रियं मा हन्तुमर्हसि॥

Devaki said: "O brother who wishes me well! This girl is like your daughter-in-law, and is a female. You should never kill a woman."

(Bhagavat Purana, Skandha–10, Chapter–4, Shloka–4)

Had this custom not been so prevalent, Devaki wouldn't have tried to emphasise a future relationship when the girl child had just been born. Details of some of the marriages in Krishna's family between first cousins, which have been mentioned in the texts, are listed below:

i) Bhadra: Bhadra was the daughter of Krishna's aunt Shrutikirti, who was married to the king of Kaikai. Krishna was married to Bhadra after his marriage to Rukmini.

ii) Mitravinda: Mitravinda was the daughter of Krishna's aunt Rajadhidevi, who was married to the king of Avanti. While returning from Draupadi's *swayamvar*, Krishna had attended the *swayamvar* of Mitravinda, and the princess had herself chosen Krishna from amongst hundreds of kings and put the garland around his neck.

iii) Subhadra: Arjuna, Krishna's first cousin, had a love marriage with Subhadra, and for this, he sought the help of Krishna himself.

iv) Shubhangi: During her *swayamvar*, this daughter of Rukmi, the brother-in-law of Krishna, chose to marry Krishna's son Pradyumna, who was her first cousin.

v) Rukmavati: Rukmi, in order to end the hostility between him and Krishna, proposed his granddaughter Rukmavati's marriage to Krishna's grandson Aniruddha. Krishna accepted the proposal on Rukmini's request. It was during this wedding between Rukmavati and Aniruddha that Rukmi was killed by Balarama.

vi) Vatsala (or Shashirekha): This daughter of Balarama was married to Subhadra's son Abhimanyu.

Here are some other marriages between first cousins, which took place in the olden days:

i) Yashoda: A feudal landlord from Vaishali called Samarveer had married his daughter, Yashoda to his nephew Mahavir, the God of the followers of Jainism.

ii) Yashodhara: Gautama Buddha's wife, Yashodhara was the daughter of his paternal aunt Pramita.

Comment: So, marriages among first cousins were quite common during that period, and it was not a taboo at all.

58. Who was present with Krishna during his final moments?

After the Yadavasthali incident, Krishna went into the forest, where a hunter named Jara shot an arrow at him, mistaking him for a deer and wounding him grievously. When the hunter approached closer to collect his prey, he was horrified to see his king in a wounded state. This hunter was present with Krishna till his last breath. This entire incident is described in detail in the Mahabharata and the Vishnu Purana, but there is not a single shloka mentioning it in the Harivansha Purana. The Brahmavaivarta Purana and Garga Samhita do not mention it either. Let us first see what the Mahabharata states:

मत्वात्मानमपराद्धं स तस्य पादौ जरा जगृहे शंकितात्मा।
आश्वासयंस्तं महात्मा तदानीं गच्छन्नूर्ध्वं रोदसी व्याप्य लक्ष्म्या।।

Vaishampayan said: "Now, thinking that he had committed a grave crime, the hunter was terrified, so he immediately grabbed Shri Krishna's feet. Then, the great soul Shri Krishna reassured him, and infusing the earth and the sky with his radiance, he departed for the higher sphere."

(Mahabharata, Mausala Parva, Chapter–4, Shloka–24)

The Vishnu Purana describes this episode in this manner:

अजानता कृतमिदं मया हरिणशंकया।
क्षम्यतां मम पापेन दग्धं मां त्रातुमर्हसि।।

The hunter said to Krishna: "I have committed this crime unwittingly, thinking that I was hunting a deer. Please forgive me! My sin is burning me; please protect me."

(Vishnu Purana, Part–5, Chapter–37, Shloka–71)

गते तस्मिन्सभगवान्संयोज्यात्मानमात्मनि।
ब्रह्मभूतेऽव्ययेचिन्त्ये वासुदेवमयेऽमले।।
जन्मन्यमरे विष्णवाप्रमेयेऽखिलात्मनि।
तत्याज मानुषं देहमतीत्य त्रिविधां गतिम्।।

Sage Parashar said to Sage Maitreya: "After the hunter called Jara left, Shri Krishna merged his soul into the Eternal Godhead, transcended the three-dimensional realm and discarded this human body."

(Vishnu Purana, Part–5, Chapter–37, Shloka–74-75)

According to the Bhagavat Purana, after being struck by the arrow, Krishna sent back the hunter, Jara, who was trembling with fear, after having reassured him. Then, he told Daruka, his charioteer, to go to Dwarka:

गच्छ द्वारवतीं सूत ज्ञातीनां निधनं मिथः।
संकर्षणस्य निर्याणं बन्धुभ्यो ब्रूहि मद्दशाम्।।

Shri Krishna said to Daruka: "Daruka! Go to Dwarka and tell everyone about the internecine killing of the descendants of the Yadava clan, the demise of brother Balarama and my death."

(Bhagavat Purana, Skandha–11, Chapter–30, Shloka–44)

So, contrary to the Mahabharata and the Vishnu Purana, the Bhagavat Purana states that it was Krishna's charioteer, Daruka who was present with him during his final moments.

59. Did Krishna steal the famed Syamantaka gem from Satrajit?

Wherever this incident has been discussed, it has been stated unanimously that the cunning Satrajit had accused the innocent Krishna of stealing the gem. However, based on the discrepancies found in the description of events in these texts, it is inferred that whatever has been written about this event is not the entire truth. At one point, the Garga Samhita describes this event in the following manner:

सत्राजिताय सूर्येण दत्तः साक्षात्स्यमंतकः।
उग्रसेनाय स मणिः श्रीकृष्णेनाभियाचितः।।
सत्राजितस्तं न ददौ द्रव्यलोभेन मैथिल।
दिनेदिने स्वर्णभारानष्टौ यः सृजति स्वतः।।

Narada says: "Mithileshwar! A reputed Yadava named Satrajit from amongst Mathura's elite was given the Syamantaka gem by the Sun himself. Krishna had sought that gem for Mathura's King Ugrasen, but Satrajit refused to give it to him due to his greed for wealth, as that gem produced eight *bhara*[10] of gold per day."

(Garga Samhita, Dwarka Khanda, Chapter–8, Shloka–2-3)

Actually, the gifts of honour received from several kings and the treasure that was discovered on the Gomanta Hill largely contributed to Krishna's prosperity, but this wealth was not sufficient to build Dwarka from the ground up and make it prosper. Such being the case, the shlokas quoted above make the reader skeptical about the assertion made in the texts. On the other hand, the texts depict Shatdhanva, Kritvarma and Akrura as the ones who stole the gem. They had stolen the gem from Dwarka itself. So, the question arises, how did that gem arrive in Dwarka? Well, later on, when the gem was seized from Akrura, it was decided that this gem would remain with Akrura only; meaning, it would not be kept in Dwarka. But if one observes the circumstances in Dwarka from that point onwards, several aspects become clear. Any person reading the texts can comprehend that Dwarka had begun to decline gradually after this incident. It is thus evident that the Syamantaka gem had contributed to the prosperity of Dwarka; this fact may not have been mentioned in the texts, but it is definitely accepted by experts.

60. What were Krishna's primary hobbies?

After an in-depth study of almost all the texts related to Krishna's life, it can be authoritatively stated that for Krishna, harbouring a hobby did not mean allowing any emotion, task or object to dominate or overpower him. In fact, this practice of remaining detached was by itself a hobby for him. He always lived in the present as it was. Krishna did not harbour any 'hobby' in the sense that this question means it. Other than that, if he wished to play music but did not have a flute with him, he would just pluck a few leaves from a tree and create music from them, by fashioning the leaves into a musical instrument. If the ornaments his mother adorned him with were not enough for him, he would adorn himself with peacock feathers or fruits and flowers with equal passion.

10. One bhara = 8,000 tola = 1 quintal

Therefore, it is not appropriate at all to bind Krishna to merely a couple of hobbies. Even after studying the colossal life he led and a cartload of books, one cannot pick out a single activity or object that could be termed as Krishna's hobby. He was an adept at adapting himself to the situation; he had no reservations about anything. Therefore, those who think that playing the flute, wearing the *pitambar,*[11] enjoying the *Chhappan Bhog*, riding chariots, indulging in politics, and so on were his hobbies, are totally ignorant about Krishna. If every act of Krishna is considered to be his hobby, then the list of his hobbies would become much longer than this. So, in a nutshell, he accepted everything; there was nothing that he abstained from.

61. How was Satrajit related to Krishna?

Satrajit was the father of Krishna's wife Satyabhama, and the owner of the Syamantaka gem. He was Krishna's arch-rival and was always hostile to Krishna, never letting him be at peace, from Mathura to Dwarka, and right up to his death. He was an extremely wealthy man from amongst the Yadava elite, and commanded as much respect in the kingdom of Mathura as Vasudeva. After Kansa's death, the ambitious Satrajit desperately wished to become the king of Mathura, and he even employed a slew of tricks to topple Ugrasen from the throne. But to his misfortune, Krishna's stature in Mathura had grown several times higher than him after Kansa's death, and that is why he remained hostile to Krishna throughout his life. This is the gist of their mutual relationship.

62. Did Krishna get the opportunity to become the king of Mathura?

Yes, after he had killed Kansa, Krishna got the opportunity to become the king of Mathura, which he declined. The Harivansha Purana clearly describes this episode, whereas the other Puranas only mention Ugrasen's ascension to the throne.

पुत्रो निर्यातितः क्रोधान्नीतो... x...कृपणः पश्चिमां क्रियाम्॥

Kansa's father Ugrasen said: "Krishna! You wreaked vengeance on my son for his crime; you have righteously achieved fame and made your mark on this earth. Your glory has dazzled all the kings and they will

11. Yellow-coloured garment

all take refuge in you. Krishna! Accept this invincible army of Kansa replete with elephants, horses, chariots and foot soldiers. After the annihilation of the enemy, you have automatically become the master of the women of the palace, the treasure, the vehicles and everything else that is present here. Now, all of us Yadavas are under your refuge. Please heed our request and grant permission to conduct the last rites of all those killed here, including Kansa."

(Harivansha Purana, Vishnu Parva, Chapter–32, Shloka–18-30)

Ugrasen said this because in those days, tradition dictated that any person who killed the king—whether he was another king or a commoner—would generally replace the dead king, thereby becoming the new king of that kingdom. Therefore, Ugrasen, following the same tradition, proposed that Krishna should become the king of Mathura. However, Krishna politely declined his offer and said:

न हि राज्येन मे कार्यं नाप्यहं नृप कांक्षितः।
न चापि राज्यलुब्धेन मया कंसो निपातितः॥
किं तु लोकहितार्थाय कीर्त्यर्थं च सुतस्तव।
व्यंगभूतः कुलस्यास्य सानुजो विनिपातितः॥
अहं स एव गोमध्ये गोपैः सह वनेचरः।
प्रीतिमान् विचरिष्यामि कामचारी यथा गजः॥
एतावच्छतशोऽप्येवं सत्येनैतद् ब्रवीमि ते।
न मे कार्यं नृपत्वेन विज्ञाप्यं क्रियतामिदम्॥
भवान राजास्तु मान्यो मे यदूनामग्रणीः प्रभुः।
विजयायाभिषिच्यस्व स्वराज्ये नृपसत्तम॥
यदि ते मत्प्रियं कार्यं यदि वा नास्ति ते व्यथा।
मया निसृष्टं राज्यं स्वं चिराय प्रतिगृह्यताम्॥

Krishna said: "O King! I do not need a kingdom. Neither do I aspire for it, nor have I killed Kansa out of greed for this kingdom. I have killed your son, who was a rotten part of this family, only in the interest of the greater good and as a meritorious deed. I will remain the same forest dweller and continue to happily perambulate with the cowherds, among the cows. I swear by the truth and repeat these words a hundred times and tell you, I have nothing to do with the kingdom; please announce this publicly. You are the eminent master of the Yadavas and honourable for me too, so you must become the king. O,

Supreme Among Kings! Conduct your own coronation as the ruler of this kingdom. Victory to you! If you wish to please me in some way, and if you are not distressed because of me, then accept this kingdom returned by me for a long term."

(Harivansha Purana, Vishnu Parva, Chapter–32, Shloka–48-53)

In the Mahabharata:

आहुकः पुनरस्माभिर्ज्ञातिभिश्चापि सत्कृतः।
उग्रसेनः कृतो राजा भोजराजन्यवर्धनः॥

Krishna said: "Then, all of us family members together honourably enthroned Ahuk Ugrasen, who would ensure the welfare of the Kshatriyas of the Bhoja clan, as the king."

(Mahabharata, Udyoga Parva, Chapter–128, Shloka–38)

In the Bhagavat Purana:

एवमोशास्य पितरौ भगवान्देवकीसुतः।
मातामहं तूग्रसेनं यदूनामकरोन्नृपम्॥
आह चास्मान्महाराज प्रजाश्चाज्ञप्तुमर्हसि।

Shukdeva says: "Shri Krishna thus reassured his parents and made his maternal grandfather Ugrasen the king of the Yadavas and said to him, 'We are your subjects; establish your rule on us.'"

(Bhagavat Purana, Skandha–10, Chapter–45, Shloka–12-13)

In the Vishnu Purana:

उग्रसेनं ततो बन्धान्मुमोच मधुसूदनः।
अभ्यषिञ्चत् तथैवैनं निजराज्ये हतात्मजम्॥

Parashara said: "Then, Madhusudan Krishna freed Ugrasen from captivity and enthroned him as his king, after his son Kansa was killed."

(Vishnu Purana, Part–5, Chapter–21, Shloka–9)

Similar descriptions are found in other Puranas and Samhitas too. So, Krishna did get the opportunity to become the king of Mathura, which he declined. And rejecting such a tremendous opportunity at the age of 18 is enough to indicate how large-hearted he was.

63. What was the name of Krishna's charioteer?

The name of Krishna's charioteer was Daruka, who was his childhood friend from Mathura. After the Yadavasthali incident, only Krishna and his charioteer had survived from among all those who were present.

दारुकः कृष्णपदवीमन्वीच्छन्नधिगम्यताम्।
वायुं तुलसिकामोदमाघ्नायाभिमुखं ययौ॥

Shukdeva said: "Shri Krishna's charioteer, Daruka kept walking ahead, trying to find his (Krishna's) location, sniffing the air and following the fragrance of basil worn by Krishna and guessing his whereabouts."

(Bhagavat Purana, Skandha–11, Chapter–30, Shloka–41)

64. Why did Krishna choose to become Arjuna's charioteer, as opposed to some other Pandava's?

Just as Arjuna was one of the best archers of Aryavarta, Krishna was one of the best charioteers of Aryavarta. The Kaurava army had four archers equivalent to Arjuna's calibre—Bhishma, Karna, Drona and Ashwathama. However, Arjuna was the only archer in the Pandava army; and except Bhima, none of his brothers were highly proficient at wielding their weapons. As for Bhima, once he reached the battlefield, he did not even need a chariot, as he was more comfortable on foot. But of course, mace-fighting had its limitations, for, one could use it only to fight an opponent standing at an arm's distance. In other words, the mace was useless if the enemy was positioned at a considerable distance. Therefore, the Pandavas' victory in the war depended entirely on Arjuna. Hence, it was he who needed the best chariot, the best horses and the best charioteer. That is why Krishna was made the charioteer of Arjuna.

65. Did Sage Durvasa really curse Krishna?

No, that is absolutely untrue. This story is based on Chapter 159 of the Anushasan Parva of the Mahabharata, which has been added later, and is clearly an embellishment. The chapter begins by demonstrating the superiority of Brahmins:

युधिष्ठिर उवाच

ब्रूहि ब्राह्मणपूजायां व्यूष्टिं त्वं मधुसूदनः।
वेत्ता त्वमस्य चार्थस्य वेद त्वां हि पितामहः॥

Yudhishthira asked: "O Madhusudan! What is the result of worshipping a Brahmin? You alone must explain this, because you are well versed in this subject, and my Grandsire also considers you to be an expert in this subject."

(Mahabharata, Anushasan Parva, Chapter–159, Shloka–1)

In response to this, Krishna recounted a story to Yudhishthira about how his son Pradyumna had once quarrelled with the Brahmins and was furious with them. Krishna had then explained to his son that it was wrong to believe that they were superior to the Brahmins just because they were kings. *(Mahabharata, Anushasan Parva, Chapter–159, Shloka–11).* The Brahmins are the most supreme in the three worlds, and they are worshiped everywhere. They have the ability to burn this world to ashes *(Mahabharata, Anushasan Parva, Chapter–159, Shloka–12)*. Then, Krishna narrated a story to his son Pradyumna, telling him that once upon a time, when Sage Durvasa had come to Dwarka on a visit, no one had invited him to stay in their house, because they were familiar with his short temper. Eventually, he stayed at Krishna's palace, but in a few days' time, he made everyone's life miserable. In fact, one day, he even yoked Rukmini to a chariot, instead of tethering a horse to the chariot. But Krishna remained obedient to the Brahmin without losing his calm. One day, Durvasa ordered for *kheer*[12] to be prepared and when it was served to him, he ate a little and returned the rest of it to Krishna, ordering him to smear it on his entire body; and if some of it was left over, then Krishna had to smear it on Rukmini. Krishna told Pradyumna that even though he obeyed Durvasa, the sage was enraged because he had not smeared the *kheer* on his feet and soles. Then, the furious Durvasa cursed him, saying, "You did not obey the command properly, so your death will arrive from your feet."

*(Mahabharata, Anushasan Parva,
Chapter–159, Shloka–14-55)*

Comment: At the very outset, it is evident that the story narrated above is fictional. It is a malicious attempt to illustrate the superiority of Brahmins, by adding this twist to the incident of the arrow piercing Krishna's foot. Here, I have given only a brief outline of the story, and after reading the original story in the Mahabharata, any person can see for himself that for a petty, selfish motive, a story has been exaggerated to such absurd proportions that what it narrates is just not possible

12. Rice and milk porridge

in nature. And people who have done this have exaggerated not only the scriptures related to Krishna, but almost all the scriptures and in every way. Readers must comprehend that the scriptures were written by Brahmins, after all. Therefore, they have left no stone unturned to depict themselves as superior, while showing others as inferior. But all such assertions have always been far from reality. One must remember that every person, irrespective of his caste or creed, is a constituent of the society; everyone duly contributes to it and enjoys due respect too. Besides, one cannot even imagine that Krishna, who respected women immensely, would have acquiesced to have his wife, Rukmini yoked to a chariot.

66. Was Balarama habituated to liquor?

Yes, Balarama used to consume liquor regularly. Evidence of his fondness for liquor is found in the scriptures, right from the time when he and Krishna had taken refuge on the Gomanta Hill. This episode is described in the Harivansha Purana as follows:

तृष्णा चैनं विवेशाशु वारुणीप्रभवा तदा।
शुशोष च मुखं तस्य मत्तस्येवापरेऽहनि।।
स्मरितः स पुरावृत्तममृतप्राशनं विभुः
तृषितो मदिरान्वेषी ततस्तं तरुमैक्षत।।
तस्य प्रावृषि फुल्लस्य यदम्भो जलजोज्झितम्।
तत्कोटरस्थं मदिरा संजायत मनोहरा।।
तां तु तृष्णाभिभूतात्मा पिबन्नार्त इवसकृत्।
मोहाच्च चलिताकारः समजायत स प्रभु।।

Vaishampayan said: "Then, Balarama started craving liquor. On the second day, his mouth began to feel parched, like that of a drunkard. Recalling the liquor he had consumed in the past, he thirstily began searching for it, and just then, his glance rested on a tree. In the monsoon season, the rain showered by the dark clouds was pouring on the blooming Kadamba, filling up a cavity of its trunk; and to Balarama, this liquid appeared like nectar. His heart was racing due to his uncontrollable thirst for liquor, and he began consuming that drink feverishly, in the manner of a drunkard. Due to excessive drinking, he became inebriated, and consequently, his steps began to falter in spite of his sturdy body."

(Harivansha Purana, Vishnu Purana, Chapter–41, Shloka–8-11)

Actually, the Gomanta Hill where Krishna and Balarama had taken refuge, after fleeing from Jarasandha, had an abundance of Mahua, Kadamba and similar trees from which intoxicating drinks could be made. As the region was devoid of human habitation, the liquid from those trees would get collected in their cavities, undisturbed, and spread their fragrance all around. When a connoisseur of liquor such as Balarama smelled it, his thirst made him restless, and he began to drink it uncontrollably, akin to a drunkard who has chanced upon liquor after a very long time. Apart from this, evidence of liquor prohibition in Dwarka is also found in the Mahabharata and the Bhagavat Purana. Thus, it is clear from the above references that Balarama used to consume liquor regularly.

67. Did the inhabitants of Dwarka consume liquor?

There is plenty of evidence in all the texts which proves that everyone in Dwarka, right from the commoners to the royal family, used to consume liquor. It was when the drinking had crossed its limit, turning into debauchery, that prohibition was imposed:

अघोषयंश्च नगरे वचनादाहुकस्य ते।
जनार्दनस्य रामस्य बभ्रोश्चैव महात्मनः।।
अद्य प्रभृति सर्वेषु वृष्ण्यन्धककुलेष्विह।
सुरासवो न कर्तव्यः सर्वैनगरवासिभिः।।
यश्च नोऽविदितं कुर्यात् पेयं कश्चिन्नरः क्वचित्।
जीवन् स शूलमारोहेत् स्वयं कृत्वा सबान्धवः।।

Vaishampayan says: "On the orders of King Ugrasen, Krishna, Balarama and Babhru, the royal officials decreed that henceforth, no resident of the city should prepare liquor in the residences of Kshatriyas hailing from the Vrishni and Andhak clans. Anyone who is found preparing liquor sneakily would be crucified alive for the crime, along with his kin."

(Mahabharata, Mausala Parva, Chapter–1, Shloka–29-30)

Some of the women freed from Narakasura's captivity lived in Dwarka as Krishna's concubines, and many of them had illicit relations with Krishna's debauched son, Saamb. It has been stated that in his palaces, wine and women were openly indulged in. *(Saamb Purana, Chapter–3)* It is clear from this evidence that even during those days in Dwarka, consumption of liquor was so rampant that the king was compelled to impose prohibition.

68. Did prostitutes also reside in Krishna's Dwarka?

Yes, evidence of this is found in the Bhagavat Purana. When Krishna had returned to Dwarka after the Mahabharata war, prostitutes had also come to the outskirts of the kingdom to welcome him, along with the members of the royal family:

वारमुख्याश्च शतशो यानैर्तद्दर्शनोत्सुका।
लसत्कुंडलनिर्भात्त कपोलवदनश्रियः॥

Shukdeva says: "Along with them, several hundred of the best prostitutes, whose faces looked radiant because of the glow of their earrings lighting up their cheeks, had also set off in their palanquins, in order to welcome him."

(Bhagavat Purana, Skandha–1, Chapter–11, Shloka–20)

The Harivansha Purana also mentions the prostitutes of Dwarka:

दैत्याधिवासं निर्जित्य यदुभिर्दृढविक्रमैः।
वेश्या निवेशिता वीर द्वारवत्यां सहस्रशः॥
सामान्यास्ताः कुमाराणां क्रीडानार्यो महात्मनाम्।
इच्छाभोग्या गुणैरेव राजन्या वेषयोषितः॥

Vaishampayan says: "The strong, valorous Yadava warriors conquered the sea, the abode of the demons, and had thousands of prostitutes settled in Dwarka. Those young women, dressed in various attires, were objects of enjoyment for the noble, young Yadava men. With their skills, they were available for amorous dalliance with all these men, as per their wishes. All those prostitutes were called Rajanya (Kshatriya) because the princes enjoyed amorous dalliance with them.

(Harivansha Purana, Vishnu Parva, Chapter–88, Shloka–8-9)

Once upon a time, a *rasa*[13] was organised in Dwarka as per Krishna's instructions, constituting a dance performance put forth by the prostitutes after the Yadavas had finished swimming:

कृष्णेङ्गितज्ञा जलयुद्धसङ्गाद् भैमा निवृत्ता दृढमानिनोऽपि।
नित्यं तथाऽऽनन्दकराः प्रियाणां प्रियाश्च तेषां ननृतुः प्रतीताः॥

---

13. Dance

The Yadavas of the Bhima clan, who quickly grasped the hints given by Krishna, ceased frolicking in the water despite their strong pride. Then, the prostitutes, who attended to the pleasure of those dear men, began dancing in an assured manner.

(Harivansha Purana, Vishnu Parva, Chapter–89, Shloka–53)

69. Why did Krishna kill Kalyavana?

When Krishna and the king of Mathura, Ugrasen learned from their spies that Jarasandha was planning to attack Mathura from several directions along with a host of allied kings, including a very powerful king, Kalyavana, they took immediate action. They quickly decided to have the inhabitants of Mathura migrate to Dwarka, which had not been fully built yet. Then, with great promptness, they organised the departure of as many residents of Mathura as possible. At the same time, to ensure that this caravan comprising a sizeable population of Mathura reached its destination, Dwarka safely, Krishna himself headed towards the location where Kalyavana's army was camping. This had become necessary because Kalyavana's huge army could have chased them and obliterated the entire caravan in just two days. So, to avoid this calamity without having to engage in a fight, Krishna, through his messenger, sent a symbolic message to Kalyavana who was marching rapidly towards Mathura:

घोरमाशीविषं कृष्णं कृष्णः प्राक्षेपयत् तदा।
ततस्तं मुद्रयित्वा तु स्वेन दूतेन हारयत्।।

Vaishampayan said: "Shri Krishna placed a fierce, black poisonous snake in an urn, sealed it from the top, and sent it to that king through his messenger."

निदर्शनार्थं गोविन्दो भीषयामास तं नृपम्।
स दूतः कालयवने दर्शयामास तं घटम्।।

"Actually, Govind (Krishna) had attempted to frighten that king by using the snake as a symbol. O King Janamejaya! That messenger opened the urn and showed the snake to Kalyavana to symbolically indicate that Krishna was as fierce as that snake."

कालसर्पोपमः कृष्ण इत्युक्त्वा भरतर्षभ।
तत्कालयवनो बुद्ध्वा त्रासनं यादवैः कृतम्।।

"Kalyavana deduced that these Yadavas have tried to frighten him by using the snake as a symbol."

पिपीलिकानां चण्डानां पूरयामास तं घटम्।
स सर्पो बहुभिस्तीक्ष्णैः सर्वतस्तैः पिपीलिकैः।
भक्ष्यमाणः किलांगेषु भस्मीभूतोऽभवत् तदा॥

"In response, Kalyavana filled that urn with ferocious ants. Overpowering the snake completely, the ants attacked it from all sides, their deadly stings killing the black snake in no time."

तं मुद्रयित्वा तं घटं तथैव यवनाधिपः।
प्रेषयामास कृष्णाय बाहुल्यमुपवर्णयन्॥

"Then, Kalyavana sealed the urn just as he had received it and returned it to Krishna, symbolically indicating the sheer numerical strength of his army."

(Harivansha Purana, Vishnu Parva, Chapter–57, Shloka–33-37)

वासुदेवस्तु तं दृष्ट्वा योगं विहतमात्मनः।
उत्सृज्य मथुरामाशु द्वारकामभिजग्मिवान्॥
वैरस्यान्तं विधित्संस्तु वासुदेवो महायशाः।
निवेश्य द्वारकां राजन्वृष्णीनोशास्य चैव ह॥
पदातिः पुरुषव्याघ्रो बाहुप्रहरणस्तदा।
आजगाम महावीर्यो मथुरां मधुसूदनः॥

Vaishampayan said: "O King! Seeing that his manoeuvre had failed, Shri Krishna immediately had the caravan of Mathura's inhabitants depart towards Dwarka under his supervision, and then Madhusudan returned to Mathura, banking only on his own strength."

(Harivansha Purana, Vishnu Parva, Chapter–57, Shloka–38-40)

Thereafter, Krishna led Kalyavana to a cave, where he killed him cleverly. Krishna's strategic manoeuvre against Kalyavana, which is mentioned above, is not available in the Mahabharata or any other Purana. This description is found only in the Harivansha Purana.

70. Was Krishna's son, Saamb, really a troublemaker?

On the basis of the Puranas, it can be said that Saamb was an extremely unruly character. According to the description given in the Puranas,

Saamb was physically attractive, but also suffered from leprosy. Indulging in impertinent behaviour and mischief was his sole activity. He did not possess even a single trait that was characteristic of a noble prince belonging to a royal family. He did not desist even from harassing the sages who frequently visited Krishna. But in spite of this, he was dear to his uncle, Balarama, because both of them were addicted to liquor. In fact, due to their fondness for liquor, both uncle and nephew were much talked about across the whole of Dwarka. Saamb was such a troublemaker that he did not even refrain from disrespecting his own father, Krishna.

Saamb's mischief was not confined to Dwarka alone; other kingdoms were also troubled by his antics. When Duryodhana had organised his daughter Lakshmana's *swayamvar*, he had sent an invitation to Balarama too, who had trained him in mace-fighting. Balarama then sent his beloved nephew Saamb to attend the *swayamvar*. Interestingly, the moment Saamb's gaze fell upon Lakshmana, he was bowled over by her beauty. But, on the other hand, Lakshmana did not even spare him a glance, as she walked past him with her wedding garland in hand. Actually, Lakshmana knew about Saamb's shenanigans, and was also aware that he was afflicted with leprosy and was debauched, so she did not pay any attention to him. However, the impertinent Saamb could not tolerate being ignored with such disdain, and consequently, he abducted Lakshmana from an assembly full of people. But, to his misfortune, the soldiers of Hastinapur overpowered him and arrested him. When the news of his capture reached Dwarka, Balarama intervened, and finally, this drama came to an end, albeit with great difficulty. Saamb was eventually married to Lakshmana.

(Harivansha Purana, Vishnu Parva, Chapter–62)

Of the 16,100 women that Krishna had freed from Narakasura's captivity, many lived in Dwarka as Krishna's concubines. Saamb had relations with many of them, and one woman named Nandini was prominent among them *(Matsya Purana, Chapter–70)*; *(Saamb Purana, Chapter–3)*; *(Bhavishya Purana, Parisarga Parva, Chapter–31)*. Even in Prabhasa, Saamb was the leader of the Yadavas who misbehaved with sages such as Vishwamitra, Kanva and Narada.

71. Did Krishna's first son Pradyumna really marry a demoness who was much older than him?

According to the description given in the Puranas, Krishna's first son, Pradyumna was married to a woman from the demon clan who was much older than him. On the seventh day of Pradyumna's birth, a demon named Shambar had abducted him from the solarium, carried him to his distant hamlet by the sea, and handed him over to a woman to raise him. The woman's name was Mayawati and she was a fisherwoman. Rukmini and Krishna's son was very attractive, and Mayawati loved the beautiful child and nurtured him with great care. When Pradyumna grew into a young boy, Mayawati told him that he was Krishna's son and that he had been abducted by Shambar. Consequently, Pradyumna killed Shambar as soon as he found the opportunity, and married Mayawati. Thereafter, he came to Dwarka along with Mayawati.

(Harivansha Purana,
Vishnu Parva, Chapter–104-108)

72. Did Krishna ever attack any king in order to capture his cows?

One such story is narrated in the Harivansha Purana. By the time Krishna was born, India had developed to a great extent, and the importance of diamonds, pearls, jewellery and so on had increased, making them an invaluable part of a person's wealth. Nonetheless, cows still remained a crucial indicator of one's wealth. In those days, it was routine for people to slip away with each other's cows, the evidence of which is available in hundreds of places in the Vedic series of texts. As for the question above, it is related to the marriage of Krishna's grandson, Aniruddha to Banasura's daughter, Usha. When Krishna learned that his grandson Aniruddha had been arrested by Banasura in the course of his love affair with Usha, Krishna, along with his son, Pradyumna—who was Aniruddha's father—attacked Shonitpur,[14] the kingdom of Banasura, with approximately hundred soldiers. A fierce battle took place, as a result of which Banasura was defeated, and consequently, Aniruddha and Usha were married to each other. After the marriage, Krishna handed over the kingdom of Shonitpur to a worthy minister of Banasura called Kushmanda and made him the head of state. For several

14. A district in present-day Assam

days after the marriage, Krishna enjoyed the warm hospitality of the kingdom as a guest along with his son, grandson, granddaughter-in-law and his soldiers. One day, Kushmanda informed Krishna that Banasura had given thousands of cows of an exceptional breed to Varuna, who was protecting and taking care of them. He also told Krishna that the milk given by these cows was very sweet and nutritious. Thus, on his return journey, Krishna launched an attack on Varuna's kingdom, and the ensuing battle with Varuna's soldiers continued for several days. Finally, when Varuna himself joined the battle with his sons, he thought it wise to first ask Krishna about the purpose of his attack. In response, Krishna asked him to hand over the cows given to him by Banasura. Varuna replied that he had promised Banasura that he would not allow anyone to snatch away his cows till his (Varuna's) last breath. He also appealed to Krishna that if he was really striving to establish righteousness without any bias, then Krishna should help him keep his promise. But if Krishna was greedy for the cows, then he should kill him and snatch them away. Additionally, Varuna pointed out that he was older than Krishna and had never indulged in any unethical act. Varuna's words silenced Krishna and he decided not to capture the cows.

(Harivansha Purana, Vishnu Parva, Chapter–127, Shloka–1-97)

73. When did the worship of Indra begin in India?

Indra has been a prominent god in the Vedic civilisation, and most of the mantras in the Rigveda are dedicated to him. He was primarily worshipped during the various sacrifices or yajnas performed by the Kshatriyas such as the Vajapeya Yajna, Ashwamedha Yajna and Rajasuya Yajna. Indra was also worshipped in the Soma Yajna performed by Brahmins. However, this worship of Indra was confined only to the yajnas, which could be conducted at any time of the year, at an astrologically determined auspicious hour. Unlike other Indian festivals, there was no specific date fixed for the festival of Indra's worship. This practice was prevalent in India till the time of Uparichar Vasu, a prominent king of north-central India, who was also the grandfather of Jarasandha. There is evidence in the Mahabharata that Uparichar Vasu, the king of Chedi kingdom, started this worship in his kingdom in order to please Indra. During his lifetime, the Hindu month of Ashwin (September–October) was considered the first month of the New Year. So, he had designated the first day of the Krishna Paksha (dark phase) of the Ashwin month as the day dedicated for Indra's worship. At that time, this ritual was performed only by kings, both of greater and lesser repute. Common people did not have to bear the burden of conducting it.

Well, Uparichar Vasu had five sons, and all of them expanded the kingdom on the strength of their capabilities. One of these five brothers, Brihadratha, conquered Magadha and established his reign over it. Later, it was this very Brihadratha who gave birth to Jarasandha, who was Kansa's father-in-law and Krishna's arch-enemy. Notably, these five brothers, including Brihadratha, established their dominance over many regions of India and propagated the festival of Indra's worship to such an extent that this royal festival grew into a community celebration in those regions. Thereafter, people from all walks of life started celebrating this festival according to their capacity. But even so, at that time, this festival still remained a community event, rather than a private, familial celebration.

(Mahabharata, Adi Parva, Chapter–63)

Thus, on the basis of the only evidence of Indrotsav, or Indra's festival, given in the Hindu religious texts, it can be said that by the time Krishna was born, this festival was not very ancient; it preceded Krishna by barely 200–300 years. And since the tradition of Indrotsav was relatively new among thousands of Hindu traditions, people celebrated it with great enthusiasm. And when Krishna put an end to it, people expressed great surprise too. Then, scores of people with varied interests and intentions began propagating this tradition by word of mouth, and it also began to be registered in the scriptures of various sects.

74. Did Krishna receive formal education?

All the texts provide evidence of Krishna and Balarama's education in the gurukul of Sage Sandipani. However, their tryst with the gurukul was much shorter than usual, as the following shlokas of some scriptures illustrate:

अथो गुरुकुले वासमिच्छन्तावुपजग्मतुः।
काश्यं सांदीपनिं नाम ह्यवन्तिपुरवासिनम्॥

Shukdeva said: "Now, both of them, desiring to live in a gurukul, went to Sage Sandipani of the Kashyap lineage, who lived in Avanti (Ujjain)."

(Bhagavat Purana, Skandha–10, Chapter–45, Shloka–31)

कस्यचित् त्वथ कालस्य सहितौ रामकेशवौ।
गुरुं सान्दीपनिं काश्यमवन्तिपुरवासिनम्॥

Vaishampayan said: "After some time, Balarama and Krishna went to Guru Sandipani, a resident of Avantipur, who was born in Kashi."

(Harivansha Purana, Vishnu Parva, Chapter–33, Shloka–3)

The two shlokas from the two Puranas mentioned above have different definitions of the Sanskrit word 'Kashya', which indicates how Indian society later became more inclined towards casteism. In the ancient Harivansha Purana, the word 'Kashya' has been taken to mean the place Kashi (modern-day Varanasi), whereas 500–1000 years later in the Bhagavat Purana, the same word is used to denote caste lineage. Well, the story of Sage Sandipani in other Puranas is as follows:

तत्सान्दीपनिं काश्यमवन्तिपुरवासिनम्।
विद्यार्थं जग्मतुर्बालौ कृतोपनयनक्रमौ॥

Parashara said: "After the thread ceremony was over, both the boys (Krishna and Balarama) went to study at (the ashram of) Sage Sandipani of Avantipur, who was born in Kashi."

(Vishnu Purana, Part–5, Chapter–21, Shloka–19)

कृष्णः सांदीपनेर्गेहं गत्वा च सबलो मुदा।
नमश्चकार स्वगुरुं गुरुपत्नीं पतिव्रताम्॥

Narayana said: "O Narada! Shri Krishna cheerfully went to the house of Sage Sandipani with Balarama, and paid obeisance to his guru and his wife."

(Brahmavaivarta Purana, Shri Krishna Janma Khanda, Chapter–102, Shloka–1)

The South Indian version of the Mahabharata mentions Krishna's education as follows:

ततस्तौ जग्मतुस्तात गुरुं सान्दीपनिं पुनः।
गुरुः शुश्रूषया युक्तौ धर्मज्ञौ धर्मचारिणौ॥

Grandsire Bhishma said: "O Yudhishthira! After that, both the righteous brothers went to Guru Sandipani at Ujjaini to study."

(Mahabharata, Sabha Parva, Chapter–54, Shloka–1)

In this manner, Krishna and Balarama's education in the ashram of Sage Sandipani has been discussed everywhere.

75. What was the relationship between Krishna and Draupadi?

Many statements have been made in the Mahabharata and the Puranas, based on which people have jumped to numerous conclusions, and from time to time, these assertions have also been propagated in the society by word of mouth. There is no evidence of a love affair between Krishna and Draupadi in the Mahabharata or any Purana. But in order to comprehend the relationship between Draupadi and Krishna, it is essential to take into consideration a few points that come across in the stories of Draupadi narrated in the Mahabharata:

i) Drupad's enmity with Dronacharya and Arjuna: Drona (the son of Bharadwaj and Ghritachi, the celestial maiden) and Drupad (the prince of Panchal) used to study and play together in Bharadwaj's ashram when they were children. They were great friends, but as they grew older, they became increasingly busy and were separated from each other for a long period of time. After the death of his father, Drupad became engaged in ruling the kingdom, while Drona went to Sage Parashuram's ashram for further training. After completing his education, when Drona met Drupad in his court, he said, "Dear friend! I am your childhood friend, Drona. Recognise me." To this, Drupad replied in a curt tone:

नाश्रोत्रियः श्रोत्रियस्य ना रथी रथिनः सखा।
ना राजा पार्थिवस्यापि सखिपूर्वं किमिष्यते।।

"How can a scholar of the Vedas be a friend of a non-scholar; how can a valiant warrior befriend one who is not a warrior, and how can a king befriend one who is not a king?"

(Mahabharata, Adi Parva, Chapter–165, Shloka–15)

Deeply hurt by Drupad's indifference, Drona set out in search of refuge, finally reaching Hastinapur. There, Grandsire Bhishma gave him refuge and appointed him to train the Kaurava and Pandava princes. On the completion of their training, when it was time for the princes to give *gurudakshina*,[15] Drona asked them to capture Drupad and throw him at his feet. Arjuna fulfilled this wish of his guru. When Drona saw Drupad in captivity, he said, "You had said that the one who is not a king cannot be a friend of a king, didn't you? Well, I have won your kingdom, but in spite of this, I am giving back half your kingdom and setting you free. You may live in the north-west of the Ganges, and I shall live in the south-eastern region." At this juncture, Drupad had no choice but to accept Drona's condition, so he agreed, but this humiliation kept gnawing at him.

(Mahabharata, Adi Parva, Chapter–165, Shloka–28)

It is clear from this entire incident that Drupad was desperate to wreak vengeance on Drona and Arjuna, but those who have added embellishments to the Mahabharata ignored this fact; on the contrary, they attempted to project that Drupad was yearning to make Arjuna his son-in-law. None of the scholars over the past several centuries have been convinced by this assertion of the Mahabharata. So, these scholars proposed a parallel story closer to the reality of the event, which goes like this: Krishna was the rising star of the Aryavarta region, and as he had performed several seemingly impossible feats, Drupad believed that Krishna was the only one who could help him wreak vengeance against Drona and Arjuna. To this end, Drupad sent his daughter's marriage proposal through a person whom Krishna would find well-nigh impossible to refuse. Drupad sent *Acharya*[16] Sandipani to Dwarka with this proposal. It was during this time that Krishna had met both Drupad and Draupadi, and Draupadi had clearly expressed her love. But despite being impressed by Draupadi's intelligence, Krishna distanced himself from her due to her colossal ego. But yes, on account of her intelligence, the two had certainly begun to share a great rapport as friends.

ii) In some sections of the Mahabharata, Draupadi expresses her love for Krishna and addresses herself as his friend: When Krishna met Draupadi in the forest after the gambling and disrobing incidents, several commoners and prominent people were present there along with Draupadi's brother Dhrishtadyumna. In the presence of everyone, Draupadi clearly tells Krishna that she loves him, so who else would she

15. An offering of gratitude made to the guru
16. Teacher

share her grief with?

सा तेऽहं दुःखमाख्यास्ये प्रणयान्मधुसूदनः।

"O Madhusudan! I love you, so I will share my grief with you alone."

कथं नु भार्या पार्थानां तव कृष्ण सखी विभो।
धृष्टद्युम्नस्य भगिनी सभां कृष्येत मादृषी॥

Draupadi said: "O Krishna! The wife of Kunti's sons, the so-called valiant heroes, Krishna's friend and Dhrishtadyumna's sister was dragged by her hair to that assembly."

(Mahabharata, Vana Parva, Chapter–12, Shloka–60-61)

चतुर्भिः कारणैः कृष्ण त्वया रक्ष्यास्मि नित्यशः।
संबंधाद् गौरवात् सख्यात् प्रभुत्वेनैव केशवः॥

Draupadi said: "O Krishna! You must protect me for four reasons. One, you are my relative; two, I am the daughter and daughter-in-law of noble families; three, I am your friend; and four, you are also capable of protecting me."

(Mahabharata, Vana Parva, Chapter–12, Shloka–127)

Comment: In short, Draupadi and Krishna were good friends. It can also be said that both of them understood each other very well.

76. Why did Draupadi trust Krishna so much?

It is evident that Draupadi was dependent on Krishna all her life. In fact, not just Draupadi, even her five husbands—the Pandavas—were dependent on Krishna. Actually, to be able to get a sense of this deep-seated trust is a big achievement in itself, because to express this level of trust in words would be akin to making an effort that is incomplete! Every pore and fibre of the five Pandavas, Kunti and Draupadi was indebted to Krishna. You can see Kunti admitting this in her own words in the Bhagavat Purana:

यथा हृषीकेश खलेन देवकी कंसेन रुद्धातिचिरं शुचार्पिता।
विमोचिताहं च सहात्मजा विभो त्वयैव नाथेन मुहुर्विपद्गणात्॥
विषान्महाग्नेः पुरुषाददर्शनादसत्सभाया वनवासकृच्त्तः।
मृधे मृधेऽनेकमहारथास्त्रतो द्रौण्यस्त्रतश्चास्म हरेऽभिरक्षिताः॥
विपदः सन्तु ताः शेशत्तत्र तत्र जगद्गुरो।
भवतो दर्शनं यत्स्यादपुनर्भवदर्शनम्॥

Kunti pleaded: "O Krishna! Just as you had protected your mother

Devaki from the wrath of Kansa, you have also repeatedly protected me and my sons. Krishna, the list is long – you have protected our clan during the incidents of poisoning and the burning of the lac house, from the demons of the forest, the dangers of exile, the numerous valiant warriors in several wars and just now, from the deadly weapon of Ashwathama. I wish we keep facing adversities so that we may always be blessed by your company."

(Bhagavat Purana, Skandha–1, Chapter–8, Shloka–23-25)

The fact that people trusted Krishna to such an extent was not a miracle; it was the selfless nature of Krishna, which compelled not just his friends, but even his enemies to trust him. And as far as Draupadi's trust in him is concerned, she had been bowled over by his personality at the time of her marriage. Draupadi had made it quite evident to Krishna that she loved him. But Krishna ignored her hint and instead married Bhadra from Nagakoot as well as Jambavati, who belonged to a forest tribe. Having said that, he never shirked his duties towards Draupadi. He had discharged them responsibly on every occasion; whether it was the establishment of Indraprastha or the execution of the Rajasuya Yajna, it was impossible to measure the extent of Krishna's contribution. In spite of the unprecedented humiliation that the Pandavas and their wife faced, none of them were willing to confront Duryodhana and his cronies. It was Krishna alone who had decided that this humiliation would not be tolerated anymore. That is why Draupadi used to place immense trust in her friend.

77. Which members of Krishna's family were present during the incident of Yadavasthali, which took place in the Prabhasa region?

There are a few differences in various texts regarding this incident, but essentially, the description of it is almost the same. Krishna's father Vasudeva, his great-grandson Vajra and some inhabitants were not present during the incident of Yadavasthali. As for Uddhava, he had already left for Badrikashram with Krishna's consent, before this incident occurred. Most of the remaining men were present at Yadavasthali. The Mahabharata describes it as follows:

Krishna's Family Members Present During the Yadavasthali Incident:

Krishna – Himself
Balarama – Brother
Gada – Younger Brother
Gada – Son
Pradyumna – Son
Saamb – Son
Charudeshna – Son
Aniruddha – Grandson
Satyaki – Friend

Apart from the names of Krishna's family members mentioned above, the Mahabharata also mentions all the Yadavas. According to the Bhagavat Purana, Krishna's son Pradyumna began fighting with his brother Saamb; their brother Gada began fighting with his own son, also named Gada; and Aniruddha had started fighting with Satyaki. Both the Mahabharata and the Bhagavat Purana state that most of the Yadavas present there were killed by Krishna himself:

भगवन्निहताः सर्वे त्वया भूयिष्ठशो नराः।

Babhru said: "O Krishna! Now everyone has been killed. Most of them have been killed by you alone."

(Mahabharata, Mausala Parva, Chapter–3, Shloka–47)

प्रत्यनीकं मन्यमाना बलभद्रं च मोहिताः।
हन्तुं कृतधियो राजन्नापन्ना आततायिनः॥
अथ तावपि संक्रुद्धावुद्यम्य कुरुनन्दन।
एरकामुष्टिपरिघौ चरन्तौ जघ्नतुर्युधि॥
ब्रह्मशापोपसृष्टानां कृष्णमायावृतात्मनाम्।
स्पर्धाक्रोधः क्षयं निन्ये वैणवोऽग्निर्यथा वनम्॥

Shukdeva said: "When Krishna asked the quarrelling Yadavas to desist from fighting, they turned hostile towards him and Balarama, and ran towards them to kill them. O Parikshit, Scion of Kurus! Then, Krishna and Balarama also began to stomp around the battlefield, as they picked fistfuls of *eraka* grass and began hurling it at them. Just as the fire produced by a bamboo devours the bamboo itself, the fury of the descendants of the Yadavas, fuelled by competition, destroyed them."

(Bhagavat Purana, Skandha–11, Chapter–30, Shloka–22-24)

78. Were the people of Dwarka debauched?

There is evidence in the Mahabharata that during the final moments, before Dwarka met its end, the Yadavas of Dwarka had stooped to the lowest levels of debauchery:

नापत्रपन्त पापानि कुर्वन्तो वृष्णयस्तदा।
प्रार्दयन्ब्राह्मणांश्चापि पितॄन्देवांस्तथैव च।।
गुरूंश्चाप्यवमन्यन्ते न तु रामजनार्दनौ।
पत्न्यः पतीनुच्चरन्ति पत्नीश्च पतयस्तथा।।

"In those days, the Vrishnis used to sin openly and were not ashamed of it. They had become hostile even towards the Brahmins, Gods and manes. They had begun to dishonour not only Krishna and Balarama but also the gurus. The wives started cheating on their husbands and vice versa."

(Gita Press Mahabharata, Mausala Parva, Chapter–2, Shloka–10-11)

79. A YouTube video states that after Krishna's separation from Radha, he never played the flute again. Is it true?

In the Mahabharata and the Harivansha Purana, there is no mention of Krishna playing the flute in his childhood or even during his political life in Dwarka. Details about Krishna and his flute are found in the Puranic texts such as the Bhagavat Purana and the Brahmavaivarta Purana. According to the Garga Samhita, Krishna played the flute throughout his life. As most texts state that Krishna played the flute, there is no reason to doubt it. At the same time, it is hard to imagine that someone like Krishna, who always dwelled in joy and knew how to utilise every moment perfectly, could have ever discarded his flute. Therefore, those who make such claims are wrong.

80. In which places did Krishna organise the *rasa* (dance)?

There is no mention whatsoever of Krishna's rasa in the Mahabharata. The Bhagavat Purana describes only one rasa celebration, which is described in detail in Skandha–10, Chapters 29–33. These five chapters are called Rasa Panchadhyayi and have been published separately as well. The Harivansha Purana briefly describes the rasa in Chapter 20 of the Vishnu Parva. And the same Harivansha Purana, in Chapters 88–89 of the Vishnu Parva, also describes the rasa that took place in Dwarka, which, when compared to other rasas, can be termed as the maharasa or the Great Dance. Apart from this, there is a description of two other rasas in the Shri Krishna Janma Khanda of the Brahmavaivarta Purana, which revolves around Radha. The first is the main rasa in Vrindavan (Chapter 28) and the second is the rasa with Radha on the banks of the Virja river (Chapter 128). The Garga Samhita also describes more than one rasa:

i) The main rasa of Vrindavan *(Vrindavan Khanda, Chapter–19-22);*

ii) When Uddhava arrived in Mathura bearing the message of the milkmaids, who were distraught because of their separation from Krishna, Krishna went to Vrindavan with Uddhava and held the rasa again *(Mathura Khanda, Chapter–20);*

iii) Rasa with Radha and all the queens in the Siddhashram *(Dwarka Khanda, Chapter–18);*

iv) Rasa with Radha and the milkmaids in an unknown location away from Dwarka *(Ashwamedha Khanda, Chapter–43-46).*

81. Did Balarama ever participate in the rasa?

Chapter–65, Skandha–10 of the Bhagavat Purana states that Balarama had gone to Vrindavan (from Dwarka) and had met Nanda, Yashoda and all the cowherds and milkmaids. Over a period of two months, Balarama drank heavily and danced freely with the milkmaids.

(Bhagavat Purana, Skandha–10, Chapter–65, Shloka–17-37)

The Garga Samhita also gives an account of Balarama's rasa, similar to the Bhagavat Purana. This Samhita also describes how Balarama drank heavily and celebrated the rasa with the milkmaids for two months in Vrindavan in the spring season.

(Garga Samhita, Balabhadra Khanda, Chapter–9)

Chapter–24, Part–5 of the Vishnu Purana also describes Balarama going to Vrindavan and indulging in rasa and other pleasure pursuits.

82. Did Krishna go back to Vrindavan ever again?

At one point, the Brahmavaivarta Purana states:

इत्याकर्ण्य ययौ गेहमुद्धवश्च महायशाः।
हरिर्जगाम स्वप्ने च गोकुलं विरहाकुलम्।।
स्वप्ने राधां समाश्वास्य दत्त्वा ज्ञानं सुदुर्लभम्।
संतोष्य क्रीडया तां च गोपिकाश्च यथोचितम्।।

Krishna said: "O Uddhava! I will surely fulfil your promise. I will go to Yashoda and the *gopis*[17] in a dream." Hearing this, Uddhava left for his home, while Krishna, in his dream, left for Gokul, which was steeped in misery and utterly distraught due to the pangs of separation. In his dream, he reassured Radha and granted her supremely esoteric knowledge. Then, he frolicked with the *gopis* and appeased them appropriately. *(Brahmavaivarta Purana, Shri Krishna Janma Khanda, Chapter–98, Shloka–42-43)* So, Krishna went to Gokul and Vrindavan in his dream but in reality, he never returned to Vrindavan.

83. Did Krishna meet his eldest son Pradyumna for the first time only in his youth?

Yes! And that is because, Krishna's eldest son Pradyumna took birth in his absence; and on the seventh day after his birth, he was abducted from the solarium by a demon named Shambar, who took the newborn baby and handed him to his maid Mayawati to raise him. This son of Krishna and Rukmini was quite attractive, and as he grew older, Mayawati's affection towards him began to increase. Ultimately, after Mayawati told him who he really was, Pradyumna killed Shambar and returned to Dwarka with Mayawati. By this time, he was a young man who was married too:

तमृक्षवन्ते नगरे निहत्यासुरसत्तमम्।।
गृह्यं मायावती देवीमागच्छन्नगरं पितुः

Vaishampayan said: "Pradyumna came to his father's city with Mayawati after killing the great demon Shambar in a city called Rukshavant."

(Harivansha Purana, Vishnu Parva, Chapter–108, Shloka–2)

जीवपुत्रा त्वयापुत्र कासौ भाग्यसमन्विता।।
किमर्थं चाम्बुदश्यामः सभार्यस्त्वमिहागतः।
अस्मिन वयसि सुव्यक्तं प्रद्युम्नो मम पुत्रकः।।

When Pradyumna and Mayawati met Rukmini in her palace, Rukmini could not recognise her son and instead enquired: "Son! Who is that

17. Milkmaids

fortunate *Jivaputra,*[18] who has given birth to a long-lived son like you? Why have you, with a deep-hued body akin to a dark cloud, come here with your wife?"

(Harivansha Purana, Vishnu Parva, Chapter–108, Shloka–15-16)

When Krishna learned that a charming but unknown young man had arrived at Rukmini's palace with a young woman, he rushed there:

सोऽपश्यत् तं सुतं ज्येष्ठं सिद्धं मन्मथ लक्षणैः।
स्नुषां मायावतीं चैव हृष्टचेता जनार्दनः।।
सोऽब्रवीत् सहसा देवीं रुक्मिणीं देवतामिव।
अयं स देवि सम्प्राप्तः सुतश्चापधरस्तव।।

Vaishampayan said: "Krishna saw his eldest son Pradyumna, endowed with attributes similar to those of Kamadeva[19] and also his daughter-in-law Mayawati. His heart was suffused with joy on seeing them, and he said to Rukmini, 'My lady, this is your son who has now come to you carrying his bow.'"

(Harivansha Purana, Vishnu Parva, Chapter–108, Shloka–21-22)

सती चेयं शुभा साध्वी भार्या वै तनयस्य ते।
मायावतीति विख्याता शम्बरस्य गृहोषिता।

Krishna said: "She is the pious, saintly wife of your son, who is endowed with auspicious qualities. Her name is Mayawati, and she has stayed in Shambarasura's house for a long time."

(Harivansha Purana, Vishnu Parva, Chapter–108, Shloka–24)

This story is also found in Bhagavat Purana *(Skandha–10, Chapter–55)* with a slight difference.

84. Did Kubja of Mathura really share a romantic relationship with Krishna?

The Mahabharata does not provide any straightforward description related to Kubja, but it is certainly found in all Puranas such as Harivansha Purana, Bhagavat Purana, Brahmavaivarta Purana as well as Garga Samhita. According to these accounts, Kubja used to work as a female attendant in the gynaeceum in Kansa's palace. Her job was to prepare garlands and cosmetic items such as fragrant powders and

18. One who is blessed with children
19. God of love

pastes for the members of the royal family, and also apply them to the royals. According to these Puranic descriptions, there was great intimacy between Krishna and Kubja. In fact, she had even moved to Dwarka after a few years.

85. Who advised the cowherds to migrate from Gokul to Vrindavan?

It was Krishna who first advised the cowherds to relocate from Gokul. In fact, it was Krishna who first noticed that the greenery around Gokul had depleted. In the Harivansha Purana, Krishna explains in great detail the reason behind this depletion to his elder brother Balarama:

अथ दामोदरः श्रीमान् संकर्षणमुवाच ह।
आर्य नस्मिन वने शक्यं गोपालैः सहक्रीडितुम्।।

Vaishampayan said: "Then, one day, Damodar Shri Krishna said to his brother Balarama and other cowherds, 'Arya! Now, it is no longer possible to play with the young cowherds in this forest.'"

अवगीतमिदं सर्वमावाभ्यां भुक्तकाननम्।
प्रक्षीण तृणकाष्ठं च गोपैर्मथित पादपम्।।

He said: "We have destroyed the beauty and wealth of this forest by utilising it. The grass here has been grazed and the wood has been cut. The cowherds have mutilated every tree here."

घनीभूतानि यान्यासन् काननानि वनानि च।
तान्याकाशनिकाशानि दृश्यन्तेऽद्य यथाऽसुखम्।।

"The woods and forests, which were lush green earlier, now appear as barren as the sky. One does not derive joy in seeing them anymore."

XXX XXX XXX

संनिकृष्टानि यान्यासन् काष्ठानि च तृणानि च।
तानि दूरावकृष्टासु मार्गितव्यानि भूमिषु।।

"The grass and wood, which were in close proximity earlier, are now so scarce that one has to look for them in the vast tracts of plowed land."

अरण्यमिदमल्पोदमल्पकक्षं निराश्रयम्।
अन्वेषितव्यविश्रामं दारुणं विरलद्रुमम्।।

"There is very little water in this forest now, the dry wood and grass have depleted too, and this place is no longer useful to provide shelter. One has to search for a spot to rest here; there are very few trees left, and they are in quite a dismal state too."

अकर्मण्येषु वृक्षेषु स्थितविप्रस्थितद्विजम्।
संवासस्यास्य महतो जनेनोत्सादितद्रुमम्॥

"The trees here are no longer useful. The birds that lived on them have now gone elsewhere. The people of this large hamlet have destroyed the trees."

XXX XXX XXX

शैलानां भूषणं घोषो घोषानां भूषणं वनम्।
वनानांभूषणं गावस्ताश्चास्माकं परा गतिः॥

"The beauty of the mountains lies in the small villages and hamlets; the beauty of these villages and hamlets lies in the forests; and what makes the forests beautiful are the cows. These cows are our only support."

तस्मादन्यद् वनं यामः प्रत्यग्रयवसेन्धनम्।
इच्छन्त्यनुपभुक्तानि गावो भोक्तु तृणानि च॥

Krishna concluded with an advice: "So, let us go to another forest which has abundant, fresh grass as well as fuel. Our cows wish to graze on fresh grass, which has not been grazed yet."

(Harivansha Purana, Vishnu Parva, Chapter–8, Shloka–8-18)

All the shlokas mentioned above indicate the early development of Krishna's wisdom. This proves that the insight to gauge a situation before it could go out of hand, had begun developing in him right from childhood.

86. Why was Krishna called 'Ranchhod'?

He was called 'Ranchhod' because he had fled from the battle that Jarasandha was about to launch. However, it is crucial to know the reason behind his desertion. What kind of a situation had developed in Mathura, which compelled Krishna to flee?

When the spies of Mathura reported that Jarasandha was about to launch an attack, the royal palace was terrified. Actually, Jarasandha was attacking the kingdom only to kill Krishna; otherwise he had no enmity against Mathura. But an attack is an attack, and when it is launched by a powerful king such as Jarasandha, it is a serious matter indeed. However, despite this, the soldiers and inhabitants of Mathura were reassured, as they recalled Krishna's past exploits; but the palace had to prepare, because, after all, a war is a war. On the other hand, most of the influential and prominent Yadavas of Mathura considered Krishna as their rival, and they wanted to drive away both Krishna and his brother, Balarama, from Mathura, so that they could eliminate the very root of their problems. Some even held the opinion that the two brothers should be taken into custody and handed over to Jarasandha so that Mathura could be assured of lasting peace. Even Krishna's father Vasudeva wanted Krishna and Balarama to be driven out of Mathura. In such a situation, Krishna deemed it wise to flee from the battle. He knew that if they were not present in Mathura, Jarasandha would not attack the city. This was the sole reason behind Krishna's decision to flee from the battle.

(Harivansha Purana, Vishnu Parva, Chapter–38, Shloka–56-61, Chapter–39, Shloka–2-3)

In the Harivansha Purana, this is what Krishna said about the incident in his own words:

अरथौ पत्तिनौ युद्धे निस्त्तनुत्रौ निरायुधौ।
जरासंधोद्यमभयात् पुराद् द्रावेव निःसृतौ।।

Krishna said: "We brothers do not have chariots to fight the war, so we are on foot. We do not wear armour, and we do not have weapons in our hands. It is only the two of us who have left the city out of fear of an attack by Jarasandha."

(Harivansha Purana, Vishnu Parva, Chapter–39, Shloka–42)

The Bhagavat Purana describes Krishna and Balarama's desertion from Mathura as follows:

विलोक्य वेगरभसं रिपुसैन्यस्य माधवौ।
मनुष्यचेष्टामापन्नौ राजन्दुद्रुवतुर्द्रुतम्।।
विहाय वित्तं प्रचुरमभीतौ भीरुभीतवत्।
पद्भ्यां पलाशाभ्यां चेलतुर्बहुयोजनम्।।

Shukdeva says: "O Parikshit! On seeing the lightning speed at which the enemy army was approaching, Krishna and Balarama quickly fled. Even though they were fearless, they feigned fear and leaving all their wealth behind, they kept running on foot for several *yojana.*[20]"

(Bhagavat Purana, Skandha–10, Chapter–52, Shloka–7-8)

The Vishnu Purana narrates this incident very briefly, but in a different manner:

---

20. 1 yojana is approximately 12 km

साम चोपप्रदानं च तथा भेदं च दर्शयन्।
करोति दण्डपातं च क्वचिदेव पलायनम्।।

Sage Parashar said: "At times, they employed the strategy of consensus, gratification, causing divisions among their enemies, or punishment; and at other times, they themselves fled from the scene."

(Vishnu Purana, Part–5, Chapter–22, Shloka–17)

87. Were Pradyumna and Satyaki considered to be the reason behind the destruction of the Yadavas?

This is what the Mahabharata, the text that provides the most authentic information on the life of Krishna, states about this assertion:

यो तावर्जुनशिष्यौ ते प्रियौ बहुमतौ सदा।
तयोरपनयात्पार्थ वृष्णयो निधनं गताः।।

Vasudeva said: "Arjuna! It was only because of those two (Pradyumna and Satyaki), who were your favourite disciples and whom you respected greatly, that the descendants of the Vrishnis were annihilated."

यौ तौ वृष्णिप्रवीराणां द्वावेवातिरथौ मतौ।
प्रद्युम्नो युयुधानश्च कथयन् कत्थसे च यौ।।

"O Arjuna! The two among the prominent heroes of the Vrishni clan, who were considered extremely valiant, and the ones whose praises you sang after deliberately mentioning them in conversations."

तौ सदा कुरुशार्दूल कृष्णस्य प्रियभाजनौ।
तावुभौ वृष्णिनाशस्य मुखमास्तां धनंजय।।

"O Dhananjaya, Supreme among the Kurus! Those who were dear to both you and Krishna, are the very persons who have now caused the annihilation of the Vrishni clan."

*(Mahabharata, Mausala Parva,
Chapter–6, Shloka–6-8)*

Comment: Vasudeva reveals his agony in the shlokas mentioned above. In those days, Dwarka was in such a deplorable state that all its inhabitants had become impertinent, while their sons and grandsons did not obey anyone either. Thus, when the genocide took place because of this, Vasudeva first vented his ire on those closest to him. This is the sentiment behind these shlokas; whereas the reality is that all the inhabitants of Dwarka were collectively responsible for this genocide. It was their alcoholism and depravity that had resulted in the destruction of Dwarka.

88. From where did Krishna get the conch shell 'Panchajanya'?

Krishna's famous conch shell 'Panchajanya' was actually the property of a demon of the sea, King Panchajan, whom Krishna had killed during his mission to bring back his guru's son from the demon's captivity; and it was after the demon's death that Krishna had acquired the conch:

न चाहर्षमहं देव दैत्यः पंचजनो महान्।
अन्तर्जलचरः कृष्ण शंखरूपधरोऽसुरः॥
आस्ते ते नाहतो नूनं तच्छ्रुत्वा सत्वरं प्रभुः।
जलमाविश्य तं हत्वा नापश्यदुदरेऽर्भकम्॥
तदंगप्रभवं शंखमादाय रथमागमत्।

The sea, in a human form, said: "O Krishna! I have not taken that child. Far into the sea, a formidable Asura named Panchajan, from the Daitya clan, lives in the form of a conch shell. Surely, he alone must have stolen that child." Hearing this, Krishna went far into the sea and killed the Asura. Then, Krishna took his conch and returned in his chariot.

(Bhagavat Purana, Skandha–10, Chapter–46, Shloka–40-42)

स तु पंचजनं हत्वा शंखे लेभे जनार्दनः।
यस्तु देवमनुष्येषु पांचजन्य इति श्रुतः॥

Vaishampayan said: "After killing Panchajan, Shri Krishna took a conch, which is famous among the gods and humans as the 'Panchajanya'."

(Harivansha Purana, Vishnu Parva, Chapter–33, Shloka–17)

There is no description of this incident in the Mahabharata. However, the epic certainly mentions several instances of Krishna blowing on the Panchajanya conch.

89. What happened to Krishna's family after his death?

After the unfortunate incident of Yadavasthali, Vasudeva, who had given up food several days earlier, died the next day after Arjuna's arrival in Dwarka. Then, Arjuna had his cremation performed by Vajra, after which he organised the mass cremation of all the other Yadavas, who had lost their lives in Prabhasa:

यथाप्रधानतश्चैव चक्रे सर्वास्तथा क्रियाः।
ये हता ब्रह्मशापेन मुसलैरेरकोद्भवैः॥

Vaishampayan said: "Then, Arjuna went to the place where that horrific genocide had taken place. There, in order of their age, he cremated the Yadavas, killed by the pounders that were created out of *eraka* grass due to Lord Brahma's curse."

(Mahabharata, Mausala Parva, Chapter–7, Shloka–30)

ततःशरीरे रामस्य वासुदेवस्य चोभयोः।
अन्वीक्ष्य दाहयामास पुरुषैराप्तकारिभिः॥
स तेषां विधिवत्कृत्वा प्रेतकार्याणि पाण्डवः।
सप्तमे दिवसे प्रायाद्रथमारुह्य सत्वरः॥

Vaishampayan continued: "Then, after getting his trusted men to locate the bodies of Balarama and Krishna, Arjuna had them cremated too. Thereafter, he set forth from Dwarka on the seventh day."

(Mahabharata, Mausala Parva, Chapter–7, Shloka–32-33)

अश्वयुक्तै रथैश्चापि... X... समन्ताज्जनमेजय॥

Vaishampayan further said: "The women of the valorous warriors of the Vrishni clan, wailing and mourning on the way, left with him on chariots pulled by horses, oxen, donkeys, camels and so on. Following Arjuna's instructions, the servants, warriors and soldiers of the Andhaks and the Vrishnis, created a protective circle around all the elders, women and children as they walked. Constituting a few thousands, they were all following Krishna's great grandson Vajra. Even as they continued to evacuate the land of Dwarka, the sea began submerging it behind them. On seeing this, they spontaneously exclaimed, 'Strange are the ways of Destiny!' Well, Arjuna took all those people along, camping at various places from time to time; travelling in this manner, he reached Panchanad (Punjab) and made a halt after identifying an appropriate clearing. However, when a band of thieves saw that Arjuna was the sole protector of the numerous women and enormous wealth that was being carried by them, they were overcome by greed. They deliberated among themselves, 'Brothers, look! This Arjuna, who is all alone, and these demoralised soldiers, are passing through our area with this orphaned community, so they should be attacked.' And the next moment, thousands of thieves attacked Arjuna's convoy, sneaking up behind them. Then, Arjuna rushed to the end of the caravan with servants and soldiers in tow, and challenging the thieves, he tried to launch a counter-attack on them. But alas, he was helpless when confronted with those thieves. Then, right before his eyes, those bandits started dragging and taking those beautiful women away. Some women, fearing that the bandits would touch them, quietly acquiesced and went along. Janamejaya! Thus, Arjuna was left gaping, while those lowly bandits abducted all the beautiful women of the Andhak and Vrishni clans, including those from Krishna's family."

(Mahabharata - Gita Press Edition - Mausala Parva, Chapter–7, Shloka–34-63)

एवं कलत्रमानीय वृष्णिनां हृतशेषितम्।
अन्यवेशयत कौरव्यस्तत्र तत्र धनंजयः॥

"And finally, Arjuna, the scion of the Kurus, helped the few women, who had been saved from being abducted, in settling down at various places."

(Mahabharata, Mausala Parva, Chapter–7, Shloka–68)

हार्दिक्यतनयं पार्थो नगरे... X...संविभज्यैनान् वज्रे पर्यददज्जयः॥

"He helped the son of Kritvarma and the women of Bhojraj's family settle down in the city of Martikavat, while he had all the elderly people, children and the remaining women who had lost their brave ones settle down in Indraprastha. Satyaki's son was put in charge of the region around the banks of River Saraswati, and some elderly people and women were also sent to stay with him. Then, Arjuna appointed Vajra as the king of Indraprastha. In spite of Vajra's insistence that they should not go, the women of Akrura's family left for the forest to perform penance. Krishna's wives Rukmini, Bhadra and Jambavati immolated themselves, while the rest of his wives, including Satyabhama, left for the forest to perform penance. In this manner, all the people of Dwarka who had arrived with Arjuna were appropriately segregated and handed over to Vajra."

(Mahabharata, Mausala Parva, Chapter–7, Shloka–69-75)

The Bhagavat Purana does not mention anything about the abduction of women by the bandits, and this entire incident has been mentioned in a single shloka:

स्त्रीबालवृद्धानादाय हतशेषान् धनञ्जयः।
इंद्रप्रस्थं समावेश्य वज्रं तत्राभ्यषेचयत्॥

Shukdeva says: "Dear Parikshit! After the post-cremation rituals, Arjuna returned to Indraprastha with the surviving women, children and elderly men, and there he made everyone settle down in a proper manner and crowned Vajra, the son of Aniruddha, as the king."

(Bhagavat Purana, Skandha–11, Chapter–31, Shloka–25)

In Chapter–38, Part–5 of the Vishnu Purana, the description of this event is similar to that in the Mahabharata, except for a slight difference. The difference is that according to this Purana, all the wives of Krishna, Balarama, Ugrasen and Vasudeva had immolated themselves with their husbands.

The Garga Samhita or Brahmavaivarta Purana do not mention this event at all, but on the basis of all the evidence found in the texts, it can be seen that after Krishna's demise, his family was more or less in a dismal state.

90. In the battlefield of Kurukshetra, did Krishna ignore the rules and resort to skulduggery?

Here are Krishna's actions in the battlefield of Kurukshetra which are termed as his skulduggery:

i) It is often said that it was Krishna who urged the Pandavas to ask Grandsire Bhishma himself how he could be killed. But in the Mahabharata, the truth is different:

समयस्तु कृतः कश्चिन्मम भीष्मेण संयुगे।
मन्त्रयिष्ये तवार्थाय न तु योत्स्ये कथंचन॥
दुर्योधनार्थं योत्स्यामि सत्यमेतदिति प्रभो।
स हि राज्यस्य मे दाता मन्त्रस्यैव च माधव॥
तस्माद्देवव्रतं भूयो वधोपायार्थमात्मनः।
भवता सहिताः सर्वे प्रयाम मधुसूदन॥
तद्वयं सहिता गत्वा भीष्ममाशु नरोत्तमम्।
रुचिते तव पृच्छामि मन्त्रं वार्ष्णेय माचिरम्॥
स वक्ष्यति हितं वाक्यं सत्यमस्माज्जनार्दन।
यथा च वक्ष्यते कृष्ण तथा कर्तास्मि संयुगे॥

Yudhishthira said: "O Krishna! I have an agreement with Bhishma. He promised me and said, 'I can give you advice that will be in your favour, but I will not fight on your behalf in any manner. I will fight for Duryodhana only.' Lord! This is true. Therefore, O Madhav! Bhishma will grant me both the kingdom and the beneficial advice. So, O Madhusudan! Why don't all of us, along with you, go and ask Grandsire Bhishma himself how he could be killed? O Janardhana! If we ask him, he will give us advice that is truthful and beneficial. In this war, I will do exactly what he tells me to."

(Mahabharata, Bhishma Parva,
Chapter–107, Shloka–45-49)

Comment: It is completely clear from the shlokas above that Krishna had not suggested the idea of asking Bhishma himself how he could be killed. It was Yudhishthira who had devised this plan.

ii) The allegation that in order to have Narakasura's son, Bhagadutta killed during the Mahabharata war, Krishna had revealed confidential details about him to Arjuna, and had got him killed by deceit:

ततो गाण्डीवधन्वानमभ्यभाषत केशवः।
अयं महत्तरः पार्थ पलितेन समावृतः।।
वलीसंछन्ननयनः शूरः परमदुर्जयः।
अक्ष्णोरुन्मीलनार्थाय बद्धपट्टो ह्यसौ नृपः।।
देववाक्यात्प्रचिच्छेद शरेण भृशमर्जुनः।
छिन्नमात्रेंऽशुके तस्मिन्रुद्धनेत्रो बभूव सः।।
तमोमयं जगन्मेने भगदत्तः प्रतापवान्।
ततश्चन्द्रार्धबिम्बेन बाणेन नतपर्वणा।।
बिभेद हृदयं राज्ञो भगदत्तस्य पाण्डवः।
स भिन्नहृदयो राजा भगदत्तः किरीटिना।।

Then, Krishna said to Arjuna who wielded the bow: "O Son of Kunti! This Bhagadutta is quite old, all his hair has turned grey, and his eyes mostly remain closed, because the eyelids keep drooping due to the wrinkles in his forehead and other places. He is brave and extremely formidable. To keep his eyes open, this king has strapped his eyelids to his forehead with a cloth." The moment Krishna said this, Arjuna fired arrows to tear off the piece of cloth tied to the king's eyelids, due to which Bhagadatta could not keep his eyes open anymore. And since he could no longer see anything, Arjuna immediately pierced his heart with a crescent moon arrow.

(Mahabharata, Drona Parva, Chapter–29, Shloka–44-48)

Comment: In a battlefield, the responsibility of the charioteer is multidimensional. He not only has to obey the instructions of the one who is commanding the chariot, but he also has to protect, serve and guide him. This is why the charioteers of great warriors were kings themselves, who were also valiant warriors in addition to being well versed in war strategy. For instance, in the same battle of Mahabharata, while Krishna, the king of Dwarka, was the charioteer of Arjuna; Shalya, the king of Madra, was the charioteer of Karna. Similarly, there were several kings who had become the charioteers of other great warriors in that war. Therefore, if Krishna had given Arjuna any information or advice related to the war, then he had merely performed his duties; there was no trace of deceit in it.

91. Why did Krishna rush to kill Grandsire Bhishma?

According to the Mahabharata, there were two occasions in the battle of Kurukshetra when Krishna felt agitated enough to kill Grandsire Bhishma, even if it meant that he had to break his pledge to not wield weapons in the war.

On the third day of the war:

पार्थस्य दृष्टवा मृदुयुद्धतां च।
भीष्मं च संख्ये समुदीर्यमाणम्।।

Sanjaya said: "When Krishna saw that Arjuna was not being aggressive enough while fighting Grandsire Bhishma, while the latter was fighting with increasing intensity in this battle."

(Mahabharata, Bhishma Parva, Chapter–59, Shloka–82)

तमाद्रवंतं प्रगृहीतचक्रं दृष्ट्वा देवं शान्तनवस्तदानीम्।
असम्भ्रमं तद् विचकर्ष दोर्भ्यां महाधनुर्गाण्डिवतुल्यघोषम्।।

Sanjaya said: "O King! Seeing Krishna rush towards him with the Sudarshan discus, Bhishma, the son of Shantanu, without feeling any fear or panic at that time, and with both hands, began pulling his bow, which had a deep sound similar to that of a Gandeeva bow."

(Mahabharata, Bhishma Parva, Chapter–59, Shloka–95)

On the ninth day of the war:

वासुदेवस्तु संप्रेक्ष्य पार्थस्य मृदुयुद्धताम्।
भीष्मं च शरवर्षाणि सृजन्तमनिशं युधि॥

Sanjaya said: "Vasudeva Krishna saw that Arjuna was not fighting wholeheartedly and was being lenient towards Grandsire Bhishma. Whereas Bhishma was standing in the centre of the army and was constantly showering arrows, blazing like the sun."

(Mahabharata, Bhishma Parva, Chapter–106, Shloka–53)

उत्सृज्य रजतप्रख्यान्हयान्पार्थस्य मारिष।
वासुदेवस्ततो योगी प्रचस्कन्द महारथात्॥
अभिदुद्राव भीष्मं स भुजप्रहरणो बली।
प्रतोदपाणिस्तेजस्वी सिंहवद्विनदन्मुहुः॥

Sanjaya said: "When Krishna could not bear it, he released (the reins of) the silver-white horses of Arjuna, jumped from that huge chariot, and using his arms alone as weapons, raised the whip, and roaring repeatedly, rushed towards Grandsire Bhishma with great speed."

(Mahabharata, Bhishma Parva, Chapter–106, Shloka–56-57)

Comment: On the whole, it can be said that on several occasions, Krishna had not only broken his promise, but had also violated the rules of war.

92. Apart from Radha and Kubja, did any other woman come close to Krishna?

In the Puranas, Samhitas and the Mahabharata, there is no mention of any woman in Krishna's life except Radha, Kubja and his wives. In fact, even in a voluminous epic such as the Mahabharata, in which Shishupala condemns Krishna for the pettiest of things pertaining to his life, he does not name Radha or Kubja even once. Out of the Puranas that were written later, the Harivansha Purana, which is said to be a supplementary of the Mahabharata, mentions Kubja but not Radha. The same is the case with the Bhagavat Purana, which revolutionised Krishna's worship. Even this text mentions Kubja but not Radha. Therefore, in a nutshell, the answer to this question is that based on all the texts available so far, one can conclude that no woman—other than Radha, Kubja and his wives—had come into Krishna's life.

93. Did Krishna ever have to display his marksmanship like Arjuna?

Yes, Krishna had to display his marksmanship on one occasion. Lakshmana, one of the eight principal queens of Krishna, tells Draupadi how she was married to Krishna:

यथा स्वयंवरे राज्ञि... X ...सूर्ये चाभिजिति स्थिते॥

Lakshmana said: "Queen Draupadi! Just as your father had set a fish as the target for precision shooting in your *swayamvar*, my father had done the same. The difference being, the fish in our competition was covered from outside, and its reflection could be seen only in the water below. With the desire to marry me, kings from various kingdoms wielded the bow and arrow and made their attempts, but all in vain. O Queen! Among those kings, your husband, Arjuna with his Gandeeva bow, Karna, Jarasandha, the king of Ambasth, Bhima, Duryodhana and others were also present. Your husband, Arjuna could locate the fish in the water, but his arrow missed the fish by a whisker. O Queen! Thus, when the pride of all those noteworthy, arrogant people was shattered, Shri Krishna rose from his seat, effortlessly strung the bow, saw the reflection of the fish in the water at first glance, and shot it down. It was the second *pahar*[21] of the day, during the course of the Abhijit *muhurta.*"

(Bhagavat Purana, Skandha–10,
Chapter–83, Shloka–19-26)

Comment: From the above shlokas, it is evident that Krishna not only knew archery but was also an adept at it. He was no less proficient than his famed, contemporary archers.

94. Which ornaments did Krishna love to wear?

Neither the Mahabharata nor the Puranas mention Krishna's fondness for a particular ornament or attire. He was as fond of adornments made from fruits, flowers and peacock feathers in Gokul, as he was of the gold jewellery from Dwarka's treasury. None of the texts mention that Krishna unfailingly wore a particular ornament. Besides, the description of Krishna's jewellery in the ancient texts is very limited; while the Puranas, composed in the medieval period, and the compositions of his poet-devotees begin by depicting Krishna as laden with ornaments.

21. A unit of time equalling three hours

Therefore, it is a waste of time to conduct a research on Krishna's favourite ornaments. And this shows that most of the popular notions about Krishna are baseless, which is indeed unfortunate.

95. Did Krishna run a business in Mathura?

The Harivansha Purana mentions a shloka in which Krishna, while fleeing towards the Gomanta Hill, apprises Sage Parshurama of the reason for his escape:

पितरं तस्य तत्रैव स्थापयित्वा जनेश्वरम्।
स्वमेव कर्म चारब्धौ गवां व्यापारकारकौ।।

"After killing Kansa, I made his father ascend the throne. Then, we brothers, whose occupation has always been related to cattle-rearing, started our business in Mathura itself."

(Harivansha Purana, Vishnu Parva, Chapter–39, Shloka–39)

Such evidence which is recorded at various points in the ancient texts, but is neglected for centuries, is actually extremely useful, because it is from this that we can obtain a true picture of the life of great men. For instance, if we consider the shloka given above, then it comes to light that Krishna and Balarama used to earn a living through their business in Mathura.

96. Did Krishna blindly favour the Pandavas?

Gauging the manner in which Krishna supported the Pandavas throughout his life, this is what people suspect. Apart from this, there are also a couple of shlokas in the Mahabharata, based on which such people do not miss the opportunity to deride Krishna:

यः शत्रुः पाण्डुपुत्राणां मच्छत्रुः स न संशयः।
मदर्था भवदर्था ये ये मदीयास्तवैव ते।।

Krishna said: "He who is an enemy of the Pandavas is my enemy too; there is no doubt about it. Your friends are my own and my friends are your own."

तव भ्राता मम सखा सम्बन्धी शिष्य एव च।
मांसान्युत्कृत्य दास्यामि फल्गुनार्थे महीपते।।

Krishna said: "O King Yudhishthira! Your brother Arjuna is my friend, relative and disciple too, so for Arjuna, I will even sever my flesh."

एष चापि नरव्याघ्रो मत्कृते जीवितं त्यजेत्।
एष नः समयस्तात तारयेम परस्परम्।।

Furthermore, Krishna said: "Arjuna, who is like a lion, and supreme among men, can also sacrifice his life for me. Taat (Elder one)! We have resolved that we will help each other overcome any crisis."

स मां नियुंक्ष्व राजेन्द्र यावत्सज्जो भवाम्यहम्।
प्रतिज्ञातमुपप्लाव्ये यत्तत्पार्थेन पूर्वतः।।
पातयिष्यामि गांगेयमित्युलूकस्य संनिधौ।
परिरक्ष्यमिदं तावद्वचः पार्थस्य धीमतः।।

Krishna said: "Rajendra! Assign me work in the war; I will be your warrior. Before the commencement of the war, in the presence of everyone in the town of Upalavya, Arjuna had promised that he would kill Grandsire Bhishma, the son of Ganga. It is necessary for me to fulfil that promise made by the intelligent Partha (Arjuna)."

अनुज्ञातेन पार्थेन मया कार्यं न संशयः।

Krishna said: "It is my duty to ensure that Arjuna's promise is fulfilled; there is no doubt about that."

(Mahabharata, Bhishma Parva, Chapter–107, Shloka–32-37)

There are many other similar incidents in the Mahabharata and the Puranas, wherein Krishna appears to be the protector, supporter and advocate of the Pandavas. However, this illusion of readers is dispelled after deliberating upon the entire Mahabharata without the shadow of prejudice. The question here is really about wisdom, and the depth of Krishna's wisdom cannot be fathomed without elevating oneself to his level. Therefore, people would be better off if they avoided such questions, because it is impossible for supreme men such as Krishna to unnecessarily favour someone.

97. According to the TV series 'Mahabharata', apart from Arjuna, Krishna alone could break the Chakravyuha formation. Is it true?

Well, that could be the view of the makers of the TV series, but according to the Mahabharata, there were four people who were capable of penetrating the Chakravyuha that Dronacharya had devised:

त्वं वाऽर्जुनो वा कृष्णो वा भिन्द्यात्प्रद्युम्न एव वा।
चक्रव्यूहं महाबाहो पञ्चमो नोपपद्यते।।

Yudhishthira said to Abhimanyu: "O, One with Mighty Arms! It is only you, Arjuna, Krishna and Pradyumna who can penetrate the Chakravyuha. There is no fifth warrior who is capable of accomplishing this task."

(Mahabharata, Drona Parva, Chapter–35, Shloka–15)

These are the words of Yudhishthira, the very person whose truthfulness has been extolled throughout the Mahabharata, so the claim made by the makers of the TV series only indicates their ignorance. The correct answer to this question is that according to the Mahabharata, only four people were capable of penetrating the Chakravyuha.

98. How many sons did Krishna's brother Balarama have?

According to the Mahabharata and all the Puranas, Balarama had only two sons: Nishath and Ulmook.

(Bhagavat Purana, Skandha–11, Chapter–30, Shloka–17)

99. Was Balarama involved in the war of Mahabharata?

No, Balarama had distanced himself from the Mahabharata war. His biggest reason for shunning the war was domestic and internal conflict. Actually, in the matter of supporting the Kauravas and the Pandavas, Krishna's family was split into two factions, which had become evident on many occasions. Several members of Krishna's family across generations had been relatives of many members of the royal dynasty of Hastinapur. But as Krishna was more inclined towards the Pandavas for a host of reasons, Balarama had spontaneously become inclined towards Duryodhana. The moment Duryodhana realised this, the astute politician that he was, he had begun serving Balarama with greater dedication, showing great deference to him. All these facts have already been stated in this book as answers to various questions, so they need not be repeated. Thus, coming straight to the present question, the Mahabharata states why Balarama did not participate in the war:

उभौ शिष्यौ हि मे वीरौ गदायुद्धविशारदौ।
तुल्यस्नेहोऽस्म्यतो भीमे तथा दुर्योधने नृपे।।

Balarama said: "Both Bhimsen and Duryodhana are my disciples and are adepts at mace-fighting; therefore, I have the same affection for both of them."

(Mahabharata, Udyoga Parva, Chapter–157, Shloka–33)

ध्रुवो जयः पाण्डवानामिति मे निश्चिता मतिः।
तथा ह्यभिनिवेशोऽयं वासुदेवस्य भारत॥

He continued: "I am positive that the Pandavas will win this war. Because O Bharata! Shri Krishna has taken a solemn vow to ensure this."

(Mahabharata, Udyoga Parva, Chapter–157, Shloka–31)

तस्माद् याम्यामि तीर्थानि सरस्वत्या निषेवितुम्।
न हि शक्ष्यामि कौरव्यान् नश्यमानानुपेक्षितुम्॥

He also said: "Since I will not be able to ignore the condition of the Kauravas when they are annihilated, I will head to the pilgrimage centres on the banks of River Saraswati and perform worship."

(Mahabharata, Udyoga Parva, Chapter–157, Shloka–34)

It was because of these reasons that Balarama had avoided participating in the Epic War. Had he fought, he would have done so along with Dwarka's army, which Duryodhana had acquired. And this would have led to his direct confrontation with Krishna. But he loved Krishna so much that he was always ready to dispatch every detractor of Krishna to hell! These are the reasons why he deemed it wise to refrain from participating in the war.

100. Is it true that at the time of Shishupala's birth, Krishna had promised his mother that he would forgive his ninety-nine transgressions and slay him on the hundredth one?

According to the Mahabharata, at the time of Shishupala's birth, he had four hands and three eyes, and his parents were terrified on seeing this. They doubted whether this strange child would even survive! Now, worried as they were along with the entire royal family, they were in for a greater shock when they heard a celestial prophecy that the slayer of this child had already been born, and apart from him, no one else would be able to kill this child. The parents were somewhat relieved, but they also became curious to know who that slayer was. Just then, they heard another celestial prophecy:

अन्तर्भूतं ततो भूतमुवाचेदं पुनर्वचः।
यस्योत्संगे गृहीतस्य भुजावभ्यधिकावुभौ॥
पतिष्यतः क्षितितले पंचशीर्षाविवोरगौ।
तृतीयमेतद्बालस्य ललाटस्थं तु लोचनम्॥
निमज्जिष्यति यं दृष्ट्वा सोऽस्य मृत्युर्भविष्यति।

"The one in whose lap his two extra hands with ten fingers will instantly fall off, and in whose lap the third eye on his forehead will disappear into the forehead, will be his slayer."

(Mahabharata, Sabha Parva, Chapter–43, Shloka–9-11)

Then, people started streaming in from far and wide to behold this strange child, and if this was not enough, kings and emperors also arrived to see him, at the invitation of King Damghosh. The king and his wife cleverly put the child in the lap of each king, but the signs they were looking for were nowhere in sight.

एतदेव तु संश्रुत्य द्वारवत्यां महाबलौ॥
ततश्चेदिपुरं प्राप्तौ संकर्षणजनार्दनौ।
यादवौ यादवीं द्रष्टुं स्वसारं तौ पितुस्तदा॥

"Then, when this news reached Dwarka, both Krishna and Balarama arrived to see that child."

(Mahabharata, Sabha Parva, Chapter–43, Shloka–14-15)

Comment: One must note here that when Shishupala had participated in Rukmini's *swayamvar* as a contender for Rukmini's hand in marriage, even before the establishment of Dwarka, how could he possibly be born after Dwarka was built? The details about this mentioned in the significant text, Harivansha Purana—which is called a supplementary of the Mahabharata and whose 16,000 shlokas are considered as part of the Mahabharata—are contrary to this story. According to the Harivansha Purana, Rukmini's *swayamvar* was held at a time when Dwarka was not even discussed, and Rukmini's brother Rukmi was determined to marry her to Shishupala. In this Purana, this entire episode is narrated in great detail in five chapters. Krishna had barged into Rukmini's *swayamvar* to protest against the disregard of Mathura, which was a royal transgression, and it was due to Krishna's painstaking efforts that the *swayamvar* was annulled. All these facts are available in Chapters 47–51 of the Vishnu Parva in the Harivansha Purana. Well, keeping this in mind, read the story ahead in the Mahabharata:

न्यस्तमात्रस्य तस्यांके भुजावभ्यधिकावुभौ।
पेततुस्तच्च नयनं न्यमज्जत ललाटजम्।।
तद्दृष्ट्वा व्यथिता त्रस्ता वरं कृष्णमयाचत।
ददस्व मे वरं कृष्ण भयार्ताया महाभुज।।
त्वं ह्यार्तानां समोशासो भीतानामभयप्रदः।
एवमुक्तस्ततः कृष्णः सोऽब्रवीद्यदुनन्दनः।।
मा भैस्त्वं देवि धर्मज्ञे न मत्तोऽस्ति भयं तव।
ददामि कं वरं किं च करवाणि पितृष्वसः।।
शक्यं वा यदि वाऽशक्यं करिष्याणि वचस्तव।
एवमुक्ता ततः कृष्णमब्रवीद्यदुनन्दनम्।।
शिशुपालस्यापराधान्क्षमेथास्त्वं महाबल।
मत्कृते यदुशार्दूल विद्ध्येनं मे वरं प्रभो।।
कृष्ण उवाच।
अपराधशतं क्षाम्यं मया ह्यस्य पितृष्वसः।
पुत्रस्य ते वधार्हस्य मा त्वं शोके मनः कृथाः।।

Grandsire Bhishma said: "Then, Shishupala's mother, Shrutashrava put her strange son straight into Krishna's lap. The moment he was placed in Krishna's lap, the child's extra hands fell off and the third eye disappeared into the forehead. On seeing this, the child's mother was terrified, and she started asking Krishna for a boon. She said, 'Krishna! I am distraught with fear, so please grant me a boon for this child's life.' Krishna said, 'Aunt! There is no need to be afraid of me. Tell me, what boon should I grant you?' Shrutashrava said, 'O mighty Krishna, the pride of the Yadavas! You must forgive all the transgressions of this child for the sake of your aunt.' Then, Krishna said, 'Aunt! Even if this son of yours deserves to be killed by me on account of his faults, I will forgive a hundred of his transgressions.'"

(Mahabharata, Sabha Parva, Chapter–43, Shloka–18-24)

Comment: Now, no one knows whether all of this has been said to justify Shishupala's slaying by Krishna or for some other reason. Actually, so much has been added to the Mahabharata later on that one cannot even find the threads of several stories. Every detail about Shishupala and Krishna that is available in the texts has been laid out here. So, it is up to your prudence to decide what is true.

101. Why was Krishna upset with Karna?

In the battlefield of Kurukshetra, where Krishna listed every single misdeed of Karna, one can get a glimpse of the clear-cut reasons why Krishna was upset with him. When Karna's chariot was stuck in the mud in the battlefield and he alighted from the chariot to pry it out, Krishna ordered Arjuna to continue shooting arrows at him. At this, Karna started ranting against Arjuna, reminding him of ethics and righteousness.

प्रकीर्णकेशे विमुखे ब्राह्मणेऽथ कृतांजलौ।
शरणागते न्यस्तशस्त्रे याचमाने तथाऽर्जुन।।
अबाणे भ्रष्टकवचे भ्रष्टभग्नायुधे तथा।
न विमुंचन्ति शस्त्राणि शूराः साधुव्रते स्थिताः।।
त्वं च शूरतमो लोके साधुवृत्तश्च पाण्डव।
अभिज्ञो युद्धधर्माणां तस्मात्क्षममुहूर्तकम्।।
दिव्यास्त्रविदमेयात्मा कार्तवीर्यसमो युधि।

Karna said: "Arjuna! The one who stands with his hair untied, has beaten a retreat from battle, is a Brahmin, has surrendered to you with folded hands, has laid down his arms, is begging for his life, whose arrows, armour and other weapons have been destroyed... such a man is never attacked with weapons by valiant warriors who follow best practices. O Scion of Pandu! You are known across the world as a great warrior and a virtuous person. You are well versed with the ethics of war and have studied the Vedanta too. You possess the knowledge of divine weapons, and are endowed with a strong will power, and are as valorous as *Kartavirya* Arjuna."

(Mahabharata, Karna Parva, Chapter–90, Gita Press, Shloka–111-114)

On hearing Karna sermonise on ethics and righteousness, Krishna was enraged and he began listing every single one of his misdeeds:

संजय उवाच

अथाब्रवीद्वासुदेवो... **X** *...धर्माभिगुप्तैः सततं नृसिंहैः।।*

Sanjaya said: "O King! Then, sitting in the chariot, Shri Krishna said, 'O Son of Radha! How convenient it is that, standing here in this battlefield, you are now preaching about righteousness. It is often seen that when ignoble people fall into trouble, they condemn their destiny, but not their misdeeds.

• Karna! When you, Duryodhana, Dushasana and Shakuni, the son of Subal, had ordered a menstruating Draupadi, who was then clad in a single garment, to come to the royal court, did you not think of righteousness and ethics?

• Where were your ethics when Shakuni, in the assembly of Kauravas, deliberately cheated and defeated King Yudhishthira, who had no knowledge of the game of dice?

• Karna! Where were your ethics when you did not return the Pandavas' kingdom to them, even after the thirteenth year of exile?

• Where were your ethics when King Duryodhana, paying heed to your advice, fed poisoned food to Bhimsen and had him bitten by snakes?

• Where were your ethics when you had tried to burn the Pandavas alive, while they were sleeping in the house of lac in Varanavatnagar?

• Karna! Where were your ethics when, in a packed assembly, you derided a menstruating Draupadi, who was in the clutches of Dushasana?

• O Son of Radha! Where were your ethics when, from close quarters, you were ogling at Draupadi who was being tormented by the ignoble Kauravas?

• Do you remember what you had said to Draupadi? Weren't you the one who had said, 'O Krishnaa (Draupadi)! The Pandavas have now been destroyed; they have fallen into hell forever. So, choose another husband!' Where were your ethics while making such statements and ogling at the beautiful Draupadi with your eyes wide open?

• Karna! Where were your ethics when, fuelled by your greed for the kingdom and following Shakuni's advice, you invited the Pandavas for a game of gambling once again?

• Where were your ethics when, joining hands with many warriors, you killed the innocent child, Abhimanyu, in battle?

If your ethics were not present on those occasions, what is the use of you ranting about ethics and righteousness in the battlefield today? Charioteer! No matter how many ethical deeds you perform here, you cannot be spared as long as you are alive.

Just as King Nala had reclaimed his lost kingdom on the strength of his valour, the greedless Pandavas will also regain their kingdom on the strength of their muscle power. The ethics of the Pandavas protect them at all times, so do not preach ethics to them. Dhritarashtra's sons will surely perish!'"

(Mahabharata, Karna Parva, Chapter–91 Gita Press, Shloka–1-14)

Comment: Krishna had praised Karna's bravery, philanthropy and many other qualities on several occasions. But Karna's active participation in Draupadi's humiliation and the fact that he not only gave his consent to Duryodhana's misdeeds but also wholeheartedly supported them, were some of his deeds which had obliterated all his virtues. Thus, it was inevitable for Krishna to become enraged at Karna, who preached a lot but possessed no wisdom.

102. Why does Barbareek's name crop up in discussions pertaining to the Mahabharata war?

Actually, the story of Barbareek is a folklore which was added later to the Skanda Purana. This story appears in Chapters 59–66 in the Kumarika Khanda under the Maheshwar Khanda of the Skanda Purana. This Purana gives an elaborate account of Ghatotkachha's marriage to a young girl named Maurvi, and a son born to them, named Barbareek. On reading the story that spans eight lengthy chapters, any reader will soon realise that this entire tale is an embellishment, a mere fabrication. Barbareek has been discussed in this particular Purana only; no mention of him is found in any other Purana or the Mahabharata. Secondly, the discourse on non-violence in the middle of these eight chapters by a Digambara Jain sage in Chapter 61 also proves that this story has been written after Jainism gained popularity in India. And as Barbareek's name is not mentioned in any other text, it is absolutely certain that just like the numerous stories of Krishna's miracles, this story has also been added later on, and has no connection whatsoever with reality.

103. What was Krishna's opinion about Ashwathama when he tried to destroy Uttara's womb by using the *Brahmastra*?

In the Bhagavat Purana and the Mahabharata, there is a difference in the interpretation of this incident, so it is necessary to examine the contents of both the texts, one by one. So, let us first take a look at the Bhagavat Purana.

When Ashwathama killed Draupadi's sons as well as the soldiers who were asleep, Arjuna and Krishna set out to hunt him down. On locating him, they engaged in a long and arduous duel with him, after which Arjuna subjugated him, tied him up and led him towards his camp. Then, Krishna said to Arjuna:

मैनं पार्थार्हसि त्रातुं ब्रह्मबंधुमिमं जहि।
यो असौ अनागसः सुप्तान् अवधीन्निशि बालकान्।।
मत्तं प्रमत्तमुन्मत्तं सुप्तं बालं स्त्रियं जडम्।
प्रपन्नं विरथं भीतं न रिपुं हन्ति धर्मवित्।।
स्वप्राणान्यः परप्राणैः प्रपुष्णात्यघृणः खलः।
तद् वधस्तस्य हि श्रेयो यद् दोषाद्यात्यधः पुमान्।।
प्रतिश्रुतं च भवता पांचाल्यै शृण्वतो मम।
आहरिष्ये शिरस्तस्य यस्ते मानिनि पुत्रहा।।
तदसौ वध्यतां पाप आततायात्मबंधुहा।
भर्तुश्च विप्रियं वीर कृतवान् कुलपांसनः।।
सूत उवाच।
एवं परीक्षता धर्मं पार्थः कृष्णेन चोदितः।
नैच्छद् हन्तुं गुरुसुतं यद्यप्यात्महनं महान्।।

Krishna said: "Arjuna! It is not right to spare this ignoble Brahmin, so just kill him. He has murdered children who were asleep at night! Righteous people never kill children, women, or those who are unmindful, sleeping, inebriated, mentally retarded, ignorant, refugees, those without a chariot; and they never kill even a terrified enemy. But when a person nurtures his own life by killing others, then slaying him is actually in his best interest. Arjuna! You have also made a promise to Draupadi, so kill this *kulangar.*[22] Suta says: *"Actually, Shri Krishna gave such advice to test Arjuna's righteousness, but Arjuna was large-hearted. Although Ashwathama had killed his sons, Arjuna could not bring himself to kill the son of his guru."*

(Bhagavat Purana, Skandha–1, Chapter–7, Shloka–35-40)

After reading the italicised words in the context above, it becomes clear how much Bhagavat Purana upholds and nurtures the primacy of Brahmins. Furthermore, let us see what Draupadi says in this Purana:

22. The one who is a curse to his own clan

उवाच चासहन्त्यस्य बंधनानयनं सती।
मुच्यतां मुच्यतां एष ब्राह्मणो नितरां गुरुः॥

Suta says: "Draupadi could not bear to see the guru's son tied up and brought to the camp in this manner. So, she said, 'Release him, release him! He is a Brahmin and for us, he is extremely honourable.'"

(Bhagavat Purana, Skandha–1, Chapter–7, Shloka–43)

It is clear from this evidence that depicting Krishna's straightforward and unambiguous anger as a test for Arjuna, and belittling even the pain of a mother, is a devious conspiracy to nurture the idea of Brahmanism. Therefore, it is also necessary to peruse the details of this incident as given in the Mahabharata, where Draupadi resolved to give up food until she saw her sons' killer being put to death:

तस्य पापकृतो द्रौणेर्न... X...पुमानस्तीह कश्चन॥

Draupadi warned all the Pandavas including Yudhishthira: "If you do not invoke your valour and kill the sinful son of Drona along with his relatives, then I will end my life by fasting right here. Listen to me carefully! If Ashwathama does not get punished for his sinful deed, then I will give up my life right here!" Saying this, she started observing a fast in Yudhishthira's presence. Then, Yudhishthira consoled her saying that since all her sons and relatives had attained martyrdom in the crusade, she should not grieve like this. "O Draupadi! That sinner has fled to the forest after killing everyone; and even if he is killed there, would you really believe it?" Then, Draupadi said that she had heard that there was a gem lodged in that sinner's forehead, which he was born with. So, if that gem was brought to her after killing him, she would believe that he had, indeed, been killed. She then told Bhima that just as Indra had killed Shambarasura, he too should fulfil her desire by killing the sinful Ashwathama.

(Mahabharata, Sauptika Parva, Chapter–11, Shloka–14-23)

Then, taking Bhima along with them, Krishna and Arjuna went to the forest, where a fight ensued, in which *Brahmastra* and celestial weapons were used. Finally, to their utter surprise, Veda Vyasa and Narada reached the place, and Ashwathama's life was traded at the price of the said gem. There is also a discussion in the shloka above about tying this gem, which was said to be inborn:

यमाबध्य भयं नास्ति शस्त्रव्याधिक्षुधाश्रयम्।
देवेभ्यो दानवेभ्यो वा नागेभ्यो वा कथंचन॥
न च रक्षोगणभयं न तस्करभयं तथा।
एवंवीर्यो मणिरयं न मे त्याज्यः कथंचन॥

"Tying it liberates a person from the fear of weapons, disease, hunger, gods, giants, snakes, demons and thieves. Such is the wonderful effect of this gem of mine! So, I shall never discard it under any circumstances."

(Mahabharata, Sauptika Parva, Chapter–14, Shloka–29-30)

Therefore, it is clear that in order to uphold Brahmanism and the Varna system, the story of this imaginary gem has been conjured in the Mahabharata. No one has questioned these writers on the point that, if Ashwathama was invincible due to the gem, then why did he need to run to the forest out of fear? Well, several stories have been created in this manner, especially in the later scriptures, and it is, indeed, difficult to make sense of anything. Therefore, it is better to focus only on those truths recorded in the scriptures that explain the deeper meaning of life, and ignore all spurious details and claims.

104. How was Krishna related to the Pandavas?

Krishna was a Yadava, while the Pandavas hailed from the Kuru dynasty, and the root of both the clans, that is, the father was the same—King Yayati. As generations progressed, the sub-divisions between the two families grew wider, and matrimonial relations also began to form within these families. Shantanu, the king of Hastinapur, had an elder brother who ruled in the Bahlik region[23] and in the texts, he is also known by the name Bahlik. Five daughters of this Bahlik's family were Krishna's stepmothers, among whom Balarama's mother, Rohini was the eldest. It was on the basis of this relationship that Vidura used to call Vasudeva his brother-in-law:

कच्चित् कुरूणां परमः सुहृन्नो
भामः स आस्ते सुखमंग शौरिः।
यो वै स्वसॄणां पितृवद् ददाति
वरान् वदान्यो वरतर्पणेन॥

Vidura asked Uddhava: "Is Vasudeva, the brother-in-law of the Kuru

23 Present-day western Afghanistan

dynasty, doing well? The one who takes care of his sisters, Kunti and others, in the manner of a father, the best among the honourable ones, Vasudeva is doing well, isn't he?"

(Bhagavat Purana, Skandha–3, Chapter–1, Shloka–27)

Kunti, the mother of the Pandavas, was the biological sister of Vasudeva. The former king of Mathura, Shursen had ten sons including Vasudeva and five daughters including Kunti. The complete details about this have been given in the answer to a previous question, and hence they need not be repeated here. King Shursen gave his elder daughter, Pritha, to his childless friend, King Kuntibhoja, as his adopted daughter. In the house of Kuntibhoja, this Pritha was named Kunti. In her youth, she was married to Pandu, the younger brother of King Dhritarashtra, and later became the mother of three Pandavas. That is the reason why Krishna repeatedly addresses Arjuna as Prithaputra (son of Pritha) in the celebrated scripture Bhagavad Gita and the Mahabharata.

Rohini's daughter Subhadra, who was a daughter of the Kuru family, was married to Arjuna, also a descendant of the Kuru dynasty. That is not all! According to the folklore prevalent in south India, Subhadra's son Abhimanyu married Shashirekha, the daughter of his maternal uncle Balarama, as well as Uttara, the daughter of Virata.

Lakshmana, the daughter of Arjuna's cousin Duryodhana, was married to Saamba, Krishna's son, in a dramatic manner. These are the details of the relations only between the prominent people of these two dynasties. But apart from these, there may have been numerous such relations between the lesser-known people of these two families, about whom no details are available in historical records. In other words, it can be said that there were multifarious relations between Krishna and the Pandavas.

105. Was Krishna the guru of Arjuna's son Abhimanyu?

There is no statement in the Mahabharata or the Puranas on the basis of which it can be said that Krishna had ever trained Abhimanyu as a guru. However, the Mahabharata does mention that Abhimanyu's childhood was spent in Dwarka, where he received his education. He was dear to his maternal grandfather Vasudeva, and Krishna was also highly impressed by his conduct and his eagerness to learn; but nowhere is it said that Krishna had tried to teach him anything on his own. Of course, it is a different matter if Abhimanyu had learnt a thing or two from his maternal uncle, Krishna on account of his own insatiable curiosity; otherwise, Krishna barely stayed in Dwarka, no more than two to four months at a stretch, due to the exile of the Pandavas and also because he was engaged in other political activities in the Aryavarta region. Those who know about the life of Krishna are aware that he never tried to formally teach anything to anyone. Whatever he learnt in life was due to his insight, and whatever he said was in keeping with the demand of the circumstances. It was not in Krishna's nature or mindset to especially insist on teaching something to someone.

106. Was Kansa really bald, the way it is depicted in the TV series on Krishna?

This is not mentioned in the Mahabharata, any Purana of the Hindus, or even in the Jain scriptures such as Harivansha Purana, Padma Purana and Tirsath Shalaka Purusha, in which Krishna and the legendary personalities associated with him are described in detail. No mention of this is found even in the Buddhist texts. Therefore, this is a complete fabrication designed by the people of this era. The truth is, when Krishna and Balarama killed several wrestlers of Kansa in the wrestling arena of Mathura, Kansa lost his mental balance. And in his frenzy, he ordered the imprisonment and killing of Nanda, Vasudeva, Devaki and other Yadavas. In order to save the lives of all these people, Krishna instantly jumped onto the platform where Kansa was seated, and clutching at his braid, he toppled him from the throne:

स कृष्णेनायतं कृत्वा बाहुं परिघ संनिभम्।
मूर्धजेषु परामृष्टः कंसो वै रंगसंसदि॥

Vaishampayan said: "In the arena, Krishna stretched out his muscular arm and caught Kansa's braid."

(Harivansha Purana, Vishnu Parva, Chapter–31, Shloka–76)

भ्रंशितेनोत्तरीयेण सहसा वलिताननः।
चेष्टमानः समाक्षिप्तः कंसः कार्ष्णेन तेजसा॥

"Kansa, who was pulled with force by Krishna, fell on to the floor and started writhing."

(Harivansha Purana, Vishnu Parva, Chapter–31, Shloka–81)

चकर्ष च महारंगे मंचान्निष्क्रम्य केशव:।
केशेषु तं बलाद् गृह्य कंसं क्लेशार्हतां गतम्।।

"Kansa was in an extremely miserable state. Once again, Krishna vigorously grabbed his hair and began dragging him into the vast arena."

(Harivansha Purana, Vishnu Parva, Chapter–31, Shloka–82)

समाजवाटे क्रीडित्वा विकृष्य च गतायुषम्।
कृष्णो विसर्जयामास कंसदेहमदूरत:

"In the arena, Krishna disdainfully dragged the lifeless Kansa's body and dropped it nearby."

(Harivansha Purana, Vishnu Parva, Chapter–31, Shloka–84)

The Bhagavat Purana also mentions that Krishna grabbed Kansa's hair and dragged him down from the throne:

प्रगृह्य केशेषु चलत्किरीटं
निपात्य रंगोपरितुंगमंचात्।
तस्योपरिष्टात् स्वत्स्वयमब्जनाभ:
पपात विशाश्रय आत्मतंत्र:।।

Shukdeva says: "Just then, Kansa's crown fell off and Krishna clutched his hair and pulled him down from the high platform into the arena. Then, Krishna, the supremely liberated one and the one who grants refuge to the entire world, jumped on him."

(Bhagavat Purana, Skandha–10, Chapter–44, Shloka–37)

Thus, it is clear from this evidence that Kansa was not bald. Krishna had turned Kansa's hair itself into the first weapon to attack him. Therefore, in this case, the image portrayed by the makers of the TV series is completely wrong.

107. Why was Krishna annoyed with Yudhishthira?

This incident occurred before the mace fight between Bhima and Duryodhana, after the Mahabharata war had ended. Yudhishthira's truthfulness and his supreme devotedness has been extolled and highlighted throughout the Mahabharata. Indeed, there was no one who abided by truth and ethics the way he did; and this fact has been highlighted with great pride at various points in the text. But for Krishna, the great enlightened one who had a deep understanding of the workings of time, these qualities held no significance. He was of the view that what needed to be done at a given moment, just had to be done; and what needed to be avoided at a given moment, simply had to be avoided.

So, when Duryodhana, who had lost the Mahabharata war, was hiding in a pond, unarmed, and the Pandavas were looking for him, a few tribals and hunters who had spotted him in their path, conveyed the news of his whereabouts to the Pandavas. On hearing the news that Duryodhana was hiding in a pond, the Pandavas along with Satyaki, Krishna and some eminent soldiers from Panchal reached the pond and challenged Duryodhana to come out and fight. At this, Duryodhana called out from inside the pond, saying that he is chariotless and unarmed, so the challenge was meaningless at that moment. Then, Yudhishthira, inebriated with the pride of being truthful and ethical, said:

आमुंच कवचं वीर मूर्धजान्यमयस्व च।
यच्चान्यदपि ते नास्ति तदप्यादत्स्व भारत।।
इममेकं च ते कामं वीर भूयो ददाम्यहम्।
पंचानां पाण्डवेयानां येन त्वं योद्धुमिच्छसि।।
तं हत्वा वै भवाराजा हतो वा स्वर्गमाप्नुहि।
ऋते च जीविताद्वीर युद्धे किं कुर्म ते प्रियम्।।

Yudhishthira said: "Brave scion of Bharata, Duryodhana! You should don your armour and tie your hair well; and take with you anything that is essential for you. O Brave One! I further promise you that on choosing any one of us five Pandavas to fight with, if you kill him, you can become the king; and if you die, you will attain heaven. Brave one! Tell me, what is that one desirable thing that we can do for you, except saving your life in this duel?"

(Mahabharata, Shalya Parva, Chapter–32, Shloka–60-62)

Krishna was enraged on hearing these words uttered by Yudhishthira. For, the fact that he had asked Duryodhana to choose any one of the five Pandavas for a duel—and promised him the kingdom of Hastinapur if he killed that Pandava brother—was nothing but rank foolishness.

युधिष्ठिरस्य संक्रुद्धो... X ...सृष्टा भैक्ष्याय वा पुनः॥

• Reprimanding him, Krishna said, "Yudhishthira! What would happen if Duryodhana chose you, Arjuna, Nakula or Sahadeva in this duel?

• How could you be so impetuous as to say that he can become the king of Hastinapur after killing just one of us?

• I do not think that you can overpower Duryodhana, who wields the mighty mace. O King! He has practised mace-fighting for thirteen years on an iron statue made to look like Bhimsen, with a burning desire to kill him.

• How can we possibly accomplish our task now? For, you have acted recklessly because of your pride.

• I do not think anyone is worthy of fighting Duryodhana except Bhimsen, and the problem is that even he (Bhimsen) has not practised much.

• You have now started playing the game of gambling once again. But this gamble of yours is far more cataclysmic in nature than Shakuni's game of dice.

• Admittedly, Bhimsen is extremely powerful, but Duryodhana has practised intensively. And everyone knows that even when a strong person is pitted against one who has practised well for a fight, it is the latter who is more likely to gain the upper hand.

• You have put your enemy in a strong position, bringing him on par with you. You have not only put yourself in trouble, but have also put all of us in jeopardy.

• Who could be so foolish as to defeat all his enemies, and then, in the scenario of only one of them remaining alive and that too in trouble, he wagers the kingdom he has just conquered and gambles it away, offering it on a platter to the enemy? In such circumstances, who could be so foolish as to prefer a one-on-one combat?

• I do not see any warrior in the world, even among the gods, who can beat Duryodhana in a mace-fight today.

• None of you brothers, be it Bhima, Arjuna, Nakula or Sahadeva, can defeat Duryodhana in a fair mace-fight, because he has practised intensively.

• Yudhishthira! In light of all this, how did you say that he could engage in a mace-fight and become the king after killing one of us?

• Even if Bhimsen is asked to fight using the mace, I doubt his victory, because Duryodhana has practised long and hard.

• In spite of this, you repeatedly said that Duryodhana could become the king after killing just one of us. Therefore, it has now been proved beyond doubt that the children of King Pandu and Kunti do not deserve to enjoy the kingdom. The Almighty has given them this birth only to be exiled or to keep begging forever."

(Mahabharata, Shalya Parva,
Chapter–33, Shloka–1-17)

After this, Bhima tried to pacify Krishna by assuring him of his valour and reminding Krishna of his long-standing rivalry with Duryodhana.

108. How true is the story that Duryodhana's waist was rendered weak because he moved away from Gandhari's gaze?

This is folklore, and there is no mention of such an incident either in the Mahabharata or any Purana. The popular folklore states that after the Mahabharata war had ended and just before Duryodhana's mace-fight with Bhima had begun, Gandhari had sent a message to Duryodhana to appear completely naked before her. But before he could do so, Krishna learned about this and advised him to at least wrap a banana leaf around his waist, as he was a grown-up man. Duryodhana followed Krishna's advice and as a result, Gandhari could not see his waist, due to which it remained vulnerable and ultimately became the cause of his death. The Mahabharata states something different in this regard:

त्वां च प्राप्य रणे पापो धार्तराष्ट्रो विनंक्ष्यति।
त्वमस्य सक्थिनी भंक्त्वा प्रतिज्ञां पालयिष्यसि॥

Krishna said: "The sinner Duryodhana will surely be destroyed fighting against you in the battlefield, and you will break both his thighs and fulfil your promise."

(Mahabharata, Shalya Parva, Chapter–33, Shloka–27)

It is evident that Krishna is talking about Bhima's resolve, which he had made when Draupadi was humiliated. In Chapter 60 of this same Parva, the curse of Sage Maitreya is said to be the reason behind Bhima breaking Duryodhana's thighs:

मैत्रेयेणाभिशप्तश्च पूर्वमेव महर्षिणा।
ऊरू ते भेत्स्यते भीमो गदयेति परन्तप।।

Krishna said: "O Balarama, who torments the enemies! Sage Maitreya had already cursed Duryodhana that Bhimsen would break both his thighs with his mace."

(Mahabharata, Shalya Parva, Chapter–60, Shloka–18)

Thus, it is clear from this evidence that the tale of Duryodhana's body becoming indestructible on account of Gandhari's gaze is nothing but folklore. It neither has a historical basis nor can anyone be blamed or criticised for it. However, those who wish to know the truth behind historical events would be better off if they trust only the ancient historical contexts.

109. Was Krishna a non-Aryan?

A conflict between the Aryans and the non-Aryans in India has been prevalent since ancient times, possibly even before the period of the Mahabharata. The distinctive feature of the Aryans has been their *Varna*[24] system and various types of yajnas or sacrifices. Indra has been their principal deity, while the non-Aryans, that is, the ancient inhabitants of Aryavarta, have been naturalists. It was due to the conflict between Krishna and Indra that Duryodhana, on the verge of dying, calls him non-Aryan in the battlefield of Kurukshetra:

त्वया पुनरनार्येण जिह्ममार्गेण पार्थिवाः।
स्वधर्ममनुतिष्ठन्तो वयं चान्ये च घातिताः।।

"A non-Aryan like you has resorted to cunning means and got us killed along with other kings who were abiding by their duties."

(Mahabharata, Shalya Parva, Chapter–61, Shloka–38)

110. Was Abhimanyu particularly dear to Krishna?

There is no evidence which proves that Abhimanyu's guru was Krishna, but both Krishna and Abhimanyu's father, Arjuna adored him, and evidence of this is available in the Mahabharata:

दयितो वासुदेवस्य बाल्यात् प्रभृति चाभवत्।
पितृनामिव सर्वेषां प्रजानामिव चन्द्रमा।।

24. Caste

"Just as all manes and common people love the moon, Abhimanyu had become very dear to Krishna ever since his childhood."

जन्मप्रभृति कृष्णश्च चक्रे तस्य क्रिया शुभाः।
स चापि ववृधे बालः शुक्लपक्षे यथा शशीः॥

"Krishna had made wonderful arrangements for his upbringing right since his birth. The child, Abhimanyu, began to grow like the moon of the bright phase."

(Mahabharata, Adi Parva,
Chapter–221, Shloka–70-71)

Abhimanyu was trained in the use of weapons by his father, Arjuna:

चतुष्पादं दशविधं धनुर्वेदमरिन्दमः।
अर्जुनाद्वेद वेदज्ञः सकलं दिव्यमानुषम्॥
विज्ञानेष्वपि चास्त्राणां सौष्ठवे च महाबलः।
क्रियास्वपि च सर्वासु विशेषानभ्यशिक्षयत्॥
आगमे च प्रयोगे च चक्रे तुल्यमिवात्मना।
तुतोष पुत्रं सौभद्रं प्रेक्षमाणो धनंजयः॥

"That child had acquired knowledge of the complete science of artillery, with all its four sections and ten divisions, including the use of divine and human weapons, from his father, Arjuna. He was also imparted special training in the science of weapons, including how to wield them with dexterity as well as the principles governing them. Arjuna had made Abhimanyu his equal, in the knowledge and use of weapons. He used to feel quite content on seeing Abhimanyu, the son of Subhadra."

(Mahabharata, Adi Parva, Chapter–221, Shloka–72-74)

It is clear from the evidence above that a gifted nephew like Abhimanyu was particularly dear to Krishna.

111. Was Yudhishthira addicted to gambling?

On the basis of the descriptions that appear at various points in the Mahabharata, it is evident that Yudhishthira was a gambler, and his enemies were also aware of this:

द्यूतप्रियश्च कौन्तेयो न च जानाति देवितुम्।
आहूतश्चैष्यति व्यक्तं नित्यमेवाह्वयत्स्वयम्॥

Shakuni said: "Kunti's son Yudhishthira loves gambling, but he does not know how to play, and is quite inept. If he is invited for a game of gambling or war, he will come running."

(Mahabharata, Sabha Parva, Chapter–49, Shloka–39)

Draupadi was also distressed with Yudhishthira's addiction to gambling.

ऋजोर्मृदोर्वदान्यस्य ह्रीमतः सत्यवादिनः।
कथमक्षव्यसनजा बुद्धिरापतिता तव।

Draupadi had even said to Yudhishthira once, "You are simple, gentle, generous, self-effacing and truthful. I wonder how this addiction for gambling has gripped your mind."

(Mahabharata, Vana Parva, Chapter–30, Shloka–19)

112. What kind of political relations did Krishna share with his father-in-law and Rukmini's father Bhishmak, the king of Vidarbha?

King Bhishmak, father of Krishna's first wife, Rukmini, and his entire family admired Jarasandha. Before the Rajasuya Yajna, Krishna gave Yudhishthira a description of the kings in favour of and opposed to the Bharatas:

चतुर्थभाग् महाराज भोज इन्द्रसखो बली।
विद्याबलाद्यो व्यजयत्स पाण्ड्यक्रथकैशिकान्।।
भ्राता तस्याकृतिः शूरो जामदग्न्यसमोऽभवत्।
स भक्तो मागधं राजा भीष्मकः परवीरहा।।
प्रियाण्याचरतः प्रह्वान्सदा सम्बन्धिनस्ततः।
भजतो न भजत्यस्मानप्रियेषु व्यवस्थितः।।

Krishna said: "O King! The one who is the lord of one quarter of the earth, who is a friend of Indra, who is strong, who has conquered the kingdoms of Pandya, Kratha and Kaishika with his knowledge of weapons, whose brother Akruti is as valorous as Parshurama, the son of Jamadagni; that destroyer of enemies, King Bhishmak of the Bhoja clan is a devotee of King Jarasandha despite being my father-in-law. We always do everything that pleases him, we are gentle to him and we are his kin; but in spite of this, he does not consider us (his devotees) as his own, and instead, he fraternises with our enemies."

(Mahabharata, Sabha Parva, Chapter–14, Shloka–21-23)

Among all the princesses whom Krishna had married, Rukmini was the only one whose father, King Bhishmak, was the most powerful; but politically, his relations with Krishna were bitter due to Jarasandha. The shlokas given above are proof of this fact. Contrary to the evidence provided in the Mahabharata in this regard, everything that the Puranas state, that King Bhishmak and his family was a devotee of Krishna, is false and not worth believing.

113. Which were the major slayings that Krishna had undertaken?

To provide a thorough answer to this question, one is better off studying Krishna's entire biography by dividing it in two parts. His life before his arrival in Mathura is completely different from the one he lived in Mathura and beyond. There is a clear distinction between the tasks Krishna had accomplished in those two periods, and the people who got killed by him in the process. Another point that needs to be noted here is that in the Puranas, the descriptions of events have been exaggerated to absurd levels; and almost everyone is aware of this. For instance, the writers of the Puranas have exaggerated even the killing of the heron, turning it into the killing of the demon Bakasura, who could assume several forms and was apparently sent by Kansa. Similar exaggerated accounts have turned a python into the demon Aghasura, a donkey into Gadarbhasura, and a bull into Arishtasura. Therefore, those killings by Krishna are not being counted in the answer to the present question.

Slayings undertaken by Krishna in his early life:

i) Putana: The Puranas and Samhitas provide differing information about Putana. One says that she was Kansa's sister, while the other says that she was his maid. So, no matter who she was, it is true that a woman named Putana did come into the life of the newborn Krishna and was also killed by him:

पूतना लोकबालघ्नी राक्षसी रुधिराशना।
जिघांसयापि हरये स्तनं दत्त्वाप सद्गतिम्॥

Shukdeva said: "Putana was a demon. She killed children and drank their blood. It was because of her desire to kill Krishna that she had breastfed him."

(Bhagavat Purana, Skandha–10, Chapter–6, Shloka–35)

ii) Trinavarta: He was a private servant of King Kansa of Mathura, according to a description given in the Bhagavat Purana:

दैत्यो नाम्ना तृणावर्तः कंसभृत्यः प्रणोदितः।

"There was a demon named Trinavarta, and he was Kansa's private servant. It was on Kansa's insistence that he had come to Gokul."

(Bhagavat Purana, Skandha–10, Chapter–7, Shloka–20)

His name is not mentioned in the Harivansha Purana.

iii) Pralamba: This Asura was a child who could run at great speeds. Kansa had sent him to Vrindavan to abduct Krishna:

पशूंश्चारयतोर्गोपैस्तद्वदने रामकृष्णयोः।
गोपरूपी प्रलम्बोऽगादसुरस्तज्जीहीर्षया।।

Shukdeva said: "One day, when Balarama, Krishna and the other cowherds were looking after the cows as they grazed in the forest, an Asura named Pralamba arrived there, disguised as a young cowherd. He had come with the desire to abduct Krishna and Balarama."

(Bhagavat Purana, Skandha–10, Chapter–18, Shloka–17)

Comment: He was killed by Balarama, not Krishna.

iv) Keshi: This demon, who was a cannibal, lived near Vrindavan in the hills of Govardhana, but did not harm the people of Vrindavan. He was a demon under Kansa's guardianship, and the latter used to employ him on special assignments:

प्रागेव च नरेन्द्रेण माथुरेणौग्रसेनिना।
केशिनः प्रेषितो दूतो वधायोपेन्द्रकारणात्।।
स च दूतवचः श्रुत्वा क्लेशी क्लेशकरो नृणाम्।
वृन्दावनगतो गोपान् बाधते स्म दुरासदः।।

Vaishampayan said: "Even before sending Akrura to Vrindavan, Kansa, the son of King Ugrasen of Mathura, sent a messenger to Keshi and ordered him to kill Krishna. After hearing the messenger's words, the evil demon Keshi, the tormentor of humans, went to Vrindavan and began harassing the cowherds."

(Harivansha Purana, Vishnu Parva, Chapter–24, Shloka–5-6)

व्यादितास्यो महारौद्रः सोऽसुरः कृष्णबाहुना।
निपपात यथा कृत्तो नागो हि द्विदलीकृतः।।

Vaishampayan said: "Split into two parts, that dreadful demon, whose face Shri Krishna had smashed with his arm, fell to the ground, akin to an elephant cut into two pieces."

(Harivansha Purana, Vishnu Parva, Chapter–24, Shloka–47)

Slayings undertaken by Krishna after coming to Mathura:

v) Rajak: He was an impertinent washerman and dyer living in Mathura:

तलेनाशनिकल्पेन स तं मूर्द्धन्यताडयेत्।
स गतासुः पपातोर्व्यां रजको व्यस्तमस्तकः।।

Vaishampayan said: "Shri Krishna slapped him on his forehead, and the blow was no less than a thunderbolt. As soon as he was struck, Rajak's forehead burst open and he fell dead to the ground."

(Harivansha Purana, Vishnu Parva, Chapter–27, Shloka–16)

vi) Kansa: He was Krishna's maternal uncle, whose atrocities had distressed Krishna himself, the Yadavas of the kingdom of Mathura and the forest-dwelling cowherds. He was pulled, dragged and killed by Krishna in a packed assembly:

तस्य तद् वदनं श्यामं सुप्ताक्षं मुकुटं विना।
न विभाति विपर्यस्तं विपलाशं यथाम्बुजम्।।
असंग्राम हतः कंसः स बाणैरपरिक्षतः।
केशग्राहान्निरस्तासुः वीरमार्गान्निराकृतः।।

Vaishampayan said: "His body had become contorted due to his broken neck. His eyes were closed and his dark face, sans the crown, looked pale, much like a lotus flower without petals. Kansa was killed without a battle. His body was not wounded due to arrows. He was dragged by his hair, because of which he died, deprived of the heroic path."

(Harivansha Purana, Vishnu Parva, Chapter–30, Shloka–86-87)

vii) Panchajan: In order to bring back Acharya Sage Sandipani's son as *gurudakshina,*[25] Krishna went to the kingdom of the demon Panchajan, and killed him in order to rescue his guru's son from imprisonment. Simultaneously, Krishna acquired the famous conch 'Panchajanya', which became an integral part of his personality and remained so all his life:

स तु पंचजनं हत्वा शंखं प्रेभे जनार्दनः।
यस्तु देवमनुष्येषु पांचजन्य इति श्रुतः।।

Vaishampayan said: "After killing Panchajan, Janardana Shri Krishna

25. Offering of gratitude made to a guru

acquired a conch which is famous among gods and humans as Panchajanya."

(Harivansha Purana, Vishnu Parva, Chapter–33, Shloka–17)

viii) Shrugaal or Shringlava: He was the king of Karvirpur, a kingdom located near the Gomanta Hill, in the southern region of India. He was killed by Krishna:

तं रथस्य प्रमाणस्थं शृगालं युद्धदुर्मदं।
जघान समरे चक्रं जातदर्पं महाबलम्॥
ततः सुदर्शनं चक्रं पुनरायाद् गुरोः करे।
चक्रेणोरसि निर्भिन्नः स गतासुर्गतोत्सवः।
प्रपात क्षतजस्रावी शृगालोऽद्रिरिवाहतः॥

Vaishampayan said: "The mighty Shrugaal who had deliberately started the battle, sat in his chariot arrogantly and did not move from his place. It was then that Krishna's discus wounded him gravely on the chest, after which it returned to its preceptor Krishna's hand. Struck by the discus, Shrugaal's chest was ripped open and he fell down, with blood gushing out in a torrent; and in this manner, he was shorn of life and joy."

(Harivansha Purana, Vishnu Parva, Chapter–44, Shloka–28-29)

ix) Kalyavana: This king was killed by Krishna in a cave outside Mathura, when its inhabitants were migrating to Dwarka. The Puranas state that Kalyavana was burnt to ashes the moment Muchkund's eyes fell on him inside the cave. This narrative is more fiction than truth.

x) Narakasura: This king of Pragjyotishpur had captured thousands of beautiful women from his own kingdom and from those nearby, and was subjecting them to inhuman atrocities. Krishna went to his kingdom and killed him.

अथोग्रचक्रश्चक्रेण प्रदीप्तेनाकरोद् द्विधा।
चक्र द्विधाकृतं तस्य शरीरमपतद् भुवि॥

Vaishampayan said: "The furious Shri Krishna, wielding his discus, fought with Narakasura for a few moments. Then, he slashed his body into two pieces with the fiery discus. Narakasura's body, cut into two by the discus, fell to the ground."

(Harivansha Purana, Vishnu Parva, Chapter–63, Shloka–121)

xi) Shishupala: He was Krishna's cousin and the king of Chedi. Krishna had killed him during Yudhishthira's Rajasuya Yajna.

xii) Shaalva: He was the king of Madhya kingdom, and a supporter and ally of Jarasandha. To avenge the deaths of Jarasandha and Shishupala, he had attacked Dwarka in the absence of Krishna, and had caused great loss of life and property. He was eventually killed by Krishna upon his return.

xiii) Dantavakra: He was Krishna's cousin and the king of Kamarupa. He was deeply pained by the decimation of all the kings from Jarasandha's camp, either directly or indirectly by Krishna; and one day, he came to fight Krishna with a small army of his own. Krishna killed him too.

xiv) Poundrak: He was the king of Pundra, and a friend of the king of Kashi. He attacked Dwarka along with Eklavya, but was killed by Krishna.

xv) Eklavya: He was killed by Krishna even before the Mahabharata war had begun. Krishna wanted to ensure Arjuna's victory at all costs, but Eklavya could have posed a major hindrance in it. So, Krishna killed him, thus clearing the obstacle in Arjuna's path.

All of the above slayings were carried out by Krishna himself, but in addition to these, several more slayings had taken place in that period, and the Itihaasas and Puranas state that Krishna was the instigator of these killings. Actually, he wished to see a different kind of Aryavarta, and if he sensed that someone was posing an obstacle to this vision of his, Krishna either killed that person himself or got him killed by others.

114. What is Rajasuya Yajna?

According to the Mahabharata, the Rajasuya Yajna was newer compared to other Vedic yajnas, and it started after the widespread genocide by Parshurama:

जामदग्न्येन रामेण क्षत्रं यदवशेषितम्।
तस्मादवरजं लोके यदिदं क्षत्रसंज्ञितम्।।
कृतोऽयं कुलसंकल्पः क्षत्रियैर्वसुधाधिप।
निदेशवाग्भिस्तत्तेह विदितं भरतर्षभ।

Krishna said: "In the past, when Kshatriyas were massacred by Parshurama, the son of Jamadagni; the Kshatriyas who survived after hiding are all inferior compared to their predecessors. Thus, at present, the ones who are alive are Kshatriyas in name only. These Kshatriyas have collectively made a rule in accordance with their ancestors' statement that the one who conquers all the Kshatriyas will be the emperor. O Yudhishthira, supreme among the Bharatas! You too are probably aware of this."

(Mahabharata, Sabha Parva, Chapter–14, Shloka–2-3)

This revelation by Krishna in the Mahabharata makes it clear that the Rajasuya Yajna was a so-called religious act to establish domination and supremacy. But it was used less for noble purposes, and misused more often.

115. How powerful was King Jarasandha, the arch-enemy of Krishna?

The biggest obstacle in the path of Yudhishthira becoming the imperial ruler was Krishna's enemy, Jarasandha, because he dominated three-fourths of the Aryavarta region. And one can gauge how powerful he was from this very fact. Indeed, without killing him, the success of Yudhishthira's Rajasuya Yajna was not only doubtful, but well-nigh impossible. The complete details of this in the Mahabharata's Sabha Parva are as follows:

इदानीमेव वै राजन् जरासन्धो महीपतिः... X ...सर्वे स्म प्रतीचीं दिशमाश्रिताः॥

Krishna said: "O King Yudhishthira! King Jarasandha has just passed through the kingdoms of all those Kshatriya families and has been crowned as the Emperor by the kings; and with all his force and might, he is attacking them, thereby becoming the supreme ruler of all the kings. Jarasandha prefers the policy of 'divide and rule'. Today, the whole of Aryavarta is under his control. Shishupala and Dantavakra are his disciples. The mighty Hansa and Dimbhaka have also surrendered to him. The chief king of the western kingdoms, King Bhagadatta loves you, but he is inclined towards Jarasandha. In the west, only Kuntibhoja Purujit, the king of your maternal home, is overtly supporting you. Banga, Pundra, Kirat and all other kings are in his control. My father-in-law King Bhishmak is also his admirer. Shursen, Bhadrakara, Bodha and other kings have fled to the south due to their fear of him. As I had killed his son-in-law and my maternal uncle Kansa, he is after my life and my brother's too. When he did not cease to attack us despite losing several times, we left Mathura in fear and took refuge in Dwarka. In Jarasandha's view, we have wronged him, so despite being powerful, we have fled fearing him."

(Mahabharata, Sabha Parva, Chapter–14, Shloka–7-49)

न तु शक्यं जरासन्धे... X ...कात्स्र्येन कर्तुं मतिमतां वर॥

Krishna said: "Therefore, O King! In my opinion, you cannot successfully complete the Rajasuya Yajna as long as the mighty Jarasandha is alive. He has conquered all the kings and imprisoned them in Girivraj, and is about to sacrifice them all in a yajna. O King, we too have left Mathura and have gone to Dwarka, fearing his wrath. So, if you wish to complete the Rajasuya Yajna successfully, then try to free those imprisoned kings and kill Jarasandha. The Rajasuya Yajna cannot be completed without doing this."

(Mahabharata, Sabha Parva, Chapter–14, Shloka–62-69)

The shlokas of the Mahabharata quoted above suggest that if Grandsire Bhishma, Drona, Duryodhana, Karna, Arjuna, Bhima and others were invincible warriors in the Kuru dynasty, then the King of Magadha, Jarasandha, from the eastern part of Aryavarta, was also considered to be an incredibly powerful and highly influential king as well as an astute politician in Aryavarta and its surrounding areas. Thus, he was the primary competitor in the eyes of Hastinapur and Indraprastha. That is verily what this statement of Krishna implies.

116. What was Draupadi's state of mind after losing the game of dice?

If one were to believe the details provided in the Mahabharata, Draupadi never forgot her humiliation after that gruesome, watershed episode of gambling, and she always goaded her husbands into showing manliness and avenge that atrocity.

न निर्मन्युः क्षत्रियोऽस्ति लोके निर्वचनं स्मृतम्।
तदद्य त्वयि पश्यामि क्षत्रिये विपरीतवत्॥
यो न दर्शयते तेजः क्षत्रियः काल आगते।
सर्वभूतानि तं पार्थ सदा परिभवन्त्युत॥

Draupadi said to Yudhishthira: "There is no Kshatriya in the world who is devoid of anger; the very word 'Kshatriya' has been coined in such a way as to indicate that the person possesses anger. But seeing the absence of anger in you, even when the occasion demands it, I doubt whether you are truly a Kshatriya. O Son of Kunti! If a Kshatriya does not display his power even when the need arises, then he is always scorned by all beings."

(Mahabharata, Vana Parva, Chapter–27, Shloka–37-38)

नमो धात्रे विधात्रे च यौ मोहं चक्रतुस्तव।
पितृपैतामहे वृत्ते वोढव्ये तेऽन्यथा मतिः।।

A few days later, Draupadi once again said to her husband Yudhishthira: "O King! I salute God and destiny that have corrupted your intellect. Now, you do not seem inclined to even shoulder the responsibility of continuing the custom of your forefathers."

(Mahabharata, Vana Parva, Chapter–30, Shloka–1)

यदिदं वैशदेवान्ते सायम्प्रातः प्रदीयते।
तद्दत्त्वातिथिभृत्येभ्यो राजन्शेषेण जीवसि।।
इष्टयः पशुबन्धाश्च काम्यनैमित्तिकाश्च ये।
वर्तन्ते पाकयज्ञाश्च यज्ञकर्म च नित्यदा।।
अस्मिन्नपि महारण्ये विजने दस्युसेविते।
राष्ट्रादपेत्य वसतो धार्मस्ते नावसीदति।।
अेशमेधो राजसूयः पुण्डरीकोऽथ गोसवः।
एतैरपि महायज्ञैरिष्टं ते भूरिदक्षिणैः।।
राजन्परीतया बुद्ध्या विषमेऽक्षपराजये।
राज्यं वसून्यायुधानि भ्रातृन्मां चासि निर्जितः।।

Cursing furiously once again, Draupadi said: "O King! You never failed to perform your righteous duties. You always ate only after feeding the guests and other beings in your house. Worship, animal sacrifice, Kamya Yajna, Naimittika Yajna, Paka Yajna and Nitya Yajna[26] used to be conducted regularly in your household. In fact, even now, when you are away from your kingdom, living in exile in this large, deserted forest rife with bandits, you have not failed to discharge even a single righteous and pious duty. But O King! Of what use is the execution of all these rituals and the pursuit of righteous practices when they could not prevent your mind from becoming corrupted during that fraudulent game of gambling, as a result of which you lost not only your kingdom,

26. Various types of sacrifices, oblations

wealth, weapons and your brothers, but also lost me after putting me at stake?"

(Mahabharata, Vana Parva, Chapter–30, Shloka–14-18)

आर्ताहं प्रलपामीदमिति मां विद्धि भारत।
भूयश्च विलपिष्यामि सुमनास्तन्निबोध मे।।
कर्म खल्विह कर्तव्यं जातेनामित्रकर्शन।
अकर्माणो हि जीवन्ति स्थावरा नेतरे जनाः।।

Unleashing her fervid, feminal rage, Draupadi says: "Bharata! I am saying this because my anguish has made me edgy. And I will not calm down just by saying all this; I will continue to vent my anger, and you will have to listen to me patiently. O Scorcher of enemies! Even a wise person must engage in action in this world. Only stationary beings such as the mountains and trees can live without performing actions, not others."

(Mahabharata, Vana Parva, Chapter–32, Shloka–2-3)

These are a few key highlights of Draupadi's statements, which indicate her state of mind.

117. Did Duryodhana perform the Rajasuya Yajna, similar to Yudhishthira?

Yes, Duryodhana had also performed the Rajasuya Yajna, but since it has been disregarded even in the Mahabharata, how could any information pertaining to it reach the people? According to the Mahabharata, when the Pandavas and Draupadi were trekking in the valleys of the Himalayas during their exile, Duryodhana received information of their whereabouts and entertained the idea of killing them in the forest itself. When he deliberated upon and discussed this plan with his well-wishers Shakuni, Karna, Dushasana and others, all of them supported him. Then, on the pretext of taking a leisure trip to the forest, they all departed from Hastinapur along with men and arms, and reached the inaccessible valleys of the Himalayas. But upon reaching there, they were confronted by the Gandharvas, rather than the Pandavas. Consequently, a war broke out between them which was so fierce that even a warrior like Karna had to flee from battle, while Duryodhana was taken captive. When the Pandavas, who were trekking nearby, heard about this incident, Yudhishthira ordered Arjuna to help Duryodhana as much as possible and rescue him from captivity. Following his brother's orders, Arjuna fought those Gandharvas and after defeating them, he rescued Duryodhana.

As for Duryodhana, he was so ashamed of this incident that he decided to fast unto death in the forest itself, and ordered that Dushasana be crowned the king in his stead. But after much persuasion by Karna, Shakuni, Bhurishrava and others, he finally agreed to return to Hastinapur. After their return to Hastinapur, Karna decided to alleviate his friend's embarrassment by vanquishing all kingdoms, and returned to Hastinapur after conquering the entire Aryavarta except Dwarka.

(Mahabharata, Vana Parva, Chapter–248-254)

But despite this, when his friend Duryodhana could not cast away his debilitating sense of shame, Karna asked him what else he could do for him. Duryodhana then stated his wish and said:

राजसूयं पाण्डवस्य दृष्ट्वा क्रतुवरं तदा।
मम स्पृहा समुत्पन्ना तां संपादय सूतज।।

Duryodhana said: "O Son of charioteer! Seeing that supreme deed, the great Rajasuya Yajna of Pandu's son Yudhishthira, I too feel the desire to perform that Yajna. You must fulfil this wish of mine."

एवमुक्तस्ततः कर्णो राजानमिदमब्रवीत्।
तवाद्य पृथिवीपाला वश्याः सर्वे नृपोत्तम।।
आहूयन्तां द्विजवराः संभाराश्च यथाविधि।
संभ्रियन्तां कुरुश्रेष्ठ यज्ञोपकरणानि च।।

Hearing Duryodhana, Karna said to him: "O Supreme among kings! At present, all the kings are under your control. O Supreme one among the Kuru clan! Summon the best Brahmins and arrange for all the materials and implements for the yajna in accordance with the prescribed methods."

(Mahabharata, Vana Parva, Chapter–255, Shloka–6, 7-8)

After this, a single chapter (256) describes the entire Rajasuya Yajna. This part of the Mahabharata appears to be original, not an embellishment; but as the authors of this text were inclined towards the Pandavas, Duryodhana's Rajasuya Yajna has barely been given importance and has been described in just one chapter.

118. Did Krishna ever recite the Gayatri Mantra?

There is no mention of Krishna chanting the Gayatri Mantra either in the Mahabharata or any Purana. In response to other questions in this book, it has been explained in detail that Krishna was against Vedic beliefs and their establishment, and this was the reason for his recurring conflicts with Indra. Therefore, there is no question of Krishna being a supporter of Vedic mantras.

119. Did Krishna consume liquor?

There is no question of such a thing being mentioned in the major Puranas, because Krishna is depicted as a pure, Vaishnava avatar in them. Even in the portions of the Mahabharata that have been added after Veda Vyasa, Krishna has been depicted as an incarnation of Vishnu. However, some original portions still exist as they are, from which some authentic facts about Krishna can be gleaned. One such section comprises a few chapters of the Udyoga Parva. In the entire Mahabharata, there is only one instance wherein Krishna is shown consuming liquor along with Arjuna, in the presence of their respective wives, Satyabhama and Draupadi.

After the end of the incognito exile of the Pandavas, when Sanjaya went to them bearing Dhritarashtra's message, he returned to Hastinapur and apprised him of everything that he witnessed there. And in his narration, he mentioned the fact of Krishna drinking along with Arjuna:

पादांगुलिरभिप्रेक्षण् प्रयतोऽहं कृतांजलिः।
शुद्धान्तं प्राविशं राजन्नाख्यातो नरसिंहयोः।।
न चाभिमन्युर्न यमौ तं देशमभिजग्मतुः।
यत्र कृष्णौ च कृष्णा च सत्यभामा च भामिनी।।
उभौ मध्वासवक्षीबा वुभौ वरचन्दनरूषितौ।
स्रग्विणौ वरवस्त्रौ तौ दिव्याभरणभूषितौ।।
नैकरत्नविचित्रं च कांचनं च वरासनम्।
नानास्तरणसंस्तीर्णं यत्रासाते नरर्षभौ।।
अर्जुनांकगतौ पादौ केशवस्योपलक्षये।
अर्जुनस्य च कृष्णायाः शुभायाश्चांकगावुभौ।।
कांचनं पादपीठं तु पार्थो वै प्रादिशन्मुदा।
दासीभ्यामाहृतं मह्यं स्पृष्ट्वा भूमावुपाविशम्।।

Sanjaya said to Dhritarashtra: "O King! To convey your message to the god among humans, Shri Krishna, and Arjuna, I reined in my mind, locked my gaze on my toes and with folded hands, went to their inner chamber, where Shri Krishna, Arjuna, Draupadi and the honourable Satyabhama were seated. It was a place where even Abhimanyu, Nakula and Sahadeva were not allowed. At the time, both the friends, indulging in liquor, were on a high. Their bodies were anointed with sandalwood paste, and they were bedecked with fine clothes, lush garlands and exquisite ornaments. The two heroes—the destroyers of their enemies—were seated on a luxurious seat made of gold and plush upholstery. I saw that both feet of Shri Krishna were in the lap of Arjuna, while one leg of Arjuna was in Draupadi's lap and the other was in Satyabhama's lap. Kunti's son, Arjuna pointed towards a golden seat and gestured me to sit, but I merely touched it with my hand and sat on the floor."

(Mahabharata, Udyoga Parva, Chapter–59, Shloka–3-8)

In addition, there is a Purana that revolves around the Sun called the Saamba Purana. This Purana also mentions Krishna's sybaritic life with his queens.

तत्रास्मिन् दीयते तासाम् श्रेष्ठं पानं सुरासवम्।
मणिकांचनपात्रेषु नानापुष्पाधिवासितम्।।
वृत्तैश्च सहकाराणां भग्नैर्नीलोत्पलैरपि।
एतस्मिन्नन्तरे बुद्ध्वा मद्यमत्ता इति स्त्रियः।।

Sage Vashishta said to King Brihadbal: "Several women with beautiful bodies stripped off their clothes in order to indulge in amorous activity, covering themselves with lotus leaves. All of them were being served liquor in gold vessels so that they could become intoxicated."

(Saamba Purana, Chapter–2, Shloka–30-31)

120. What was Devaki and Vasudeva's physical appearance like?

Praising Vasudeva's looks, the Harivansha Purana states:

मनुष्यलोके कृत्स्नेऽपि रूपे नास्ति समो भुवि।
यस्यासीत्पुरुषाग्जएयस्य कान्तिश्चन्द्रमसो यथा।।

Vaishampayan said: "The sublime radiance of the body of Vasudeva, the foremost among men, was akin to the moon. There was no one as attractive as him in the entire world of humans."

(Harivansha Purana, Harivansha Parva, Chapter–34, Shloka–20)

Nothing is written about Devaki's physical appearance in any of the texts.

121. What kind of food did the Pandavas partake of during their exile?

It is described briefly but specifically in the Mahabharata:

वानेयं च मृगांश्चैव शुद्धैर्बाणैर्निपातितान्।
ब्राह्मणानां निवेद्याग्रमभुञ्जता महारथाः।
तांस्तु शूरान्महेष्वासांस्तदा निवसतो वने।
अन्वयुर्ब्राह्मणा राजन्साग्नयोऽनग्नयस्तथा॥
ब्राह्मणानां सहस्राणि स्नातकानां महात्मनाम्।
दश मोक्षविदां तद्वद्यान्बिभर्ति युधिष्ठिरः॥
रुरून्कृष्णमृगांश्चैव मेध्यांश्चान्यान्मनोरमान्।
बाणैरुन्मथ्य विविधैर्ब्राह्मणेभ्यो न्यवेदयत्॥

"The Pandavas used to consume the flesh of deer and other forest animals that were killed by arrows, apart from roots, tubers, fruits and grains cultivated in village farms. Wherever the Pandavas went, the Agnihotris - Brahmins who maintained the sacred fire during fire rituals - and Anagnihotris - Brahmins who did not maintain the sacred fire - of that forested region used to begin living with them. The Pandavas used to kill the Ruru antelope, black buck and other wild animals that could be killed, and bring them as food for themselves and those Brahmins. They also used the hide of these animals for various purposes."

(Mahabharata, Vana Parva, Chapter–50, Shloka–4-7)

122. Did the game of gambling played between Yudhishthira and Shakuni conform to the rules?

Absolutely not! In fact, Yudhishthira himself had raised an objection to the game being played against the rules. It is a generally accepted rule that a game of gambling is played only by those who can wager money themselves; no gambler can gamble on behalf of someone else. But that is exactly what happened in that fraudulently played gambling game of Hastinapur, wherein no one supported Yudhishthira's argument, nor did anyone oppose Duryodhana's assertion when he said:

अहं दातास्मि रत्नानां धनानां च विशाम्पते।
मदर्थे देविता चायं शकुनिर्मातुलो मम।।

Duryodhana said: "King Yudhishthira! I will give the money and gems to be wagered, but my uncle, Shakuni will play on my behalf."

To which, Yudhishthira objected and said:

अन्येनान्यस्य वै द्यूतं विषमं प्रतिभाति मे।
एतद् विद्वन्नुपादत्स्व काममेवं प्रवर्तताम्।।

"Someone else gambling for a person seems very out of place to me. So, all the wise people present here! First, you must understand this, and only then should this game begin."

(Mahabharata, Sabha Parva, Chapter–59 Gita Press, 84 South Indian version, Shloka–20-21)

However, no one paid heed to Yudhishthira's words, and that is how that disastrous game of gambling commenced.

123. Had the Yadava elite of Mathura boycotted Kansa?

According to the evidence available in the Mahabharata, the Yadava elite had boycotted Kansa in Mathura. Actually, Kansa had become quite impudent due to the backing he received from his father-in-law Jarasandha, an extremely powerful king of Aryavarta. Consequently, he used to blatantly humiliate anyone he pleased; and that is why the Yadavas had stopped involving him in their mutual affairs as far as possible. It is described in the Mahabharata as follows:

विदितं मे महाप्राज्ञ भोजेष्वेवासमंजसम्।
पुत्रं संत्यक्तवान्पूर्वं पौराणां हितकाम्यया।।
अन्धका यादवा भोजाः समेताः कंसमत्यजन्।
नियोगात्तु हते तस्मिन्कृष्णेनामित्रघातिना।।

Vidura said: "O King Dhritarashtra! I know that in the past, a king of the Bhoja dynasty had abandoned his son who had gone astray, keeping in mind the welfare of his kingdom's inhabitants. The Andhaks, Yadavas and Bhojas had collectively abandoned Kansa, and it was on their instructions that Shri Krishna, the slayer of enemies, killed him."

(Mahabharata, Sabha Parva, Chapter–52 Gita Press, 86 South Indian version, Shloka–7-8)

The shunning of Kansa by the Yadavas has been described in the Harivansha Purana as follows:

एवं भवत्सु युक्तेषु मम चित्तानुवर्तिषु।
वर्धमानो ममानर्थो भवद्भिः किमुपेक्षितः॥

"You are so capable and you are always well-disposed towards me, but at present, my sins are on the rise despite your presence; I do not know why you have been neglecting me."

(Harivansha Purana, Vishnu Parva, Chapter–22, Shloka–20)

A terrified Kansa held a meeting of the Yadavas of Mathura and tried to garner their support by talking about the trouble he faced as well as the betrayal by Vasudeva. The shloka quoted above is a statement made by Kansa in the same assembly.

124. Was Krishna a good charioteer?

Five thousand years ago, people had only two alternatives if they wished to travel fast—a horse or a chariot. Horses were available even to the common people, but it was only the wealthy, the elite and the kings that could avail of chariots. After killing Kansa in Mathura, Krishna's life took a drastic turn and became quite hectic. Thus, it was only natural for him to become an expert charioteer. And Arjuna was perhaps quite impressed with Krishna's incredible prowess as a charioteer; that is why he had dreamt of making Krishna his charioteer:

सारथ्यं तु त्वया कार्यमिति मे मानसं सदा।
चिररात्रेप्सितं कामं तद् भवान् कर्तुमर्हति॥

Arjuna said: "I have harboured a long-cherished desire to make you my charioteer – to hand over the reins of my life to you. You must fulfil my long-cherished desire."

उपपन्नमिदं पार्थ मत् स्पर्धसि मया सह।
सारथ्यं ते करिष्यामि कामः सम्पद्यतां तव॥

Krishna said: "Partha! Your competitive attitude towards me is good for you. I will become your charioteer. Let this wish of yours be fulfilled!"

(Mahabharata, Udyoga Parva,Chapter–7, Shloka–37-38)

In the second shloka above, the word 'competitive' needs special attention. According to the authors of the Mahabharata, perhaps Krishna felt that Arjuna, who was convinced that he was a great archer, was skeptical of Krishna's ability to ride the chariot perfectly, despite being impressed by his astounding prowess as a charioteer. That was the reason why Krishna had made this statement.

125. Did Dhritarashtra reluctantly permit Duryodhana to go ahead with the fraudulent gambling or was he equally involved in the conspiracy?

According to the Mahabharata, Dhritarashtra was wholeheartedly involved in the gambling conspiracy with his son Duryodhana and brother-in-law Shakuni. When Yudhishthira was losing huge portions of wealth in every round, Dhritarashtra kept asking Vidura excitedly and repeatedly, 'What have we won in this round?'

किं ते तद्विस्मृतं पार्थ यदेष कुलपांसनः।
दुर्बुद्धिर्विदुरं प्राह द्यूते किं जितमित्युत॥

Bhima said to Arjuna: "Partha! Did you forget how this destroyer of his own clan, the imprudent Dhritarashtra had got the game of gambling started and had repeatedly asked Vidura, 'What have we won in this round?'"

(Mahabharata, Ashramvaasika Parva, Chapter–11, Shloka–24)

126. Before the wrestling fight between Bhima and Jarasandha, did Krishna reveal his own identity and that of the two Pandavas?

According to the Mahabharata, it is true that before the wrestling bout between the two began, Krishna had revealed to Jarasandha his own identity and that of Bhima and Arjuna too:

युयुक्षमाणास्त्वत्तो हि न वयं ब्राह्मणा ध्रुवम्।
शौरिरस्मि हृषीकेशो नृवीरौ पाण्डवाविमौ।
अनयोर्मातुलेयं च कृष्णं मां विद्धि ते रिपुम्॥

Krishna said to Jarasandha: "We, who desire to fight with you, are certainly not Brahmins. I am Hrishikesh, the son of Vasudeva, and these two valiant ones are Bhima and Arjuna, sons of Pandu. I am their maternal uncle's son and your famous enemy Krishna. Recognise me well!"

(Mahabharata, Sabha Parva, Chapter–22, Shloka–25)

This is also mentioned in the Bhagavat Purana:

असौ वृकोदरः पार्थस्तस्य भ्रातार्जुनो ह्ययम्।
अनयोर्मातुलेयं मां कृष्णं जानीहि ते रिपुम्।।

Krishna said: "Look, this is Bhimsen, the son of Pandu, and this is his brother Arjuna, and I am their cousin and your long-standing enemy, Krishna."

(Bhagavat Purana, Skandha–10, Chapter–72, Shloka–29)

The story of Krishna, Bhima and Arjuna entering Magadha in disguise and revealing their identity to Jarasandha is found only in these two texts. There is no mention of any such incident in the Harivansha Purana, Garga Samhita or other texts.

127. Did King Virata attend Yudhishthira's Rajasuya Yajna? If so, why did he not recognise the Pandavas during their incognito exile?

According to the Mahabharata, King Virata had attended Yudhishthira's Rajasuya Yajna along with his two sons:

बाह्लिकाश्चापरे शूरा राजानः सर्व एव ते।
विराटः सह पुत्राभ्यां मावेल्लश्च महाबलः।।

"Bahlik, other valiant kings, King Virata with his two sons, and kings and rulers of Mavell and other kingdoms had arrived there."

(Mahabharata, Sabha Parva, Chapter–34, Shloka–13)

It is clearly described here that not only King Virata but his two sons had also attended Yudhishthira's Rajasuya Yajna. That yajna had lasted for months and the five Pandava brothers used to personally meet all the visiting kings from time to time and ensure that the best hospitality was being extended to them. Similarly, the Pandavas had also stayed with King Virata and his family, not just for a couple of days or weeks, but for an entire year. So, how the Pandavas were able to hide their identity despite this, and stay in that closely guarded palace, is a question that can perhaps be answered only by the authors of the Mahabharata.

128. Did Krishna's brother Balarama believe that the Pandavas were at fault?

Yes. In fact, Balarama especially considered Yudhishthira to be the root cause of all the trouble. This is mentioned in the Udyoga Parva of the

Mahabharata. After the incognito exile of the Pandavas had ended, several eminent kings of Aryavarta were invited with Krishna's consent on the occasion of Abhimanyu's marriage with Uttara. When those kings assembled after the wedding, this is what Balarama said in the assembly:

सर्वास्ववस्थासु च ते न कोप्या ग्रस्तो हि सोऽर्थो बलमाश्रितैस्तैः।
प्रियाभ्युपेतस्य युधिष्ठिरस्य द्यूते प्रसक्तस्य हृतं च राज्यम्॥
निवार्यमाणश्च कुरुप्रवीरः सर्वैः सुहृद्भिर्ह्यमप्यतंज्ञः।
स दीव्यमानः प्रतिदीव्य चैनं गान्धारराजस्य सुतं मताक्षम्॥
हित्वा हि कर्णं च सुयोधनं च समाह्वयद्देवितुमाजमीढः।
दुरोदरास्तत्र सहस्रशोऽन्ये युधिष्ठिरो यान्विषहेत जेतुम्॥
उत्सृज्य तान्सौबलमेव चायं समाह्वयत्तेन जितोऽक्षवत्याम्।
स दीव्यमानः प्रतिदेवनेन अक्षेषु नित्यं स्वपराङ्मुखेषु॥
संरम्भमाणो विजितः प्रसह्य तत्रापराधः शकुनेर्न कश्चित्।
तस्मात्प्रणम्यैव वचो ब्रवीतु वैचित्रवीर्यं बहुसामयुक्तम्॥
तथा हि शक्यो धृतराष्ट्रपुत्रः स्वार्थे नियोक्तुं पुरुषेण तेन।
अयुद्धमाकांक्षत कौरवाणां साम्नैव दुर्योधनमोशसध्वम्॥

"The Kauravas should not be provoked under any circumstances, because they are strong, and that is precisely why they have taken control over the kingdom of the Pandavas. Secondly, it is not that Yudhishthira is absolutely innocent. It was due to his addiction to gambling that his kingdom was snatched away from him. Yudhishthira was incompetent at gambling, which is why his well-wishers had discouraged him from indulging in it. But he did not pay heed to anyone. On the other hand, Shakuni was proficient in gambling; but in spite of this, Yudhishthira kept playing with him. Ignoring Karna and Duryodhana, he had repeatedly challenged Shakuni to gamble with him. He could have defeated thousands of other gamblers who were also present in that assembly; but ignoring all of them, he invited only the son of Subal, Shakuni to play. That is why he lost the gamble. When he began playing and his dice started landing wrong, he became frenzied and yet, he did not desist from playing. He obstinately kept playing and consequently faced defeat; Shakuni is not at fault here. Therefore, the messenger who is sent should convey only a conciliatory message. Do not harbour the apprehension of a war sparking between the Kauravas and the Pandavas; invite Duryodhana only with the intention of instating a treaty or compromise."

(Mahabharata, Udyoga Parva, Chapter–2, Shloka–8-13)

The shlokas given above reveal Balarama's perception of the Kauravas and the Pandavas.

129. Was there any altercation between Satyaki and Balarama regarding the Kauravas and the Pandavas?

In the court of King Virata, when Balarama blamed Yudhishthira for gambling, Satyaki responded sharply:

यादृशः पुरुषस्यात्मा तादृशं संप्रभाषते।
यथारूपोऽन्तरात्मा ते तथारूपं प्रभाषते।।
सन्ति वै पुरुषाः शूराः सन्ति कापुरुषास्तथा।
उभावेतौ दृढौ पक्षौ दृश्येते पुरुषान्प्रति।।
एकस्मिन्नेव जायेते कुले क्लीबमहाबलौ।
फलाफलवती शाखे यथैकस्मिन्वनस्पतौ।।

Satyaki said: "Balarama! A person's words reflect how he is at heart. Your speech also reflects the kind of person you are from within. In this world, there are brave men as well as cowards, and these two qualities can be seen in men invariably. Just as one branch of a tree yields fruit, while another branch of the same tree remains barren, there are two kinds of children born in the same family; one is impotent and the other is strong, just like you and Krishna."

(Mahabharata, Udyoga Parva, Chapter–3, Shloka–1-3)

It is clear from the shlokas above that Satyaki did not like the fact that Balarama was supporting Duryodhana, which is why he made such a caustic comment.

130. What is the mystery behind Krishna being accused of stealing the Syamantaka gem and killing Satrajit? How did Krishna allay this accusation?

According to the Bhagavat Purana, when Krishna had gone to Hastinapur for some work, Akrura and Kritvarma had devised a plan to vent their ire on Satrajit, and in order to make Shatdhanva join them, they said to him:

लब्ध्वैतदन्तरं राजन्शतधन्वानमूचतुः।
अक्रूरकृतवर्माणौ मणिः कस्मान्न गृह्यते॥
योऽस्मभ्यं सम्प्रतिश्रुत्य कन्यारत्नं विगर्ह्य नः।
कृष्णायादान्न सत्राजित्कस्माद्भ्रजणतरमन्वियात्॥
एवं भिन्नमतिस्ताभ्यां सत्राजितमसत्तमः।
शयानमवधील्लोभात्स पापः क्षीणजीवितः॥
स्त्रीणां विक्रोशमानानां क्रन्दन्तीनामनाथवत्।
हत्वा पशून्सौनिकवन्मणिमादाय जग्मिवान्॥

Akrura and Kritvarma said to Shatdhanva: "Why don't you steal the gem from Satrajit? He had pledged to marry his daughter, Satyabhama to us, and now he has spurned us and got her married to Krishna. So, why shouldn't Satrajit be dispatched to the abode of *Yama,*[27] just like his brother Prasen?" Their instigation made Shatdhanva fall for their words and upon finding the opportunity, he ruthlessly killed Satrajit in his sleep, and fled with the gem.

(Bhagavat Purana, Skandha–10, Chapter–57, Shloka–3-6)

When Krishna returned to Dwarka, the atmosphere of the entire city had changed. Throughout the kingdom, whispers and hushed murmurs were abound that because of his greed for the gem, Krishna had conspired and got Satrajit killed. Even his brother Balarama and wife Satyabhama suspected Krishna of the gem's theft. Seeing this, Krishna launched a search to hunt down the killer and gem thief. Seeing that the investigation was tightening the noose around his neck, Shatdhanva sought help from Akrura and Kritvarma; but they spurned him due to their fear of Krishna. Then, the helpless Shatdhanva gave the gem to Akrura and escaped from Dwarka. Krishna and Balarama followed him and killed him in Mithila, just as he was escaping, but the gem was not found on him.

पदातेर्भगवांस्तस्य पदातिस्तिग्मनेमिना।
चक्रेण शिर उत्कृत्य वाससोर्व्यचिनोन्मणिम्॥
अलब्धमणिरागत्य कृष्ण आहाग्रजान्तिकम्।
वृथा हतः शतधनुर्मणिस्तत्र न विद्यते॥

Shukdeva said: "Krishna severed Shatdhanva's head with his discus, even as he was fleeing on foot, and searched for the gem in the folds of his clothes. But when he did not find it, he returned to Balarama and

27. God of death

said, 'We killed him in vain; he did not have the gem with him.'"

(Bhagavat Purana, Skandha–10, Chapter–57, Shloka–21-22)

अक्रूरः कृतवर्मा च श्रुत्वा शतधनोर्वधम्।
व्यूषतुर्भयवित्रस्तौ द्वारकायाः प्रयोजकौ॥

Shukdeva said: "When the main conspirators, Akrura and Kritvarma, heard that Krishna had killed Shatdhanva, they too fled from Dwarka in fear."

(Bhagavat Purana, Skandha–10, Chapter–57, Shloka–29)

ननु दानपते न्यस्तस्त्वय्यास्ते शतधन्वना।
स्यमन्तको मणिः श्रीमान्विदितः पूर्वमेव नः॥
सत्राजितोऽनपत्यत्वाद्गृह्णीयुर्दुहितुः सुताः।
दायं निनीयापः पिण्डान्विमुच्यर्णं च शेषितम्॥
तथापि दुर्धरस्त्वन्यैस्त्वय्यास्तां सुव्रते मणिः।
किन्तु मामग्रजः सम्यङ्न प्रत्येति मणिं प्रति॥
दर्शयस्व महाभाग बन्धूनां शान्तिमावह।
अव्युच्छिन्ना मखास्तेऽद्य वर्तन्ते रुक्मवेदयः॥
एवं सामभिरालब्धः शफल्कतनयो मणिम्।
आदाय वाससाच्छन्नः ददौ सूर्यसमप्रभम्॥

Shukdeva said that Krishna then summoned Akrura to Dwarka and coaxing him with great affection, he said, "Uncle! We know that the gem is with you, because these days, you are performing yajnas in which gold altars are being erected. You are anyway quite charitable. You already know that Satrajit has no son, so his post-cremation rituals will be conducted by his daughter's sons and they alone will have the right to Satrajit's property. Well, even so, you may keep this gem yourself; but just show it to brother Balarama, Satyabhama and Jambavati once, because they suspect me and do not believe me. So, just show them the gem and alleviate their doubts." When Krishna reassured and convinced him, Akrura handed over the Syamantaka gem, which was as radiant as the sun and wrapped in a cloth, to Krishna.

(Bhagavat Purana, Skandha–10,
Chapter–57, Shloka–36-40)

स्यमन्तकं दर्शयित्वा ज्ञातिभ्यो रज आत्मनः।
विमृज्य मणिना भूयस्तस्मै प्रत्यर्पयत्प्रभुः॥

Shukdeva said: "Krishna showed the Syamantaka gem to his kin, thereby wiping away the stigma of being labelled a thief, and then returned the gem to Akrura."

(Bhagavat Purana, Skandha–10, Chapter–57, Shloka–41)

Comment: Apart from the Bhagavat Purana, no description of this incident is found in the Mahabharata or any other Purana.

131. How many maternal aunts did Krishna have and whose daughters were they?

Krishna had two maternal aunts, Asti and Praapti, who were the daughters of Jarasandha, the king of Magadha and one of the most powerful kings of Aryavarta.

अस्तिः प्राप्तिश्च नाम्ना ते मागधस्य सुतेनृप॥
जरासंधस्य कल्याण्यौ पीनश्रोणिपयोधरे।
उभे कंसस्य ते भार्ये प्रादाद् बार्हद्रथो नृपः॥

Vaishampayan said: "O King Janamejaya! The king of Magadha, Jarasandha, had two blessed girls, whose names were Asti and Praapti. Both these daughters were very beautiful. Brihadratha's son, Jarasandha had given both these daughters to Kansa (in marriage). Both were Kansa's wives."

(Harivansha Purana, Vishnu Parva, Chapter–35, Shloka–5-6)

The same has been mentioned in the Mahabharata, Bhagavat Purana and other Puranas without any variance.

132. Was Krishna's wife Satyabhama extremely arrogant?

According to several Puranas as well as the Garga Samhita, Satyabhama was extremely proud of her beauty, in addition to the wealth she had received from her father and her ability to control her husband. In the Garga Samhita, one can get a glimpse of Satyabhama's arrogance through a shloka which describes her bragging about herself:

श्रीकृष्णस्य वचः श्रुत्वा सत्यभामाऽथ भामिनी... X...चैद्याद्या अनेन युयुधुर्युधि॥

"On hearing Krishna's words, Satyabhama, who was proud of her exceptional beauty and youth, said to his other wives."

• Is Radha the only one who is beautiful, am I not pretty? When I was unmarried, countless suitors had asked for my hand in marriage. I have always been revered because of my fine appearance and generosity.

• Friends! It was only because of my beauty that Shatdhanva was killed, and Akrura and Kritvarma had to flee from Dwarka.
• As part of my dowry, my father had given the Syamantaka gem, which automatically produces eight *bhara*[28] of gold every day.
• That gem has brought immense glory to my house too. With my great love, I keep Krishna in control.
• All of you women, who had been enduring hell-like torture in Narakasura's captivity in Pragjyotishpur, could set foot in Dwarka only because of me.
• It was on my behest that Krishna had brought to Dwarka the large elephants, like the Airavat elephant (of Indra) from Bhaumasura's elephant stable.
• I have kept Krishna under my thumb with my chaste and faithful conduct.
• I had given Krishna away as charity to Narada along with all other materials. No woman can enjoy the kind of glory and grandeur that I do.
• No other woman is as beautiful and magnanimous as me. Then of what is consequence is Radha?"

(Garga Samhita, Dwarka Khanda, Chapter–16, Shloka–16-28)

In other words, it is true that Satyabhama was extremely vain. At the same time, she also felt proud that she had Krishna under her thumb.

133. How many times did Krishna's son Pradyumna marry?

Krishna's eldest son, Pradyumna, was abducted when he was just seven days old. The demon named Shambar, who had abducted him, had given the child to his maidservant, Mayawati, to raise him. As the boy grew into a young man, he looked increasingly handsome, and Mayawati's attraction towards him also began to surge. After killing the demon Shambar, the young Pradyumna returned to Dwarka with Mayawati and they were duly married. Mayawati was Pradyumna's first wife, and after this, he was married to Rukmavati (Shubhangi), who was the daughter of his maternal uncle Rukmi. All the Puranas related to Krishna's life have mentioned this fact.

Thereafter, when Pradyumna heard about the unique beauty of Prabhavati, the daughter of the Asura named Vajranabha, he expressed

---

28. ancient unit of weight = 1 quintal

his desire to his uncle Gada (brother of Balarama) and brother Saamba. Then, they collectively formed a gimmick group, which camped in Vajranabha's city and began demonstrating various gimmicks. There, Pradyumna managed to gain entry into the palace with the help of Prabhavati's friends and married the princess. She was his third wife.

(Harivansha Purana, Vishnu Parva, Chapter–94)

In this manner, Pradyumna's marriages had totalled three. On the basis of Puranic texts, it can be said that Pradyumna was not rebellious or wayward in any way. In fact, on several occasions, he had even accomplished the tasks assigned to him by his father Krishna, with complete responsibility.

134. What was Krishna's reaction after abducting Rukmini?

Krishna was elated after having abducted Rukmini. And when Rukmini accepted him as her husband, he had also expressed his pleasant surprise:

राजपुत्रीप्सिता... X ...पूर्णा गेह्योर्ज्योतिरक्रियाः ॥

Krishna said:

- "O Princess! Aryavarta's great, wealthy kings, who are not only respected but also far more attractive, magnanimous and powerful, wanted to marry you.
- Your father and brother wanted you to marry one of them. In fact, they had even given their word to Shishupala. But you disregarded all of them, and accepted a person like me as your husband, a person who is not worthy of you in any way. Why did you do this?
- O Beautiful One! Look, due to our fear of Jarasandha and other kings, we have settled near the sea. We are at loggerheads with powerful kings, and are almost deprived of the right to the throne. O Beautiful One! We do not even know which path we are following or what our path is. We do not even conduct our worldly affairs properly. We do not even know how to woo women. Most of the women who marry into our family have to face hardships.
- We are perpetually poor. We never possessed anything and nor will we ever possess anything in the future. This is the reason why people who consider themselves wealthy neither love us nor serve us.

• It is said that you should be friends with or marry only those whose wealth, family background, prosperity, grandeur, physical appearance and income are similar to that of yours. You should not harbour any relations with those whose status is superior or inferior to you.
• O Princess of Vidarbha! Because of your short-sightedness, you did not consider these factors, and on hearing some beggars praise me, you unwittingly married a worthless person like me.
• Well, nothing is lost yet! You may choose a Kshatriya worthy of you and marry him so that all your hopes and desires can be fulfilled.
• O Beautiful One! You are already aware that Shishupala, Shalva, Jarasandha, Dantavakra and other kings abhor me, and so does your brother Rukmi.
• You may have noticed that even during your *swayamvar*, they were all blinded by the intoxication of their power and machismo. They believe that no one else is of consequence compared to them. I had abducted you only to destroy their ego; there is no other reason behind it.
• However, one thing is certain—we are greedless and unblemished. We are not greedy for women, children or wealth. Without harbouring any attachment to the body, we are simply passive witnesses, akin to the flame of a lamp. We are fully satiated and contented with our own self-realisation."

(Bhagavat Purana, Skandha–10, Chapter–60, Shloka–10-20)

135. To whom was Krishna and Rukmini's daughter Charumati married?

According to the Bhagavat Purana:

रुक्मिण्यास्तनयां राजन्कृतवर्मसुतो बली।
उपयेमे विशालाक्षीं कन्यां चारुमतीं किल॥

Shukdeva said: "Apart from ten sons, Rukmini also had a supremely beautiful daughter with big, lovely eyes, whose name was Charumati. She was married to Bali, son of Kritvarma, who lived in Dwarka."

(Bhagavat Purana, Skandha–10, Chapter–61, Shloka–24)

136. Why did Balarama kill Krishna's brother-in-law, Rukmi?

This incident occurred during the second marriage of Krishna's grandson

Aniruddha. After it was decided that Aniruddha would be married to Rukmi's granddaughter Rochana, Balarama and several prominent Yadavas had set out to Bhojkat with the wedding procession. Well, the wedding ceremony was a joyous affair, but thereafter, some kings who were Rukmi's acolytes, advised him to play a game of dice with Balarama. Rukmi anyway did not want to miss a single opportunity to belittle Krishna's family, so he was delighted with the proposed idea. For, although he loved his sister Rukmini, he was hostile towards Krishna. Furthermore, Balarama was as inept as Yudhishthira in gambling, and he was also a gambling addict, just like Yudhishthira. He simply needed an invitation to gamble and he would immediately agree to it, no matter who the opponent was. Well, the game commenced and Balarama started losing one round after another. And, if that was not enough, the king of Kalinga began grinning from ear to ear, ridiculing Balarama every time he lost a round. At this point, it so happened that Rukmi, encouraged by his winning streak, wagered one lakh coins in the next move; but to his misfortune, Balarama won this round. However, Rukmi suddenly became truculent, and resorting to outright cheating, he started saying that he had won this round too.

After this, the game turned entirely in Balarama's favour as he kept winning repeatedly, and with this dramatic turn of events, the ruckus around him also continued to grow. Since most of the kings present on this occasion were Rukmi's supporters, they were cheering in his favour. Thus, seeing that everyone in the assembly was on his side, Rukmi made a caustic comment that stung Balarama. He said, "Balarama! You are, after all, mere cowherds who wander in the forests. What do you really know about games played with dice and arrows? This is a game that is played by kings like us." Balarama was enraged even more, because this humiliating remark was made overtly in a packed assembly. Consequently, he picked up a *mudgar*[29] that was lying close by, and striking Rukmi fiercely with it, killed him in a single strike. Then, he also mutilated the other kings who had been ridiculing him. In this manner, Rukmi, the brother-in-law of Krishna, was killed by Balarama.

(Bhagavat Purana, Skandha–10, Chapter–61, Shloka–25-37)

(Harivansha Purana, Vishnu Parva, Chapter–61, Shloka–12-48)

---

29. A long, heavy wooden implement used for physical exercise

137. How vast was Indraprastha, which Krishna had asked the demon Maya to build for the Pandavas?

This is how the Mahabharata describes Indraprastha's establishment:

अभिप्रायेण पार्थानां कृष्णस्य च महात्मनः।
पुण्येऽहनि महातेजाः कृतकौतुकमंगलः॥
तर्पयित्वा द्विजश्रेष्ठान्पायसेन सहस्रशः।
धनं बहुविधं दत्त्वा तेभ्य एव च वीर्यवान्॥
सर्वर्तुगुणसम्पन्नां दिव्यरूपां मनोरमाम्।
दशकिष्कुसहस्रां तां मापयामास सर्वतः॥

Vaishampayan said: "He (Maya demon) decided to construct the court according to the wishes of Shri Krishna and the sons of Kunti. For this, he got all the pre-construction work completed, and then, had a section of land measuring 10,000 *haath*[30] from all sides, marked for the construction of an enchanting palace of unparalleled beauty, encompassing the salient features of all the seasons."

(Mahabharata, Sabha Parva, Chapter–1, Shloka–19-21)

Based on other accounts given in the Mahabharata and various Puranic sources, it is believed that India was at its peak during Krishna's lifetime, as humans had scaled the peaks of progress during that period. Based on this fact, the description of Indraprastha given in the Mahabharata does not seem to be an exaggeration. It is not unimaginable to have a capital or a kingdom spanning an area of 5,000-odd square kilometres.

138. Did Krishna accept the annexation of Dwarka to Yudhishthira's empire at the time of the Rajasuya Yajna?

The description given in the Mahabharata in this regard is notable. A year prior to Yudhishthira's Rajasuya Yajna, the four brothers—Bhima, Arjuna, Nakula and Sahadeva—went in all four directions to consolidate all the kingdoms under their rule. Nakula went to the west, and after defeating several kings, he arrived near Dwarka, but unlike what he did in the other kingdoms, he did not enter Dwarka directly, but instead sent an envoy:

द्वारपालं च तरसा वशे चक्रे महाद्युतिः।
रामठान्हारहूणांश्च प्रतीच्याश्चैव ये नृपाः॥

30. A unit of measurement

तान्सर्वान्स वशे चक्रे शासनादेव पाण्डवः।
तत्रस्थः प्रेषयामास वासुदेवाय भारत॥
स चास्य गतभी राजन्प्रतिजग्राह शासनम्।
ततः शाकलमभ्येत्य मद्राणां पुटभेदनम्॥

Vaishampayan said: "Nakula quickly took Dwarpalpur under his control. Nakula, the son of Pandu, took other western kingdoms like Ramath, Haar and Hun under his control with a mere order. O Janamejaya! While staying there, Nakula sent an envoy to Shri Krishna, the son of Vasudeva. And O King! Krishna too accepted Nakula's rule only out of love so that the Rajasuya Yajna could be completed without any hindrance. After that, Nakula conquered the Shakala kingdom and entered his maternal kingdom Madra."

(Mahabharata, Sabha Parva, Chapter–32, Shloka–12-14)

That means Dwarka had also accepted its annexation to Indraprastha, even if it was for the sake of a formality.

139. During Yudhishthira's Rajasuya Yajna, what was the reason behind the ruckus over Krishna being honoured as the chief guest?

The Mahabharata, citing the perpetual tradition of India, states that there are six types of people who deserve exceptional respect, and honouring them as special guests in any public gathering is mandatory. That is why Grandsire Bhishma, after the end of the yajna, instructed Yudhishthira to worship (honour) all the kings who were present by offering them *arghya*[31]:

ततो भीष्मोऽब्रवीद्राजन्धर्मराजं युधिष्ठिरम्।
क्रियतामर्हणं राज्ञां यथार्हमिति भारत॥
आचार्यमृत्विजं चैव संयुजं च युधिष्ठिर।
स्नातकं च प्रियं प्राहुः षडर्घ्यार्हान्नृपं तथा॥
एतानर्घ्यानभिगतानाहुः संवत्सरोषितान्।
त इमे कालपूगस्य महतोऽस्मानुपागताः॥
एषामेकैकशो राजन्नर्घ आनीयतामिति।
अथ तेषां वरिष्ठाय समर्थायोपनीयताम्॥

Vaishampayan said: "O King! Then, Grandsire Bhishma said to Yudhishthira, 'O Yudhishthira! Pride of the Bharatas! Now, you must honour the kings who have come here, in an appropriate manner.

31. An offering of water

Acharyas,[32] priests, relatives, graduates, dear friends and kings—these six are said to be worthy of being honoured with *arghya*. If they visit you after a year, they should be worshipped with the offering of *arghya*; this is what wise men have stated. All these kings have come to our kingdom after a very long time. Therefore, O Yudhishthira! Offer *arghya* to all of them one by one, and first of all, you must honour the one who is the best and most powerful.'"

(Mahabharata, Sabha Parva, Chapter–36, Shloka–22-25)

Then, Yudhishthira asked Grandsire Bhishma, "Kindly advise me; whom do you consider superior and the most powerful among these kings?"

ततो भीष्मः शान्तनवो बुद्ध्यानिश्चित्य वीर्यवान्।
अमन्यत तदा कृष्णमर्हणीयतमं भुवि।।

"Shantanu's mighty son, Grandsire Bhishma, with his wisdom, decided that Shri Krishna was the most revered on earth."

(Mahabharata, Sabha Parva, Chapter–36, Shloka–30)

Then, with Grandsire Bhishma's permission, Sahadeva worshipped Krishna according to the prescribed rituals. Now, although the worship of Krishna was completed, a political tug of war emerged soon after. Kings who considered age, wealth and political supremacy as the basis of superiority could not digest the fact that Krishna was honoured. Krishna's cousin, Shishupala who was his political rival and also the leader of the Jarasandha camp that was opposed to Krishna, openly objected to the honour accorded to Krishna:

त्वादृशो धर्मयुक्तो हि कुर्वाणः... X ...राजभिरिहानीतैरवमानाय भारत।।

Shishupala said: "Bhishma! A virtuous man like you is humiliated in the society of gentlemen when he behaves unctuously towards someone. Everyone knows that Krishna of the Yadava clan is not a king. Then, why did you have him honoured in spite of so many kings present here? According to you:

- If you wanted to get an elderly person honoured, then instead of Vasudeva, why did you have his son honoured?
- If you wished to have a dear friend honoured, then Drupad, the greatest well-wisher of the Pandavas, who took care of them during their difficult times and elevated their political stature, was also present here.

---

32. Teachers

• If you wished to have an Acharya honoured, then Dronacharya, the best and most respected Acharya, was also present here.
• If you wished to have a priest honoured, then Veda Vyasa, the best priest of Aryavarta, was also present here.
• If you wished to have a person with divine virtue honoured, then why did you not get yourself honoured? Because you have been granted the boon of dying at will.
• If you wished to have a scholar of scriptures honoured, then you could have chosen Ashwathama; Krishna can never be a greater scholar than him.

Yudhishthira! Krishna is neither a priest nor an Acharya or a king. So, on what basis did you honour him? Yudhishthira! If all of you are so fond of Krishna and you wished to honour him only, then what was the need to invite these kings? Was it only to humiliate them?"

(Mahabharata, Sabha Parva, Chapter–37, Shloka–4-18)

So, the main reason behind that ruckus was to oppose Krishna politically.

140. Did Krishna make arrangements for the education, training and care of the sons of Draupadi and Subhadra?

According to the Mahabharata, when the Pandavas had left for the forest along with Draupadi, after losing their kingdom in a game of dice, Krishna had made arrangements to look after Kunti, Subhadra and all the young children in Dwarka itself. When Krishna went to meet the Pandavas in the Kamyaka forest, he told Draupadi about how those children were faring:

कृष्णे धनुर्वेदरतिप्रदानास्तवात्मजास्ते शिशवः शुशीलाः।
सद्भिः सदैवाचरितं समाधिं चरन्ति पुत्रास्तव याज्ञसेनि।।
राज्ये नियुक्तैश्च निमन्त्र्यमाणाः पित्रा च कृष्णे तव सोदरैश्च।
न यज्ञसेनस्य न मातुलानां गृहेषु बाला रतिमाप्नुवन्ति।।
आनर्तमेवाभिमुखाः शिवेन गत्वाधनुर्वेदरतिप्रधानाः।
तवात्मजा वृष्णिपुरं प्रविश्य न दैवतेभ्यः स्पृहयन्ति कृष्णे।।
यथा त्वमेवार्हसि तेषु वृत्तं प्रयोक्तुमार्या च यथैव कुन्ती।
तेष्वप्रमादेन तथा करोति तथैव भूयश्च तथा सुभद्रा।।
यथाऽनिरुद्धस्य यथाऽभिमन्योर्यथा सुनीथस्य यथैव भानोः।
तथा विनेता च गतिश्च कृष्णे तवात्मजानामपि रौक्मिणेयः।।

गदासिचर्मग्रहणेषु शूरानस्त्रेषु शिक्षासु रथोशयाने।
सम्यग्विनेता विनयेदतन्द्रीस्तांश्चाभिमन्युं च सदा कुमारान्॥
स चापि सम्यक्प्रणिधाय शिक्षां शस्त्राणि चैषां विधिवत्प्रदाय।
तवात्मजानां च तथाऽभिमन्योः पराक्रमैस्तुष्यति रौक्मिणेयः॥
यथा विहारं प्रसमीक्षमाणाः प्रयान्ति पुत्रास्तव याज्ञसेनि।
एकैकमेषामनुयान्ति यत्र रथाश्च यानानि च दन्तिनश्च॥

Krishna said to Draupadi: "Krishnaa! Your sons are quite affable. They are also keenly interested in the science of archery. All the children are well-behaved and disciplined. Krishnaa! Your father and brothers invited them several times by tempting them with royal luxuries and comforts. But your children did not wish to stay at their maternal grandparents' home. They do not like it there. They have a clear-cut inclination towards archery. All of them live in Dwarka and do not feel like going anywhere else. Krishnaa! The kind of training that you can impart to your children, can also be provided by Aunt Kunti, and that is verily the kind of training that Subhadra is giving them.

Krishnaa! Just as my son Pradyumna is training his son Aniruddha, Subhadra's son Abhimanyu, and Sunith, Bhanu and the others in the science of archery, he is also the teacher and mentor of your sons. Abhimanyu, an expert at imparting training and completely devoid of laziness, teaches your brave sons the nuances of fighting with the mace, sword and shield. He is also teaching them the art of chariot-riding and horse-riding, while also training them in wielding other weapons. Abhimanyu is always keenly involved in their training. Pradyumna is delighted to see the might of Abhimanyu and your sons. O *Yagyaseni!*[33] Chariots, horses, palanquins and so on are always available for your sons to travel around the city or go elsewhere."

(Mahabharata, Vana Parva,
Chapter–183, Shloka–24-31)

It is clear from the shlokas above that Krishna wanted Draupadi to cast away her worries regarding the children; he also wanted to ensure that all those children became self-sufficient Kshatriyas while there was still time. Simultaneously, the astute politician that he was, Krishna did not want to give Duryodhana any chance to compel the Pandavas in any manner by trying to trouble their children.

33. Born out of the sacrificial fire

141. Which major weapons could Krishna wield?

Krishna had undergone formal training in a gurukul, so he could wield almost all the weapons. Though his favourite weapon was the *chakra* (discus), he also used other weapons when the need arose. The scriptures mention four weapons that he possessed: the Sudarshan Chakra, the bow named Sarang, the mace named Kaumodaki and the sword named Nandaka. Some of Krishna's poet-devotees from south India have named his bow 'Kodanda' in their compositions. Meerabai also referred to Krishna as 'Kodandadhari' in her compositions, which means 'the one who carries the Kodanda bow'.

142. Did Krishna offer to attack Duryodhana, conquer Hastinapur and hand it over to Yudhishthira during the exile itself?

The Mahabharata mentions such an episode when Krishna went to the Kamyaka forest to meet the Pandavas. There, he said to Yudhishthira:

अथाब्रवीद्धर्मराजं तु कृष्णो दशार्हयोधाः कुकुरान्धकाश्च।
एते निदेशं तव पालयन्तस्तिष्ठन्तु यत्रेच्छसि तत्र राजन्॥
आवर्ततां कार्मुकवेगवाता हलायुध प्रग्रहणा मधूनाम्।
सेना तवार्थेषु नरेन्द्र यत्ता ससादिपत्त्येशरथा सनागा॥
प्रस्थाप्यतां पाण्डव धार्तराष्ट्रः सुयोधनः पापकृतां वरिष्ठः।
स सानुबन्धः ससुहृद्गणश्च भौमस्य सौबाधिपतेश्च मार्गम्॥
कामं तथा तिष्ठ नरेन्द्र तस्मिन्यथा कृतस्ते समयः सभायाम्।
दाशार्हयोधैस्तु हतारियोधं प्रतीक्षतां नागपुरं प्रभग्नम्॥
व्यपेतमन्युर्व्यपनीतपाप्मा विहृत् यत्रेच्छसि तत्र कामम्।
ततः समृद्धिप्रभवं विशोकः प्रपत्स्यसे नागपुरं सराष्ट्रम्॥

Krishna said to Yudhishthira: "O King! The warriors of Dashaarha, Kukur and Andhak clans can station themselves wherever you wish, obeying your orders. O King! The four-winged army of Mathura, replete with chariots, elephants, horses and foot soldiers, under the leadership of brother Balarama, is always ready to assist you. You may now send Duryodhana, son of the great sinner Dhritarashtra, to the same abode of death where Bhaumasura and Shaalva have gone.

Your Majesty! If you wish, you may continue to fulfil your pledge, but if you permit, the Yadava warriors can kill all the enemies and wait for your arrival in Hastinapur. O King! Cast away feelings of anger, helplessness and sorrow, and travel wherever you wish to. And thereafter, enter your famous and unsurpassed capital, Hastinapur, free of sadness and woe."

(Mahabharata, Vana Parva, Chapter–183, Shloka–32-36)

Krishna makes this offer, but Yudhishthira declines it, saying that almost twelve years of exile had already elapsed, and only one year of incognito exile was left. Therefore, it was best to wait a little longer.

143. Did Krishna enunciate the Gita to Arjuna a second time as well?

According to the Ashwamedhika Parva of the Mahabharata, Arjuna requested Krishna to recite the Gita again, but Krishna expressed his inability to enunciate it again, exactly as he had done at the time of the war, and instead started a new story. This text, from Chapter 16–51, has been publicised as the Anugita. We have discussed this earlier too in this book. Actually, this entire part of the Mahabharata is nothing but an embellishment; meaning, neither has it been composed by Veda Vyasa nor by his disciple Vaishampayan.

Well, I leave it to you to check its authenticity, and in response to the question above, my answer is—no. Let alone enunciating the Gita again, Krishna did not even engage in a general discussion on spirituality with Arjuna. After perusing the Mahabharata as well as other Puranic texts related to Krishna's life, what emerges is that after the Kurukshetra war, there was no occasion in the life of Krishna and Arjuna, whereby Krishna felt compelled to impart knowledge or wisdom to Arjuna.

Now, consider the following shlokas of this same Chapter 16:

विदितं मे महाबाहो संग्रामे समुपस्थिते।
महात्म्यं देवकीपुत्र तच्च ते रूपमैशरम्॥
यत्तु तद्भवता प्रोक्तं पुरा केशव सौहदात्।
तत्सर्वं पुरुषव्याघ्र नष्टं मे व्यग्रचेतसः॥
मम कौतूहलं त्वस्ति तेष्वर्थेषु पुनः पुनः।
भवांस्तु द्वारकां गन्ता नचिरादिव माधव॥

Arjuna said: "O One with mighty arms! Son of Devaki! When the Mahabharata war was just about to commence, I had a glimpse of your greatness and divine nature. But O Keshava! All the knowledge that you had preached to me so genially has been forgotten now, as my mind is distracted. Madhava! I yearn repeatedly to listen to (your teachings on) those subjects. You are about to leave for Dwarka soon, so please explain all those subjects to me once again."

(Mahabharata, Ashvamedhika Parva, Chapter–16, Shloka–5-7)

Then, taking a dim view of what Arjuna had just said, Krishna said:

श्रावितस्त्वं मया गुह्यं ज्ञापितश्च सनातनम्।
धर्मं स्वरूपिणं पार्थ सर्वलोकांश्च शोश्तान्।।
अबुद्ध्या यन्न गृह्णीतास्तन्मे सुमहदप्रियम्।
न च साऽद्य पुनर्भूयः स्मृतिर्मे सम्भविष्यति।।
नूनमश्रद्दधानोऽसि दुर्मेधा ह्यसि पाण्डव।
न च शक्यं पुनर्वक्तुमशेषेण धनंजय।।
स हि धर्मः सुपर्याप्तो ब्रह्मणः पदवेदने।
न शक्यं तन्मया भूयस्तथा वक्तुमशेषतः।।

"O Arjuna! At that time, I had made you listen to secret, esoteric truths. I had introduced to you the religion that represents me, and my eternal Supreme Essence, and I had also described the everlasting worlds, but you could not remember that sermon because of your imprudence; I find this highly disappointing. Now, it is well-nigh impossible to recall those truths in their entirety. O Son of Pandu! You are devoid of devotion indeed; you seem to be quite dense. Dhananjaya! Now, I cannot repeat that sermon as it was. As those truths were enough to attain the essence of God, repeating them in their entirety in the same form is not possible even for me."

(Mahabharata, Ashvamedhika Parva, Chapter–16, Shloka–9-12)

Saying this, Krishna had clearly expressed his inability to recite anything again.

144. Did Krishna really bring Abhimanyu's dead son back to life?

In the Mahabharata, the story of the birth of Abhimanyu's son, Parikshit is described in the Ashwamedhika Parva, where the words 'lethargic or passive' and 'unconscious' are hardly noticed. Almost everyone is obsessed with avatarism and stories of miracles, and as a result, these words have been deliberately ignored. In the Mahabharata, the story goes that when the five Pandavas went towards the Himalayas to raise funds for the Ashwamedha Yajna, Krishna reached Hastinapur during the same period. On his arrival, he was welcomed by the women of the Pandava family. Well, a few days later, Arjuna's widowed daughter-in-law Uttara began experiencing labour pains and soon gave birth to an unconscious child, who was neither crying nor moving its hands and feet:

स तु राजा महाराज ब्रह्मास्त्रेणावपीडितः।
शवो बभूव निश्चेष्टो हर्षशोकविवर्धनः॥

Vaishampayan said: "O King Janamejaya! Due to the devastating impact of the Brahmastra, King Parikshit was born as an unconscious child, akin to a corpse. Thus, he was the cause of the simultaneous joy and grief of his kin."

(Mahabharata, Ashvamedhika Parva, Chapter–66, Shloka–9)

Comment: Actually, it seems that the child was born malnourished. The pregnant Uttara was suffering the pain and anguish resulting out of the death of all the sons of the Pandavas and other relatives in the Mahabharata war, in addition to the pain of her husband's death, who had also been killed in the war. It seems that because of this deep anguish, the unborn child of Uttara had not developed properly. Had he really been born dead, this would have been mentioned clearly in the Mahabharata. Now, let us see what the Mahabharata states about the revival of the child:

इत्युक्तो वासुदेवेन स बालो भरतर्षभ।
शनैः शनैर्महाराज प्रास्पन्दत सचेतनः॥

"O King Janamejaya! When Shri Krishna said this, that child regained consciousness. He gradually began to move."

(Mahabharata, Ashvamedhika Parva, Chapter–69, Shloka–24)

It is clear from both the above shlokas that the child was born malnourished due to which he fainted at birth, but he was very much alive. Based on this, one can clearly say that those who love to talk about miracles have left no stone unturned in exaggerating even the smallest of incidents.

145. Did Krishna name Abhimanyu's son?

In response to this question, the actual situation at the time of the birth of Abhimanyu's son has been described in detail. When that child was born, all the Pandavas were away from Hastinapur due to some work, but fortunately, Krishna had reached there to participate in the Ashwamedha Yajna. So, naturally, the initial birth rituals were completed under his supervision, and as part of these, he had also named the child. Now, why did Krishna name that child 'Parikshit'? Regarding this, the Mahabharata states:

परिक्षीणे कुले यस्माज्जातोऽयमभिमन्युजः।
परिक्षिदिति नामास्य भवत्वित्यब्रवीत् तदा।।

Vaishampayan said: "The name of the Pandavas was about to be wiped out forever (Pareeksheen), when this child of Abhimanyu was born, so Shri Krishna said that the child should be named Parikshit."

(Mahabharata, Ashvamedhika Parva, Chapter–70, Shloka–10)

146. How did Krishna pacify Balarama and the infuriated Yadavas after getting his own sister Subhadra abducted?

When Arjuna escaped with Subhadra in Krishna's own chariot towards Indraprastha, the Yadava soldiers chased him a great distance, but they could not catch him. Consequently, all the enraged inhabitants of Dwarka began to plan an attack on Indraprastha. Thus, in order to prevent unnecessary violence and war, Krishna began pacifying the Yadavas:

*नावमानं कुलस्यास्य गुडाकेश... **X** ...वासुदेवस्य तथा कर्तुं जनाधिप।।*

Krishna said: "Arjuna has not insulted this clan; on the contrary, he has only honoured it. Arjuna is well aware that we do not take money in exchange for our daughters. He also knows that there is no guarantee that he will be able to marry the girl in a *swayamvar*. So, which brave man would wait for the *swayamvar*, and which lowly man would sell his children? I believe, Arjuna has abducted Subhadra only after considering all these aspects.

Our Subhadra is fortunate, and Arjuna, the valiant son of Kunti, has a great reputation too. So, who wouldn't want such an alliance? There is no one in this world, except Shankara, who can defeat Arjuna. At present, Arjuna has my chariot, which has horses yoked to it, racing at high speed. So, if you set out to fight with him and if he defeats you all and reaches his capital city Indraprastha, then just think, what would be the state of your self-respect, that is, the Yadava clan's reputation?

Therefore, it is not our defeat if we bring him back after reassuring him." After listening to Krishna, the Yadavas heeded his advice.

(Mahabharata, Adi Parva, Chapter–220, Shloka–2-10)

The Bhagavat Purana also describes the abduction of Subhadra, but in this text, Krishna pacifies the angry Balarama in a single shloka *(Bhagavat Purana, Skandha–10, Chapter–86, Shloka–11)*. Apart from this, the abduction of Subhadra is not mentioned in any other Purana. Thus, after perusing the evidence given in the Mahabharata, it is once again proved that Krishna possessed the capability to convince anyone with his words.

147. What was Draupadi's reaction when Arjuna reached Indraprastha after abducting Subhadra?

The Mahabharata narrates this story in a very interesting manner. After reaching Indraprastha and meeting his mother and brothers, when Arjuna went to his chamber to meet Draupadi, she said:

तं द्रौपदी प्रत्युवाच प्रणयात् कुरुनन्दनम्॥
तत्रैव गच्छ कौन्तेय यत्र सा सात्वतात्मजा।
सुबद्धस्यापि भारस्य पूर्वबन्धः श्लथायते॥
तथा बहुविधं कृष्णां विलपन्तीं धनंजयः।
सान्त्वयामास भूयश्च क्षमयामास चासकृत्॥

Draupadi said: "Son of Kunti! Why have you come here? Go where Subhadra, the daughter of the Satvata clan, is. It is true; no matter how tightly a load is fastened, the first bond becomes loose the moment the load is tied for the second time. This is verily the state of your bond of love with me." After making a few more similar comments, Krishnaa began to cry. Thereafter, Arjuna pacified her in various ways and apologised for his transgression.

(Mahabharata, Gita Press Edition, Adi Parva, Chapter–220, Shloka–16-18)

Furthermore, seeing how furious Draupadi was, Arjuna was afraid to introduce Subhadra to her. But as they all lived under the same roof, he could not help but introduce her. So, Arjuna made Subhadra dress in very ordinary attire, akin to a milkmaid, and sent her to Kunti's chamber where Draupadi was also present:

सुभद्रां त्वरमाणश्च रक्तकौशेयवासिनीम्।
पार्थं प्रस्थापयामास कृत्वा गोपालिकावपुः॥

Vaishampayan said: "Arjuna excitedly sent the unparalleled beauty, Subhadra, who was dressed in a red silk saree, to the palace, after making her dress like a milkmaid."

(Mahabharata, Gita Press Edition, Adi Parva, Chapter–220, Shloka–19)

All in all, Draupadi was certainly not happy with Arjuna's marriage to Subhadra.

148. Was Eklavya Krishna's cousin?

According to a description available in the Harivansha Purana, Eklavya was Krishna's cousin, who was abandoned by his father at the time of his birth, as he thought that his son was ill-fated. According to the Harivansha Purana:

निवृत्त शत्रुं शत्रुघ्नं देवश्रवा व्यजायत॥
देवश्रवाः प्रजातस्तु नैषादिर्यः प्रतिश्रुतः।
एकलव्यो महाराज निषादैः परिवर्धितः॥

Vaishampayan said: "Vasudeva's second brother, Devashrava gave birth to a son named Shatrughna, who was the destroyer of enemies. O King! For some reason, this son named Shatrughna was abandoned in his childhood and the *Nishadas*[34] raised him, so he became famous as Eklavya of the Nishada clan."

(Harivansha Purana, Harivansha Parva, Chapter–34, Shloka–32-33)

149. What do the texts say about the wives of Kansa?

According to the Hindu Puranas such as Bhagavat Purana, Harivansha Purana and others, Kansa had two wives, Asti and Praapti:

जिघांसुर्हि यदून् क्रुद्धः कंसस्यापचितिं स्मरन्।
अस्तिः प्राप्तिश्च नाम्ना ते मागधस्य सुते नृप॥
जरासंधस्य कल्याण्यौ पीनश्रोणिपयोधरे।
उभे कंसस्य ते भार्ये प्रादाद् बार्हद्रथो नृपः॥

Vaishampayan said: "O Janamejaya, Lord of Men! The king of Magadha, Jarasandha, had two blessed daughters, whose names were Asti and Praapti. Brihadratha's son, Jarasandha gave both his daughters to

34. A tribe

Kansa in marriage. Both of them were Kansa's wives."

(Harivansha Purana, Vishnu Parva, Chapter–34, Shloka–5-6)

अस्तिः प्राप्तिश्च कंसस्य महिष्यौ भरतर्षभ।
मृते भर्तरि दुःखार्ते ईयतुः स्म पितुर्गृहान्।।

Shukdeva said: "O Parikshit of the Bharata clan! Kansa had two queens: Asti and Praapti. They were anguished by their husband's death and left for the capital of their father's kingdom."

(Bhagavat Purana, Skandha–10, Chapter–50, Shloka–1)

But according to the Harivansha Purana written by Acharya Jinsen, a Jain teacher, Kansa had only one wife - Jeevadisha:

वाचयित्वेति विज्ञाय राजा स्वस्रीयमात्मनः।
दृष्टः कन्यां ददौ तस्मै सम्पन्नगुणसम्पदाम्।।

"After reading the signet ring, King Jarasandha understood that this Kansa is his nephew, so he rejoiced and gave him his daughter, Jeevadisha, who possessed an abundance of virtues."

(Jain Harivansha Purana, Sarga–33, Shloka–24)

It is clear from the evidence quoted above, that only two daughters of Jarasandha, named Asti and Praapti, were the wives of Kansa. In this regard, the statement made by the Jain teacher Jinsen, who lived in the 7th or 8th century, is unfounded. It is not that Jainism is new or that nothing had been written before Jinsen. Even before this, a lot had been written in the literature of Jain religion, but none of the earlier scholars of Jainism had spoken about this. So, it cannot even be said that this information has been passed on traditionally. Therefore, propagating new information about a historical fact without any sound basis, is nothing more than an attempt to indulge in guesswork and confuse people. Therefore, regarding Kansa's wives, the information available in ancient Hindu texts alone is trustworthy.

150. Was gambling a highlight of Diwali even during Krishna's time?

There are two words in this question which require separate explanations. First of all, as far as Diwali is concerned, there is no mention of it in the Mahabharata or any Purana composed in the BC era, such as the Harivansha Purana, Brahma Purana, Vishnu Purana,

Padma Purana and others. It is also said that the festival of Deepavali is celebrated to commemorate the return of the king of Ayodhya, Shri Ramchandra, from exile but there is no direct or indirect mention of Deepavali even in the Valmiki Ramayana, the first and oldest text that narrates the story of Rama. In the last Canto 131 of the Yuddha Kanda of the Valmiki Ramayana, Rama's return and his coronation immediately thereafter are described in detail; there is a description of other preparations too, but there is no description that resembles Deepavali. Furthermore, there is no mention of lighting even a single lamp in that entire preparation. Therefore, it can be said with authority that Deepavali is not based on any ancient tradition. Deepavali is mentioned briefly in the 1st–2nd Century Sanskrit drama 'Nagananda', composed during Harshavardhana's period. The play depicts how the festival of lamps is celebrated, and how the newly-wedded wife receives gifts from her in-laws. Then, in the Puranas composed in the medieval period, this festival was elevated to a divine status by creating a variety of reasons behind it or linking it to events written about in the ancient texts. In other words, it can be said that there was no Deepavali during Krishna's lifetime.

Secondly, as far as gambling is concerned, it was a long-standing hobby and addiction of the royal families and the affluent sections of the society. And there were only a few men like Krishna hailing from royal families who were not addicted to it. Other individuals who were extremely fond of gambling such as Shakuni, an expert at gambling, and the inept gambling addicts like Yudhishthira and Balarama have been discussed elsewhere in this book.

151. What is written about Krishna in the Jain scriptures?

Krishna has been accorded great prominence in the Jain religion, but various texts of this religion contradict each other. Jinsen, an 8th century Jain *Acharya,*[35] in his Harivansha Purana, has described Krishna as a practical, deceitful politician, and has placed him in hell, while describing his brother Balarama as truthful and giving him a place in heaven *(Jain Harivansha Purana, Sarga–65, Shloka–49-55)*. On the other hand, a 12th century Jain Acharya, Hemachandra, in his work on

35. Teacher

63 Shalaka *Purush,*[36] has termed Krishna, that is, Vasudeva, as a 'class' or 'category' by itself. This book portrays Vasudeva, Prati-Vasudeva and Balabhadra as three categories. According to this text, there are 63 great men in every cycle of creation, out of whom, some attain salvation in their present birth, some go to heaven, while others, after visiting hell several times, are born as human beings and then attain salvation.

According to Acharya Hemachandra, nine Vasudeva, nine Prati-Vasudeva and nine Balabhadra types of people are born in every cycle of creation. According to him, all Vasudeva and Prati-Vasudeva have gone to hell, because they were violent slaughterers, and they will attain salvation by taking birth in some human life in the future. Some Balabhadras have gone to heaven, while others are waiting for the next cycle of creation.

(Role of 63 Shalaka Purusha - 11th series of the Vijay Devasura Sangha Granthamala by Shrigaudiji Jain Temple, Pages–16-17)

152. Did a woman named Kubja really come into Krishna's life?

Almost all the Puranas describe Kubja in detail and in various styles too. Kubja is also one of the few prominent persons mentioned in the texts that describe Krishna's stay in Mathura. Whether Kubja was slim and beautiful or had a hunch back, whether she was young or old, she definitely existed. Hence, one's curiosity to find out as much as one can about Kubja is natural. Now, let us first see what the Harivansha Purana says about her:

वसुदेवसुतौ तौ च राजमार्गगतावुभौ।
कुब्जां ददृशतुर्भूयः सानुलेपनभाजनाम्।।
तामाह कृष्णः कुब्जेति कस्येदमनुलेपनम् ।
नयस्यम्बुजपत्राक्षि क्षिप्रमाख्यातुमर्हसि।।
सस्मिता सम्मुखी भूत्वा प्रत्युवाचाम्बुजेक्षणम्।
कृष्णं जलदगम्भीरं विद्युत्कुटिलगामिनी।।
राज्ञः स्नानगृहं यामि तद् गृहाणानुलेपनम्।
दृष्ट्वैव त्वारविन्दाक्ष विस्मितास्मि वरानन।।
यत्त्वमिच्छसि मे वीर त्वं गृहाणानुलेपनम्।
स्थितास्म्यागच्छ भद्रं ते हृदयस्यासि मे प्रियः।।

36. Illustrious men

कुतश्चागम्यते सौम्य यन्मां त्वं नावबुध्यसे।
महाराजस्य दयितां नियुक्तामनुलेपने॥

Vaishampayan said: "After this, both the sons of Vasudeva saw Kubja, who was carrying a vessel with fragrant paste in her hand. Krishna said, 'Kubja! Tell me quickly, for whom are you taking this?' In response, Kubja spoke in a solemn voice, akin to the murmur of a monsoon cloud, 'I am going to the king's bath; take this if you wish. I am delighted just to see you. I have stayed back for you. Come to my house. You are the Lord of my life. Where have you come from that you do not know me? I am the beloved and famed maidservant of the king. He has employed me to apply perfumes.'"

(Harivansha Purana, Vishnu Parva, Chapter–27, Shloka–25-30)

Comment: A person with a hunch is called 'Kubj' in Sanskrit. The Bhagavat Purana also depicts the first meeting between Krishna and Kubja in a similar manner. The only difference is the writing style of the two authors, otherwise the rest of the description is the same *(Bhagavat Purana, Skandha–10, Chapter–42, Shloka–1-3).* The Brahmavaivarta Purana, however, has twisted the story, because in this Purana, Kubja is depicted as an extremely old woman instead of a beautiful, young woman. But there is no question of an old woman being employed for the perfuming of a king. Well, for now, just take a look at the shlokas of this Purana:

एवंभूतां च मथुरां दृष्ट्वा कमललोचनः।
ददर्श पथि कुब्जां तां वृद्धामतियरादुराम्॥
यान्तो दण्डसहायेन चातिनम्रां नमद्गलीम्।
रूक्षितां विकृताकारां बिभ्रतीं चन्दनद्रवम्॥
कस्तूरीकुंकुमाक्तं च स्पर्शमात्रेण नारद।
सुगन्धिमकरन्देन गन्धाढ्यं सुमनोहरम्॥
सादृष्ट्वा सस्मिता वृद्धा श्रीकान्तं शान्तमीशरम्।
श्रीयुक्तं श्रीनिवासं तं श्रीबीजं श्रीनिकेतनम्॥
प्रणम्य सहसा मूधर्ना भक्तिनम्रा पुटांजलिः।
प्रददौ चन्दनं तस्य गात्रेश्यामलसुन्दरे॥

"Thus, as he was feasting his eyes on the beauty of Mathura and proceeding ahead, Krishna saw an extremely old woman standing ahead. She was walking with a stick; her waist was bent and there were wrinkles all over her body. She appeared shrivelled and deformed. She was carrying sandalwood paste mixed with musk and saffron. The old lady bowed down on seeing these two brothers and applied sandalwood to them."

(Brahmavaivarta Purana, Shri Krishna Janma Khanda,
Chapter–72, Shloka–15-19)

On the other hand, the Garga Samhita describes Kubja as a beautiful woman, similar to the description given in the other Puranas:

यांतीं स्त्रियं पद्मनेत्रां पाटीरालेपभाजनम्।
विभ्रतीं युवतीं कुब्जां पथि पप्रच्छ माधवः।।
श्रीभगवानुवाच
का त्वं कस्य प्रिया सुभ्रु कस्यार्थं चंदनं त्विदम्।
देह्यावयोर्येन तव चिरं श्रेयो भविष्यति।।
सैरंध्र्युवाच दास्यस्मि सुन्दरवर कुब्जानाम महामते।
मद्धस्तोत्थं च पाटीरं जातं भोजपतेः प्रियम्।।
अद्यापि कंसदास्यस्मि सांप्रतं तव चाग्रतः।
हस्तिशुण्डादण्डसमे भुजदण्डेऽस्ति मे मनः।।
युवां विना कोऽन्यतमोऽनुलेपं कर्तुमर्हति।
युवयोस्तु समं रूपं त्रैलोक्ये न हि विद्यते।।

"Then, both the brothers got up from there and proceeded to another street. There, a lotus-eyed young woman was passing by. She was carrying a bowl of sandalwood paste. The woman was young, but she had a hunched back. Krishna asked, 'O Beautiful One! Who are you? Whose wife are you? For whom are you taking this sandalwood? Give sandalwood to both of us too.' The woman said, 'I am Kansa's maid, and my name is Kubja. Kansa is quite fond of sandalwood paste. Although I am the maid of Kansa, I am bowled over by you, looking at your arms akin to an elephant's trunk. Who other than you in this world is entitled to apply this sandalwood?'"

(Garga Samhita, Mathura Khanda,
Chapter–6, Shloka–9-13)

Comment: In ancient times, a woman who used to earn her livelihood through craftsmanship was called 'Sairandhri'. Applying fragrant pastes and henna, tying buns, and dressing up others were some of the tasks that constituted craftsmanship for women.

153. Did Kansa employ Vasudeva to bring Krishna and Balarama from Vrindavan?

This is mentioned in the Brahmavaivarta Purana, when a minister of Kansa advised him to send Akrura, Uddhava or Vasudeva to fetch Krishna and Balarama from Vrindavan. So, Kansa first asked Vasudeva to go to Vrindavan:

तत्त्वज्ञो नीतिशास्त्राणां त्वमुपायविशारदः।
व्रज नन्दव्रजं बन्धो वसुदेव सुतालयम्॥
वृषभानं च नन्दं च बलं च नन्दनन्दनम्।
शीघ्रमानय यज्ञेऽत्र सर्वं गोकुलवासिनम्॥

Kansa said: "Dear brother Vasudeva! You are an expert in diplomacy, and you can astutely find solutions too. So, go to your son's house in Nanda-Vraj; invite Vrishabhanu, Nanda, Balarama, Krishna and all the inhabitants of Gokul for the yajna and bring them along quickly."

(Brahmavaivarta Purana, Shri Krishna Janma Khanda, Chapter–64, Shloka–33-34)

However, Vasudeva refused saying that:

नियुक्तमत्र राजेन्द्र गमनं मम सांप्रतम्।
विज्ञापितुं नन्दव्रजं नन्दं वा नन्दनन्दनम्॥
यद्यायातो नन्दपुत्रो यागो ते च महोत्सवे।
अवश्यं तद्विरोधश्च भविष्यति त्वया सह॥
तमहं च समानीय कारयिष्यामि संयुतम्।
इति मे न हि भद्रं च विघ्नस्तस्य तवापि च॥
पित्राऽऽनीतो मृतः कृष्ण इति सर्वो वदिष्यति।
वसुदेवः सुतद्वारा जघान नृपमेव च॥
द्वयोरेकतरस्यापि सद्यो मृत्युर्भविष्यति।
पतिष्यन्ति च शूराश्च नास्ति युद्धं निरामिषम्॥

"O King! It will not be right for me to go on this errand at this time. Viewed from any perspective, it would not be appropriate for me to convey the news of the yajna to my son, or Nanda's son, and bring them along with me. If the son of Nanda arrives for the celebration of your yajna, there will surely be a confrontation between you two. So, in my opinion, it is not right for me to call that child and compel him to engage in a fight here. This could prove fatal for the child and even for you! If that child is killed, then everybody will say that the father himself took Krishna along and got him killed; and if anything happens to you, then people will start saying that Vasudeva got the king killed through his son. And it is certain that one of you will die instantly. Apart from this, several more valiant fighters will also be killed, because war is never risk-free."

(Brahmavaivarta Purana, Shri Krishna Janma Khanda, Chapter–64, Shloka–37-41)

वसुदेववचः श्रुत्वा रक्तपंकजलोचनः।
खड्गं गृहीत्वा तं हन्तुं प्रययौ नृपतीश्वरः॥
हाहेति कृत्वा पुत्रं च वारयामास तत्क्षणम्।
उग्रसेनो महाराजमतीव बलवान्मुने॥
स्वपीठाद्वसुदेवश्च कोपाविष्टो गृहं ययौ।
अक्रूरं प्रेरयामास गन्तुं नन्दव्रजं नृपः॥

"On hearing Vasudeva's words, Kansa was livid with rage, and in his fury, he lunged forward to kill him with a sword. Seeing this, the mighty Ugrasen exclaimed in shock and stopped his son. Then, the angry Vasudeva also rose from his seat and left for home. Thereafter, King Kansa asked Akrura to go to Nanda-Vraj, and also sent messengers in all directions bearing the invitation."

(Brahmavaivarta Purana, Shri Krishna Janma Khanda, Chapter–64, Shloka–42-44)

154. How was Krishna's experience when he first set foot in Mathura?

There is no mention of any such incident in the Mahabharata, but the Puranas definitely provide a description of an incident involving a washerman and that of Krishna forcefully breaking the bow:

अनुशिष्टौ च तौ वीरौ... X ... रजको व्यस्तमस्तकः॥

"With Akrura's permission, both the heroes left for a tour of the city, as if two elephants desirous of battle had been unleashed from a post. On the way, they met a washerman who was dyeing a garment. When they asked him for clothes, Rajak derided them and said, 'You were born in the forest and have grown up with animals. And now, on seeing royal garments, greed has gripped you! You both are stupid and boorish.' Then, Krishna, enraged by the bitter words spoken by the washerman, struck him on the forehead. The force with which Krishna hit him was so severe that the latter's head burst open."

(Harivansha Purana, Vishnu Parva, Chapter–27, Shloka–9-16)

Now, read the description of the incident when Krishna broke the bow:

समीपं नृपतेर्गत्वा... X ...विकूजित्वा द्विधाभूतमभज्यत॥

The guards said to their king, Kansa: "Your Majesty! Listen carefully to the astonishing incident that occurred at the archery training depot. Two boys with long hair suddenly entered the depot, and no one saw them arrive. It seemed as if they had abruptly dropped there from the sky. One of them, a dark-complexioned boy, effortlessly picked up a bow which could not be lifted by even the greatest of warriors. Then, the boy tried to fasten the bow string to it, and in the process, the great iron bow broke into two pieces at the point where he had gripped it with the other hand."

(Harivansha Purana, Vishnu Parva, Chapter–27, Shloka–51-57)

The Bhagavat Purana *(Skandha–10, Chapter–41-42)*, Brahmavaivarta Purana *(Shri Krishna Janma Khanda, Chapter–71)*, and Garga Samhita *(Mathura Khanda, Chapter–6)* also narrate the same incident. But apart from these two incidents, there is no mention of any other sensation created by Krishna in Mathura.

155. When did Krishna get the opportunity to become king for the first time?

Krishna got the opportunity to become king in Mathura, right after killing Kansa. In the Harivansha Purana, it is stated that after Kansa's death, his mother Padmavati said to her husband Ugrasen:

वीर भोग्यानि राज्यानि वयं चापि पराजिताः।
गच्छ विज्ञाप्यतां कृष्णः कंससत्कारकारणात्॥

"A kingdom is enjoyed by brave men only. We are defeated now, so go inform Krishna that arrangements should be made for the last rites of Kansa."

(Harivansha Purana, Vishnu Parva, Chapter–31, Shloka–50)

इमं ते पितरं वृद्धं कृष्णस्य वशवर्तिनम्।
कथं द्रक्ष्यामि शुष्यन्तं कासारसलिलं यथा॥

Padmavati wept and said: "Your old father is now under Krishna's subjugation. How will I be able to see him as a subject, withering away like water in a drying pond?"

(Harivansha Purana, Vishnu Parva, Chapter–31, Shloka–54)

Then, Kansa's father Ugrasen walked towards Krishna and said:

हस्त्येश्वरथसम्पूर्णं... X ...कृष्ण गताः किल भवन्ति हि।।

"O Krishna! Take this invincible army of Kansa replete with elephants, horses, chariots and foot soldiers. Let your men take control of all the wealth, grains, clothes, gems and so on. Let your men also take care of all the women, vehicles and everything else. You now have complete authority over the land of Mathura. Now, you are the all-encompassing custodian for all of us Yadavas. We wish that with your grace, the last rites of Kansa should be completed. After that, I will depart for the forest with my wife and daughters-in-law."

(Harivansha Purana, Vishnu Parva, Chapter–32, Shloka–22-28)

The Bhagavat Purana simply states that Krishna crowned Ugrasen as the king:

एवमाश्वास्य पितरौ भगवान्देवकीसुतः।
मातामहं तूग्रसेनं यदूनामकरोन्नृपम्।।

"Shri Krishna thus consoled his parents and crowned his maternal grandfather Ugrasen as the king of the Yadavas."

(Bhagavat Purana, Skandha–10, Chapter–45, Shloka–12)

Even the Garga Samhita *(Mathura Khanda, Chapter–9, Shloka–5)* states in a single shloka that Krishna crowned his maternal grandfather Ugrasen as the king of Mathura. The Mahabharata does not even mention this event. But, all things considered, it can be said that Krishna, the cowherd, had got the opportunity to become the king of Mathura at the tender age of nineteen.

156. Was Krishna humiliated during Rukmini's *swayamvar*?

The Harivansha Purana narrates this incident in detail, while no other Purana or the Mahabharata mentions any such incident related to Krishna. Jarasandha, the arch-enemy of Krishna, had set rigorous conditions for the *swayamvar*, which was held under his supervision in the court of King Bhishmak of Vidarbha:

सिंहासनमनध्यास्यं पुरं चास्य न विद्यते।
कथं राजसमाजेऽस्मिन्नास्यते देवकीसुतः।।

कृष्णोऽपि सुमहावीर्यो ह्यभिमानी महाद्युतिः।
न चागमिष्यते वास्मिन् कन्यार्थे च स्वयंवरे॥
पार्थिवेषूपविष्टेषु स्वेषु सिंहासनेषु वै।
कथमास्यति नीचेषु आसनेषु महाद्युतिः॥

"No throne is fit for Krishna, because only those kings who are coronated according to the prescribed rituals can sit on a throne. Krishna has no city or capital, so how will he sit on a throne in this community of kings? Krishna is valiant and conceited; he will never come uninvited for the sake of a girl. While the kings sit on their respective thrones, Krishna will not be able to accept a seat that is less important."

(Harivansha Purana, Vishnu Parva, Chapter–50, Shloka–15-17)

So, Jarasandha had already put arrangements in place to discourage Krishna from participating in Rukmini's *swayamvar*. But when Krishna did arrive, another king called Kaishik, who was also present there, said to Krishna:

तव विश्रामहेतोर्हि कारितेदं गृहोत्तमम्।
देवानामादिदेवोऽसि सर्वलोकनमस्कृतः॥
मानुष्ये मर्त्यलोकेऽस्मिन् राजेन्द्रत्वं समाचर।
समाजे मनुजेन्द्राणां मा भूदासनसंकटम्॥

"Stay here as the king of these kings and forget about them. I have made arrangements for your rest and relaxation in a separate mansion so that no dispute arises over the non-availability of a throne for you."

(Harivansha Purana, Vishnu Parva, Chapter–50, Shloka–19-20)

This shows that arrangements were made in order to keep Krishna away from Rukmini's *swayamvar* without leading to any dispute. A few days later in Vidarbha, when Krishna met Rukmini's father Bhishmak, Krishna reproached him saying:

ममागमनमेवेह प्रायेण न हितं तव ।
अतो न कृतमातिथ्यमपात्राय नरेश्वर॥

Krishna said: "O King! Perhaps my arrival has not been favourable for you; that is why you felt that I was undeserving, and you did not extend your hospitality to me."

(Harivansha Purana, Vishnu Parva, Chapter–51, Shloka–13)

After reading this entire episode, it can be said that due to Jarasandha's influence, King Bhishmak could not even extend normal royal courtesy to Krishna.

157. Why did Kalyavana become an enemy of Krishna?

Kalyavana had no direct enmity against Krishna. He had set out from his kingdom to launch an attack on Mathura only because he was influenced by Jarasandha and other fellow kings. According to the Puranas, when Krishna returned from Vidarbha to Mathura, after the annulment of Rukmini's *swayamvar*, the kings breathed a sigh of relief. The next day, when all the kings gathered in an assembly, Bhishmak said:

स्वयंवरकृतं दोषं विदित्वा वो नराधिपाः ।
क्षन्तव्यो मम वृद्धस्य दुर्दग्धस्य फलोदयम्।।

"I adjourned the *swayamvar* because Krishna had become a hindrance to it. Please forgive me, an old man, of this misdemeanour."

(Harivansha Purana, Vishnu Parva, Chapter–52, Shloka–3)

After this, most of the kings departed for their respective kingdoms, but some of the kings from Jarasandha's camp such as Shalva, Shishupala and Dantavakra stayed back. Then, Bhishmak said to these people:

पुत्रस्य चेष्टामालोक्य त्रासाकुलितलोचनः।
मन्ये बालानिमाँल्लोकान् स एष पुरुषः परः।।
कीर्तिः कीर्तिमतां श्रेष्ठो यशश्च विपुलं तथा।
स्थापितं भुवि मर्त्येऽस्मिन् स्वबाहुबलमूर्जितम्।।

"Krishna is superior among the illustrious ones, that is, he is second to none. Whatever fame he has attained, he has done so on the strength of his own muscle power. But my son is immature; I consider him and his associates as mere children."

(Harivansha Purana, Vishnu Parva, Chapter–52, Shloka–14-15)

अलं खेदेन राजेन्द्र सुताय रिपुमर्दिने।
क्षत्रियस्य रणे राजन् ध्रुवं जयपराजयौ।।

xxx xxx xxx

अद्य तस्य रणे जेता यवनाधिपतिर्नृप।।
स कालयवनो नाम अवध्यः केशवस्य ह।
तप्त्वा सुदारुणं घोरं तपः परमदुश्चरम्।।

Then, Shalva said: "O King Bhishmak! Why do you express regret? Your son is a valiant destroyer of enemies. It is pointless to be displeased with him; rather you should be proud of him."

xxx xxx xxx

"O lord of all men! At present, Kalyavana, who is the ruler of the Yavanas, is the only one who can defeat Krishna in battle. He cannot be killed by Krishna, for, he has gained so much might and strength through his remarkable effort."

(Harivansha Purana, Vishnu Parva, Chapter–52, Shloka–19/25-26)

श्रुत्वा सौभपतेर्वाक्यं सर्वे ते नृपसत्तमाः ।
कुर्म इत्यब्रुवन् हृष्टा जरासंधं महाबलम्॥

"Hearing Shalva's words, all the kings jumped for joy and said to Jarasandha, 'That is exactly what we must do.'"

मां समाश्रित्य पूर्वस्मिन्... X ...तथास्माभिर्दूत्ये नः कृष्णविग्रहे॥

Then, Jarasandha said: "Earlier, all the kings used to come to me for protection due to their fear of other kings. And now, all the kings are advising me to seek the help of another king. Destiny is powerful indeed; it cannot be wished away. Due to Krishna's fear, I am going to seek protection from a king who is more powerful than him. Well, it is better to die than live such a life! O Kings! I will not seek protection from someone else. Whether it is Krishna, Baladeva or any king, I will unflinchingly confront anyone who attacks me; that is what I have decided. But to ensure that Krishna does not harm good kings like you, I will give my consent to sending a messenger (to Kalyavana). O Kings! The messenger must pay a secret visit to Kalyavana so that Krishna does not cause any trouble on the way. I think Shalva is the most suitable person for this assignment, because he possesses the skill to properly convey our message. Shalva must convey the message in such a manner that the king of the Yavanas, Kalyavana, joins us in case we have to engage in a battle with Krishna."

(Harivansha Purana, Vishnu Parva, Chapter–52, Shloka–34-43)

There is no mention of this episode in the Mahabharata or other Puranas. But it is clear from this sole piece of ancient evidence that Jarasandha and his friends had goaded Kalyavana into a confrontation with Krishna.

158. Why did Krishna's sons kill Vajranabha, the demon king?

The king of Vajrapur had a daughter called Prabhavati who was quite ravishing, and word about her had reached Dwarka through gimmick artists. But she was kept under heavy security, so paying an ordinary visit to her was well-nigh impossible. Hence, disguised as gimmick artists, Pradyumna went there with his brother Saamba and uncle Gada, and the three married Prabhavati and her two sisters. Later, when Vajranabha, the father of those princesses, objected to the marriage, they killed him.

(Harivansha Purana, Vishnu Parva, Chapter–92-97)

159. How did Krishna introduce himself in his first interaction with Kubja?

The Harivansha Purana narrates the episode when Krishna meets Kubja, and the two introduce themselves to each other:

वयं हि देशात्तिथयो मल्लाः प्राप्ता वरानने।
द्रष्टुं धनुर्महद् दिव्यं राष्ट्रे चैव महर्द्धिमत्॥

Krishna said: "O one with a beautiful face! Both of us brothers are wrestlers and we have come to this kingdom as guests. We have come to see the extremely huge and substantial bow in this kingdom."

(Harivansha Purana, Vishnu Parva, Chapter–27, Shloka–32)

This shloka is a significant clue for researchers, as it states that Krishna and Balarama were invited by the king of Mathura as wrestlers.

160. Did Krishna kill a host of demons in his childhood?

Before arriving at the answer to this question, it is necessary to comprehend whether Krishna was a human being or an avatar who performed miracles. If a person believes that Krishna was an avatar who performed miracles, then they need not ask such a question. That is because, for such people, everything that is written in the Puranas is true. However, as people with such beliefs are also skeptical, and are not convinced by everything written in the Puranas, the search for truth becomes essential. A comparative study becomes necessary, and it is also crucial to exercise prudence.

To answer this question, let us first take a look at the Mahabharata.

The original Mahabharata had only 8,800 shlokas and was written by Veda Vyasa. Later, his disciple Vaishampayan added 24,000 shlokas of his own, and then, several centuries later, a scholar called Ugrashrava added thousands of shlokas. One needs to grasp here that in spite of such extensive embellishment, the Mahabharata does not contain as many fabricated stories as the Puranas. And unfortunately, it is only the content of the Puranas that has inundated people's minds. Right from the Puranic period till date, thousands of stories about Krishna have been concocted in the name of devotion, which are far from reality. The events that occurred in the life of Krishna up to the time of the Rajasuya Yajna have been narrated through Grandsire Bhishma and Shishupala between Chapters 38–40 of the Sabha Parva of the Mahabharata. In these pages, there is no mention of Radha, the Rasa or Krishna's slaying of demons such as Dhenukasur, Aghasura, Bakasura and others. Stories about the serpent Kaaliya or the worship of Govardhana do find a mention, but they have certainly not been described in the manner that the Puranas have depicted them. So, when those fabricated events have not been included in the Mahabharata in spite of the extensive embellishments in it, then wherefrom did these stories crop up in all the Puranas? Therefore, it can be concluded that all those incidents are fictitious.

161. Who was Kansa's father?

It is only the Harivansha Purana that mentions this point. According to it:

न चायमुग्रसेनः स पिता... X ...दिव्येनाप्रतिगामिना।।

Narada said to Kansa: "This Ugrasen is not your father; the fiery demon Drumil who is the owner of the Saubha flying machine is your father." Hearing this, an enraged Kansa asked him, "How is that possible? Tell me the truth." Narada then explained to Kansa that when his mother had gone on a journey to Mount Suyamun, the demon king Drumil had come close to her, leading to Kansa's birth. "Hence, Ugrasen is not your father; you are the son of Drumil."

(Harivansha Purana, Vishnu Parva, Chapter–28, Shloka–53-109)

In this Purana, the story mentioned above has been narrated with unnecessary detail, which I have summarised. After reading this chapter, one can easily surmise that this story has been embellished; it is not real. Kansa himself tells a *mahout*[37] that Narada had revealed this secret to him after a forewarning. Actually, it appears that this story was created to give a miraculous and mysterious twist to the hostility between Kansa and the Yadavas, and to show that Kansa was of ignoble birth.

162. Whom did Krishna and Balarama have to fight against in the wrestling tournament organised by Kansa?

According to the Bhagavat Purana, Kansa had several wrestlers ready and waiting in the arena, to ensure that Krishna and Balarama were killed by one of them. However, after they witnessed the death of five wrestlers, including Chanur and Mushtik, the rest of the wrestlers fled from the arena:

चाणूरे मुष्टिके कूटे शले तोशलके हते।
शेषाः प्रदुद्रुवुर्मल्लाः सर्वे प्राणपरीप्सवः॥

Shukdeva said: "When the five wrestlers, Chanur, Mushtik, Koot, Shala and Toshala were dead, the remaining wrestlers fled from there to save their lives."

(Bhagavat Purana, Skandha–10, Chapter–44, Shloka–28)

The Harivansha Purana as well as the Vishnu Purana mention only three wrestlers:

अन्ध्रतोशलकौ हत्वा कृष्णसंकर्षणावुभौ।
क्रोधसंरक्तनयनौ रंगमध्ये ववल्गतुः॥
समाजवाटो निर्मल्लः सोऽभवद् भीमदर्शनः।
अन्ध्रे तदा महामल्ले मुष्टिके च निपातिते॥

"After killing Mushtik and Toshala from the kingdom of Andhra, Krishna and Balarama began jumping around in the arena, their eyes burning with rage. With Chanur and Mushtik's death, the arena, suddenly devoid of wrestlers, began to appear ominous."

(Harivansha Purana, Vishnu Parva, Chapter–30, Shloka–55-56)

कृष्णस्तोशलकं भूयो मल्लराजं महाबलम्।
वाममुष्टिप्रहारेण पातयामास भूतले॥

37. An elephant rider, trainer or keeper

चाणूरे निहते मल्ले मुष्टिके विनिपातिते।
नीते क्षयं तोशलके सर्वे मल्लाः प्रदुद्रुवुः॥

Sage Parashar said: "Thereafter, Shri Krishna punched the mighty wrestler, Toshala with his left hand and knocked him on the ground. When the supreme wrestlers, Chanur and Mushtik and the king of wrestlers, Toshala, were killed, all the wrestlers fled."

(Vishnu Purana, Part–5, Chapter–20, Shloka–79-80)

163. Was Balarama annoyed with Krishna regarding the war that occurred in Kurukshetra?

In the battlefield of Kurukshetra, while the armies of the Kauravas and Pandavas were busy in secret discussions and devising war strategy in their respective camps, Balarama reached the Pandavas' camp en route to his pilgrimage. Then, during a conversation, he expressed his thoughts:

उक्तो मया वासुदेवः पुनः पुनरुपह्वरे।
सम्बन्धिषु समां वृत्तिं वर्तस्व मधुसूदन॥
पाण्डवा हि यथास्माकं तथा दुर्योधनो नृप।
तस्यापि क्रियतां साह्यं स पर्येति पुनः पुनः॥

Balarama said: "Whenever we were alone, I had repeatedly told Krishna, 'O Madhusudan! Treat all your relatives equally, because for us, there is no difference between the Pandavas and King Duryodhana. Help him as well; he visits us frequently.'"

तच्च मे नाकरोद वाक्यं त्वदर्थे मधुसूदनः।
निर्विष्टः सर्वभावेन धनंजयमवेक्ष्य ह॥

Balarama addressed Yudhishthira: "But Yudhishthira! Madhusudan Krishna has not paid heed to my advice, only for your sake. He is focused only on Arjuna and keeps doting upon him in every way."

(Mahabharata, Udyoga Parva, Chapter–157, Shloka–28-30)

Thus, in a packed assembly, Balarama had directly accused Krishna of being biased due to his undue affection for Arjuna. Another aspect worth noting throughout the Mahabharata is that Balarama always used the word 'nripa', meaning 'king', whenever he spoke of Duryodhana, but he never used that word for Yudhishthira. This can also be seen in the shlokas quoted above, and that is the case throughout the Mahabharata.

164. Who were the principal enemies of Krishna?

In the entire history of the world, Krishna was the only great man, who had an almost equal number of admirers and detractors. No one could do anything without his direct or indirect support, but there were several of them who did not want to see Krishna anywhere near them! And some among them were even baying for his blood. Based on the facts derived from the Mahabharata and the Puranas, these are the names of the people who can be termed as Krishna's arch-enemies:
1. Kansa 2. Jarasandha 3. Shishupala 4. King Bhishmak 5. Rukmi 6. Shalva 7. Dantavakra 8. Vinda-Anuvinda 9. Satrajit 10. Shringlava 11. Kalyavana 12. Poundrak 13. Narakasura 14. King of Kashi 15. Duryodhana and others.

165. Why is Krishna called Damodar?

The word 'Damodar' is mentioned as the 758th name in the Vishnu Sahastranaam Stotra, which appears in the Padma Purana. According to it, in Krishna's childhood, his mother Yashoda had tied a rope to his stomach and fastened the other end of it to a mortar. In Sanskrit, the word 'Damodar' is a compound word constituting daam (rope) + udar (stomach). That is why Krishna was called Damodar. The Harivansha Purana contains a shloka which explains the meaning:

दाम्ना चैवोदरे बद्ध्वा प्रत्यबन्धदुलूखले।
यदि शक्तोऽसि गच्छेति तमुक्त्वा कर्म साकरोत्॥

Vaishampayan said: "Mother Yashoda tied a rope to his stomach and fastened the other end of the rope to a mortar and said, 'Now, go if you can.' And speaking thus, she became engaged in her household chores."

(Harivansha Purana, Vishnu Parva, Chapter–7, Shloka–14)

स च तेनैव नाम्ना तु कृष्णो वै दामबन्धनात्।
गोष्ठे दामोदर इति गोपीभिः परिगीयते॥

Vaishampayan said: "Krishna was called Damodar as a rope (daam) was tied to his stomach (udar). In that forest hamlet of the cowherds, the milkmaids began singing his praises using the same name."

(Harivansha Purana, Vishnu Parva, Chapter–7, Shloka–36)

166. Who cremated Krishna?

According to the evidence available in the Mahabharata and the Puranas, Krishna was cremated by Arjuna. All family members of Krishna were killed in the Yadavasthali incident, except his father, Vasudeva and his great grandson, Vajra. Vasudeva and Vajra survived because they had not gone there. According to the Mahabharata, Arjuna first cremated his maternal uncle, Vasudeva:

यस्तु देशः प्रियस्तस्य जीवतोऽभून्महात्मनः।
तत्रैनमुपसंकल्प्य पितृमेधं प्रचक्रिरे॥

Vaishampayan said: "Arjuna and the others performed Vasudeva's last rites at the place which he loved the most in his lifetime."

(Mahabharata, Mausala Parva, Chapter–7, Shloka–23)

Thereafter, he went to Prabhasa, collected the dead bodies of the killed Yadavas and cremated them:

यथाप्रधानतश्चैव चक्रे सर्वास्तथा क्रियाः।
ये हता ब्रह्मशापेन मुसलैरेरकोद्भवैः॥

"Arjuna was deeply saddened on seeing the dead bodies of the Yadavas killed in that horrific genocide. He duly cremated all the dead people in order of their age."

ततः शरीरे रामस्य वासुदेवस्य चोभयोः।
अन्वीक्ष्य दाहयामास पुरुषैराप्तकारिभिः॥

"Then, Arjuna asked his trusted men to search for the bodies of Krishna and Balarama and cremated them too."

(Mahabharata, Mausala Parva, Chapter–7, Shloka–30-31)

According to the Vishnu Purana:

अर्जुनोऽपि तदान्विष्य कृष्णरामकलेवरे।
संस्कारं लम्भयामास तथान्येषामनुक्रमात्॥

"Arjuna organised a search for the dead bodies of Balarama and Krishna and other prominent Yadavas, and performed their last rites one by one."

(Vishnu Purana, Part–5, Chapter–38, Shloka–1)

There is no mention of this event in Harivansha Purana, Brahmavaivarta Purana and the others.

167. Why is Krishna criticised so often in the scriptures?
From the evidence available in various Vedic and Puranic texts, it can be inferred that Krishna was a great man who was pragmatic, and he was a staunch opponent of futile, hypocritical and discriminatory Aryan beliefs. According to the Rigveda, he was the head of a tribal community:

अव द्रप्सो अंशुमतीमतिष्ठदियानः कृष्णो दशभिः सहस्त्रैः।
आवत्तमिन्द्रः शच्या धमन्तमप स्नेहितीर्नृमणा अधत्त॥

"On the banks of River Anshumati (Yamuna), there lived an Asura called Krishna who attacked with 10,000 troops. Indra cleverly overwhelmed the Asura who created the ruckus. Thereafter, Indra destroyed the violent army of Krishnasura for the benefit of humans."

द्रप्समपश्यं विषुणे चरन्तमुपह्वरे नद्यो अंशुमत्याः।
नभो न कृष्णमवतस्थिवांसमिष्यामि वो वृषणो युध्यताजौ॥

Indra said: "I have seen the nimble-footed Krishna. He wanders in a vast, mysterious location on the banks of River Anshumati, and sojourns like the sun. O Maruts who grant all wishes! I want you to fight and destroy him in battle."

अध द्रप्सो अंशुमत्या उपस्थेऽधारयत्तन्वं तित्विषाणः।
विशो अदेवीरभ्याचरन्तीर्बृहस्पतिना युजेन्द्रः ससाहे ॥

"Near the river Anshumati, the nimble-footed Krishna assumes a physical form, becoming effulgent. With the help of Brihaspati, Indra killed Devashunya and the approaching army along with Krishna."

(Rigveda, Mandala–8, Sukta–85, Mantra–13-15)*
*(*Sukta–96 in the Supplementary Edition)*

In the Vedic mantras above, Indra considers Krishna to be his enemy. One needs to understand here that the deities mentioned in the Vedas are all natural phenomena and are symbolic. That being the case, Indra becomes the representative of the Vedic Yajna and beliefs; and the one who considers those beliefs to be supreme, naturally sees Krishna as a great enemy in his path. This is the very reason, in the Mahabharata and various Puranas, whenever Krishna was insulted by anyone, he was condemned only on the basis of scriptural rules and Vedic beliefs, whether he was humiliated by Jarasandha, Shishupala, Rukmi, Duryodhana, Shalva, Dantavakra, Vinda or Anuvinda. All of them were strong adherents of the prescribed rules.

168. Who was Akrura and what was his relationship with Krishna?

Various Puranas make contradictory statements about the same incident or story, so it is difficult to readily believe them. However, the Harivansha Purana provides an orderly family tree of this dynasty, which can be helpful for researchers. According to this Purana, Vasudeva's grandfather, Devamidhush was one of three brothers: Anamitra, Yudhajit and Devamidhush himself. The descendants of Anamitra were Ugrasen, Kansa and others; and the grandson of Yudhajit was Shwafalk, who was the father of Akrura. Thus, Akrura was Vasudeva's nephew and Krishna's cousin:

गान्धारी चैव माद्री च... X ...अक्रूरः सुषुवे तस्माच्छ्वफल्काद्भूरिदक्षिणः॥

(Harivansha Purana, Harivansha Parva, Chapter–34, Shloka–1-11)

Compelled by circumstances, Vasudeva's sons Balarama and Krishna were living with Nanda in the forests of Gokul and Vrindavan, but the rest of the family lived in the urban environment of Mathura. Later on, Uddhava, who stayed by Krishna's side akin to his shadow, was also born in Mathura and grew up there. Uddhava was also Krishna's cousin; he was the son of Vasudeva's younger brother Devabhaga.

These shlokas of the Harivansha Purana suggest that Krishna and Akrura were cousins, but at one place in the Bhagavat Purana, Krishna addresses Akrura as 'uncle'.

ननु दानपते न्यस्तस्त्वय्यास्ते शतधन्वना।
स्यमन्तको मणिः श्रीमन्विदितः पूर्व मेव नः॥

Krishna said: "Uncle! You are the upholder of charity and ethics. We already know that Shatdhanva has left with you the Syamantaka gem, which is incredibly radiant and creates wealth."

(Bhagavat Purana, Skandha–10, Chapter–57, Shloka–36)

It is clear from the evidence quoted above that every Purana has been written by a number of people at different times based on folklore, legends and traditions prevalent in different regions. This is the reason why the descriptions, even of simple incidents, are so drastically different in each text. So, no matter what the truth is, whether Krishna and Akrura were uncle and nephew or cousins, it is certain that both of them belonged to the same family.

169. Was Akrura Krishna's supporter or opponent?

The scriptures provide an account of many facets of Akrura. When a discussion takes place in Kansa's court regarding summoning Krishna to Mathura, this is what Akrura states:

राजन् मनीषितं सध्जएयक् तव स्वावद्यमार्जनम्।
सिद्ध्यसिद्ध्योः समं कुर्याद् दैवं हि फलसाधनम्।।

Akrura said to Kansa: "Your Majesty! You want to avert your death, your misfortune, so it is right for you to think in this manner. Whether one succeeds or fails, one must perform his task with even-mindedness."

(Bhagavat Purana, Skandha–10, Chapter–36, Shloka–38)

It is clear from the shloka above that Akrura had adopted a two-pronged policy, just like any clever politician. Further proof of this can be seen in the Harivansha Purana too. On one hand, while he justifies Kansa's actions, on the other, he does not desist from provoking Krishna against Kansa.

सततं पीड्यमानं च कंसेनाशुभबुद्धिना।
दशान्ते शोषितं वृद्धं दुःखैः शिथिलतां गतम्।।

Akrura provoked Krishna saying: "Kansa has always tormented your parents. In this old age, the flesh on their body has shrivelled up, and they are also overwhelmed by pains and sorrows in various forms."

(Harivansha Purana, Vishnu Parva, Chapter–26, Shloka–6)

वृद्धौ तवाम्बापितरौ परभृत्यत्वमागतौ।
भर्त्सितौ त्वत्कृते नित्यं कंसेनाशुभबुद्धिना।।

"Your parents have become the servants of others. Because of you, that evil-minded Kansa keeps castigating them every day."

(Harivansha Purana, Vishnu Parva,
Chapter–26, Shloka–16)

The second aspect of Akrura's personality is also evident in the Puranas. He used to compete with Krishna, and that too to such an extent that he lost his senses on account of jealousy and envy. Actually, Akrura wanted to marry Satyabhama, but Satrajit married her to Krishna. A jealous Akrura then got Satrajit murdered by Shatdhanva:

लब्ध्वैतदन्तरं राजन्शतधन्वानमूचतुः।
अक्रूरकृतवर्माणौ मणिः कस्मान्न गृह्यते॥
योऽस्मभ्यं सम्प्रतिश्रुत्य कन्यारत्नं विगर्ह्य नः।
कृष्णायादान्न सत्राजित्कस्माद्भ्रातरमन्वियात्॥
एवं भिन्नमतिस्ताभ्यां सत्राजितमसत्तमः।
शयानमवधील्लोभात्स पापः क्षीणजीवितः॥
स्त्रीणां विक्रोशमानानां क्रन्दन्तीनामनाथवत्।
हत्वा पशून्सौनिकवन्मणिमादाय जग्मिवान्॥

Shukdeva said to King Parikshit: They (Akrura and Kritvarma) said to Shatdhanva, 'Why don't you steal the gem from Satrajit? Satrajit had pledged to marry his daughter, Satyabhama to us, and now he has spurned us and got her married to Krishna. So, why shouldn't Satrajit be dispatched to the abode of *Yama,*[38] just like his brother Prasen?' Their instigation made Shatdhanva fall for their words and upon finding the opportunity, he ruthlessly killed Satrajit in his sleep, and fled with the gem."

(Bhagavat Purana, Skandha–10, Chapter–57, Shloka–3-6)

Therefore, based on this evidence from the Puranas, it is clear that Akrura was a duplicitous person.

170. Was any relative of Krishna his enemy?

Not just one, but most of Krishna's relatives considered him their enemy. Here is a list of some of the prominent relatives of Krishna who tried to humiliate him all their lives, and even attempted to kill him:

Kansa – His maternal uncle, who was himself killed while attempting to get Krishna killed.

Jarasandha – Kansa's father-in-law and the valorous king of Magadha, who considered Krishna an obstacle to his political ambitions and kept baying for his blood right till the end.

Shishupala – Krishna's cousin and arch-rival, Shishupala was the king of Chedi, and he did not stop humiliating Krishna until his last breath.

Vinda-Anuvinda – Cousins from Krishna's father's side and the princes

38. God of death

of Avanti, who had been humiliating Krishna right from his days spent in the ashram of Sage Sandipani, and continued to oppose Krishna till they were killed in the battle of Mahabharata *(Bhagavat Purana, Skandha–10, Chapter–58, Shloka–30).*

Rukmi – Krishna's brother-in-law and the king of Bhojkat, who, influenced by Jarasandha's ideology, continued to oppose Krishna till he was killed by Balarama.

Bhishmak – Krishna's father-in-law and Jarasandha's blind follower *(Mahabharata, Sabha Parva, Chapter–14, Shloka–21-23).*

Satrajit – Krishna's father-in-law and an affluent Yadava of Mathura and Dwarka, who, due to his ambition, remained hostile to Krishna all his life and eventually died an inglorious death.

Duryodhana – Krishna's relative (Saamba's father-in-law) who had no personal enmity against Krishna, but because of the Pandavas, he always considered Krishna his enemy.

Dantavakra – Another cousin from Krishna's father's side and the king of Kamarupa, he was an opponent of Krishna and a supporter of Jarasandha, just like Shishupala.

Shringlava (Shrugaal) – He was a distant relative, and a hypocritical and ambitious man who began considering Krishna his rival without any reason *(Harivansha Purana, Vishnu Parva, Chapter–44, Shloka– 22).*

171. Who was Dwivid, the man who died at the hands of Balarama?

Dwivid was a friend of Narakasura and a powerful warrior of the Vanara tribe:

नरकस्य सखा कश्चिद् द्विविदो... x ... सोऽपतद् रुधिरं वमन्॥

When he heard that Narakasura had been killed by Krishna, he was livid with rage. He then came to Anarta[39] and unleashed terrible violence in the region. Within a week, the region's inhabitants were terrified due to the mayhem he had wreaked. During this period, Balarama was staying on the nearby Raivataka Mountain and was enjoying wine in the company of a bevy of beauties. When he heard about this, Dwivid reached there and created a ruckus. He also began harassing the women who had accompanied Balarama. Balarama then confronted him, but as Dwivid was quite formidable, a fight ensued between them, which

39. Present-day Kathiawar

lasted a long time; and eventually, Dwivid was killed by Balarama.

(Bhagavat Purana, Skandha–10, Chapter–67, Shloka–2-25)

172. How often do Krishna and Indra encounter each other in the scriptures?

In the Rigveda, Krishna is described as an opponent of the Aryan tradition and yajnas, and is shown to have been killed by Indra:

अध द्रप्सो अंशुमत्या उपस्थेऽधारयत्तन्वं तित्विषाणः।
विशो अदेवीरभ्याचरन्तीर्बृहस्पतिना युजेन्द्रः ससाहे ॥

"Near the river Anshumati, the nimble-footed Krishna assumes a physical form, becoming effulgent. With the help of Brihaspati, Indra killed Devashunya and the approaching army along with Krishna."

(Rigveda, Mandala–8, Sukta–85, Mantra–15)*
*(*Sukta–96 in the Supplementary Edition)*

Comment: The above mantra in the Rigveda states that Krishna was killed by Indra and the army of *Devas,*[40] while it is a well-known fact that Krishna died after being struck by an arrow. This makes it evident that whether it is the Rigveda or any other text, they are rife with embellishment.

Well, elsewhere, several Puranas describe the conflict between Krishna and Indra, when Krishna, living in Vrindavan, opposed Indra's worship:

(Bhagavat Purana, Skandha–10, Chapter–24-25)
(Harivansha Purana, Vishnu Parva, Chapter–15-19)
(Brahmavaivarta Purana, Shri Krishna Janma Khanda, Chapter–21)
(Garga Samhita, Giriraja Khanda, Chapter–3)
(Vishnu Purana, Part–5, Chapter–11-12)

The Puranas also state, Krishna and Indra had entered into a battle, when Krishna tried to bring the flowers of the Parijat tree for Satyabhama.

(Harivansha Purana, Vishnu Parva, Chapter–73)
(Bhagavat Purana, Skandha–10, Chapter–59, Shloka–39)
(Vishnu Purana, Part–5, Chapter–30)

Comment: So, while the Vedas declare that Indra was victorious, the texts revolving around Krishna describe the latter as the superior and victorious one. This clearly indicates the wide gap between Krishna and the Vedas and Yajnas.

---

40. Demigods

173. Who was Dantavakra and why was he hostile towards Krishna?

Krishna's father Vasudeva had five sisters, among whom Prithukirti was married to Vriddhasharma, the king of Karush kingdom (Kamarupa), whose son was Dantavakra. When his friends Jarasandha, Shishupala, Shalva and Poundrak were killed by Krishna one by one, he became livid with rage, and after the death of Shalva during the latter's battle with Krishna, Dantavakra entered the battlefield to fight:

शिशुपालस्य शाल्वस्य पौण्ड्रकस्यापि दुर्मतिः
परलोकगतानां च कुर्वन्पारोक्ष्यसौहृदम्॥

"After his friends were killed, that fool came to the battlefield on foot, as if he himself wished to go to the other world."

(Bhagavat Purana, Skandha–10, Chapter–78, Shloka–1)

त्वं मातुलेयो नः कृष्ण मित्रध्रुङ्मां जिघांससि।
अतस्त्वां गदया मन्द हनिष्ये वज्रकल्पया॥
तर्ह्यानृण्यमुपैम्यज्ञ मित्राणां मित्रवत्सलः।
बन्धुरूपमरिं हत्वा व्याधिं देहचरं यथा॥

Dantavakra said: "Krishna! You are my maternal uncle's son, so I shouldn't kill you; but you have killed my friends and now wish to kill me as well. That is why, you idiot! Today, I will crush you to pieces with my Vajrakarkash mace. You fool! Even though you are related to me, you are still an enemy, just like a disease that lurks in one's own body. I love these friends very much, and I am indebted to them. Now, the only way I can repay their debts is by killing you!"

(Bhagavat Purana, Skandha–10, Chapter–78, Shloka–5-6)

However, Dantavakra could not bear the force of Krishna's mace and died vomiting blood.

(Bhagavat Purana, Skandha–10, Chapter–78, Shloka–9)

174. Did all the kings of that time participate in the Mahabharata war?

In this regard, the Mahabharata, the historical text of that time, states that:

द्वावेव तु महाराज तस्माद् युद्धादपेयतुः।
रौहिणेयश्च वार्ष्णेयो रुक्मी च वसुधाधिपः॥

Vaishampayan said: "O King Janamejaya! Only two valiant warriors had abstained from that war—one was Balarama from the Vrishni clan and the other was King Rukmi."

(Mahabharata, Udyoga Parva, Chapter–158, Shloka–38)

Balarama nursed equal affection for both the Pandavas and the Kauravas, but because Krishna was explicitly in favour of the Pandavas, he, in keeping with his nature, became a supporter of Duryodhana. Even so, he could not go against his younger brother, Krishna. This is how he describes his pain:

उभौ शिष्यौ हि मे वीरौ गदायुद्धविशारदौ।
तुल्यस्नेहोऽस्म्यतो भीमे तथा दुर्योधने नृपे।।

Balarama said: "Both these valiant warriors, Bhimsen and Duryodhana, are my disciples and are adepts at mace-fighting. Therefore, I have the same affection for both of them."

(Mahabharata, Udyoga Parva, Chapter–159, Shloka–33)

न चाहमुत्सहे कृष्णमृते लोकमुदीक्षितुम्।
ततोऽहमनुवर्तामि केशवस्य चिकीर्षितम्।।

Expressing his affection for Krishna, Balarama said: "Without Krishna, I cannot even dare look at this whole world. Therefore, I abide by whatever Keshava wishes to do."

(Mahabharata, Udyoga Parva, Chapter–157, Shloka–32)

तस्माद् यास्यामि तीर्थानि सरस्वत्या निषेवितुम्।
न हि शक्ष्यामि कौरव्यान् नश्यमानानुपेक्षितम्।।

Balarama said: "Since I will not be able to ignore the condition of the Kauravas when they are annihilated, I will go and worship in the pilgrimage centres on the banks of River Saraswati."

(Mahabharata, Udyoga Parva, Chapter–157, Shloka–34)

Rukmi, on the other hand, could not participate in the war due to his arrogance and condescending behaviour. Having arrived with his huge army, he had addressed Arjuna, "If you are afraid, I will fight on your behalf."

उवाच मध्ये वीराणां कुन्तीपुत्रं धनंजयम्।।
सहायोऽस्मि स्थितो युद्धे यदि भीतोऽसि पाण्डव।
करिष्यामि रणे साह्यमसह्यं तव शत्रुभिः।।

"In an assembly of valiant warriors, Rukmi said to Arjuna, the son of Kunti, 'O son of Pandu! I have come to lend you assistance in the war, in case you are feeling terrified. In this greatest of wars, I will help you in such a manner that your enemies will find it unbearable.'"

(Mahabharata, Udyoga Parva, Chapter–158, Shloka–20-21)

Hearing such condescending words from Rukmi, which were akin to a challenge for any Kshatriya, Arjuna declined his offer of support. Then, Rukmi went to Duryodhana and spoke something similar to him, as a result of which Duryodhana also refused his help, and thus he could not join the war.

175. Did Krishna ever apprise the sages of his view on ethics and religion?

In a pilgrimage centre called Samanta Panchaka in Kurukshetra, a massive fair used to be held on the occasion of solar eclipse, evidence of which is found in the Puranas as well as the Gurugrantha Sahib composed in the 16th century. Guru Nanak Dev had also mentioned this. After renouncing the world, he had delivered his first sermon on the occasion of solar eclipse at this very fair in Kurukshetra. Well, almost all the close relatives of Krishna had gathered at this fair once. The relatives included Krishna's entire family from Dwarka, Nanda and Yashoda along with the cowherds from Vrindavan, people from Hastinapur's Kaurava family, and the Pandavas with Kunti and other queens from Indraprastha. Needless to say, thousands of sages had also arrived there. And it was there that Krishna spoke to those sages:

किं स्वल्पतपसां नृणां अर्चायां देवचक्षुषाम् ।
दर्शनस्पर्शनप्रश्न प्रह्वपादार्चनादिकम्॥

"How can those who have performed very little penance, those who are engaged in idol worship instead of perceiving God in all beings, be blessed by the company of saints like you?"

न ह्यम्मयानि तीर्थानि न देवा मृच्छिलामयाः ।
ते पुनन्त्युरुकालेन दर्शनादेव साधवः॥

"A pilgrimage centre abounding in water is not a pilgrimage centre, and the idols of clay or stone are not Gods; it is the saints and wise men that are Gods and pilgrimage centres."

नाग्निर्न सूर्यो न च चन्द्रतारका न भूर्जलं खं श्वसनोऽथ वाङ्मनः ।
उपासिता भेदकृतो हरन्त्यघं विपश्चितो घ्नन्ति मुहूर्तसेवया॥

"There is no god of fire, sun, moon, stars, earth, water, sky, air, speech and the mind. And even if there are, their worship does not obliterate sin. Their worship does not destroy the sense of duality; in fact, such worship only enhances it. But if one spends even a few moments in the company of wise people, they erase all our sins, because they are the destroyers of this sense of duality."

यस्यात्मबुद्धिः कुणपे त्रिधातुके स्वधीः कलत्रादिषु भौम इज्यधीः।
यत्तीर्थबुद्धिः सलिले न कर्हिचित् जनेष्वभिज्ञेषु स एव गोखरः॥

Krishna said: "O great souls and members of this assembly! A person who considers this corpse-like body made of the three humors—*Vata, Pitta* and *Kapha*—as his soul, that is, his 'I'-ness, who considers his wife and children as 'his own', who considers clay, stone, wood and so on as his 'presiding deity', and who considers water only, and not great men, as sacred - is a lowly donkey, even among animals."

(Bhagavat Purana, Skandha–10, Chapter–84, Shloka–10-13)

Hearing these words, the sages were perplexed, wondering what Krishna was talking about. Those ritualistic sages were mystified, because all that Krishna had uttered was akin to a blatant assault on the then prevailing hypocritical practices.

निशम्येत्थं भगवतः कृष्णस्याकुण्थमेधसः।
वचो दुरन्वयं विप्राः तूष्णीमासन् भ्रमद्धियः॥

"On hearing Krishna's cryptic speech, all the sages fell silent. They were confounded, as they just could not understand what Krishna was saying."

(Bhagavat Purana, Skandha–10, Chapter–84, Shloka–14)

All the shlokas quoted above are like an eye-opening medicine for those who worship the idol of Krishna and think that their duty ends there, or believe that they have become his followers, and wish to be called saints, merely because they have completed a pilgrimage. For, it is clear from the shlokas above that Krishna considered not only idol worship, but also yajnas as hypocrisy. And he had reiterated these truths with conviction in the Bhagavad Gita.

176. Did Eklavya and Krishna's Yadava army ever engage in a war?

The Harivansha Purana certainly mentions such an incident. Eklavya was Krishna's cousin on his father's side. He was the son of Devashrava, an uncle of Krishna, and was named Shatrughna at birth. However, a few days after his birth, he was abandoned in a forest because he was considered to be ill-fated. So, it can be said that he fell victim to hypocrisy and superstition as soon as he was born. Well, the king of the *Nishadas*[41] raised him in the forest and named him Eklavya *(Harivansha Purana, Harivansha Parva, Chapter–34, Shloka–33)*. Later, the Kauravas, Pandavas and Krishna himself had become obstacles in his path, although they did not wish to. While Arjuna had become an obstacle for Eklavya when he wished to be trained by Dronacharya, Krishna himself had prevented Eklavya from participating in Draupadi's *swayamvar*. Due to these undesirable events, it was difficult for Eklavya to attain recognition and honour in the society for his talent, because of which he used to remain frustrated. Meanwhile, after the death of his foster father, he became the king of the Nishadas and joined a third faction, distinct from the Kauravas and the Pandavas, which included the king of Kashi, Poundrak, the king of Pundra, Hans-Dimbhaka, Narakasura and others.

At the time, the progress of the Yadavas under the leadership of Krishna was unbearable for the kings of Aryavarta belonging to this faction *(Harivansha Purana, Bhavishya Parva, Chapter–94, Shloka–4)*. Hence, this group attacked Dwarka once, under the leadership of Poundrak, in order to subdue the Yadavas of the Vrishni clan. At this time, Eklavya had also arrived with Poundrak, and with his valour he had obliterated almost the entire Yadava army. Furthermore, he had also grievously wounded Nishath, Saran, Kritvarma, Ugrasen, Vasudeva, Uddhava and Akrura. Coincidentally, Krishna was not present in Dwarka at the time, so Satyaki and Balarama entered the battlefield when Ugrasen, Vasudeva and the others were injured. The battle lasted for several days, and in the meantime, Krishna reached there too. Thereafter, when Poundrak was killed by Krishna, Balarama focused his attention on Eklavya. But Eklavya fled from the battle on seeing the tide turn against him and took refuge on an island. *(Harivansha Purana, Bhavishya Parva, Chapter–102)*. Later, Krishna killed him before the commencement of the Mahabharata war, and explaining the reason

41. A tribe

behind killing him, he told the Pandavas:

एकलव्यं हि सांगुष्ठमशक्ता देवदानवाः।
सराक्षसोरगाः पार्थ विजेतुं युधि कर्हिचित्॥
किमु मानुषमात्रेण शक्यःस्यात् प्रतिविक्षितुम्।
दृढमुष्टिः कृती नित्यमस्यमानो दिवानिशम्॥
त्वद्धितार्थे तु स मया हतः संग्राममूर्धनि।
चेदिराजश्च विक्रांतः प्रत्यक्षं निहतस्तव॥

Krishna said: "O Son of Kunti! Had Eklavya's thumb been intact, he would have been invincible in battle even for the gods, the Danavas, the demons and the Nagas put together. That being the case, how could a mere human even dare to look at him? He had a strong fist; he was an adept at archery and practised it day and night. For your benefit, I killed him just before the commencement of this war. As for the mighty king of Chedi, Shishupala, he was killed right before your eyes."

(Mahabharata, Drona Parva, Chapter–181, Shloka–19-21)

177. Did any king demand tax from Krishna?

According to the Harivansha Purana, it is true that a king had dared to demand tax from Krishna. Once, the princes of Pushkar, Hans and Dimbhaka, organised a Rajasuya Yajna for their father, King Brahmadatta. And these brothers had sent their messenger to Dwarka with orders for Krishna to accept subjugation to them and pay taxes:

जरासंधस्तु धर्मात्मा बन्धुरेव सदा मम।
गच्छ प्रिय यदुश्रेष्ठं ब्रूहि मद्वचनात् त्वरन्॥
दीयतां करसर्वस्वं यज्ञार्थं सुन्दरं बहु।
लवणानि बहून्यद्य गृह्य केशव मा चिरम्॥
आगच्छ त्वरितं कृष्ण न ते कार्यं विलम्बनम्।
इति ब्रूहि यदुश्रेष्ठं याहि त्वरितविक्रमः॥

Hans said to his envoy and friend Janardana: "The great soul Jarasandha is our well-wisher, O Brahmin! Go to Krishna, the chief of the Yadavas, and with my permission, say this to him promptly, 'Keshava! Give me your entire wealth as a beautiful offering and tax for the yajna and along with that, collect huge heaps of salt and come quickly. Krishna! Do not be delayed in performing this task!'"

(Harivansha Purana, Bhavishya Parva, Chapter–113, Shloka–21-23)

178. How did Krishna respond on hearing Hans's messenger demanding tax?

When he heard the demand for the tax and salt, Krishna was enraged. He sent Satyaki to Pushkar along with the messenger, bearing a message for the brothers Hans and Dimbhaka to not conduct the yajna. When the brothers saw Satyaki arrive with their messenger, they were somewhat apprehensive and reprimanding Satyaki, they said:

भो भो यादवदायाद किमर्थं प्राप्तवानिह।
किमब्रवीन्नन्दसुतः किं वासौ मेऽदिशत् करम्॥

"O Son of Yadavas! What have you come here for? What has that son of Nanda told you? What tax has he sent for me?"

Then, Satyaki said:

इदं सत्यं वचो हंस शंखचक्रगदाभृतः।
शरैर्निशितधाराग्रैः शार्ङ्गमुक्तैः शिलाशितैः॥
दास्यामि करसर्वस्वमसिना निशितेन ते।
शिरश्छेत्स्यामि ते हंस करदानस्य संग्रहम्॥

"Hans! Listen to these true words of Shri Krishna. He says that, 'I will pay all your taxes with my sharp arrows, honed on a rock, and shot from the Sarang bow. Hans! I will sever your head with my sharp sword; it will be a good collection of tax for you.'"

(Harivansha Purana, Bhavishya Parva, Chapter–118, Shloka–30-32)

क्व नः संग्राम इत्येवं पुनराह जगत्पतिः।
पुष्करे पुण्यदे नित्यमुत गोवर्धने गिरौ॥
मथुरायां प्रयागे वा दर्शयन्तो बलानि मे।
शंखचक्रधरे देवे जगत्पालनतत्परे॥
राजसूयं महायज्ञं कर्तुमिच्छति कः स्वयम्।
वदन्वा स्वस्तिमान्मर्त्यस्त्वां विना को व्रजेत् सुखम्॥

Satyaki continued: "Shri Krishna also wants to know where the battle would take place. Will it be here in Pushkar or on the Govardhana Hill or in Mathura or Prayag? He said, 'Let the brothers show me their strength in whichever place they want.' In Shri Krishna's presence, who will dare perform a yajna like the Rajasuya Yajna on his own, without seeking his permission? Which person, other than a fool like you, would say such things and still hope to remain alive?"

(Harivansha Purana, Bhavishya Parva, Chapter–118, Shloka–45-47)

In the Mahabharata, although the names of the brothers Hans and Dimbhaka appear twice in chronicles related to Jarasandha, no such incident is mentioned. In the Puranas, there is absolutely no mention of Hans and Dimbhaka.

179. Where did the fight take place between Krishna and Hans-Dimbhaka?

The Harivansha Purana provides a description that Krishna, Balarama, Satyaki and others, while chasing Hans and Dimbhaka, had gone right up to the river Yamuna, taking some soldiers along. And that is where Krishna had killed Hans by immersing him in a pit in the Yamuna. On seeing that his brother was killed, Dimbhaka committed suicide *(Harivansha Purana, Bhavishya Parva, Chapter–128)*. After the death of both the brothers, Krishna and Balarama could not resist going to the nearby Govardhana Hill, where they had spent their childhood:

गोवर्धनेऽथ विश्रम्य बलभद्रसहायवान्।
कंचित् कालं महाराज पूर्वभुक्तमुवास ह।।

"Pleased after bringing the wicked to justice, Krishna rested on the Govardhana Hill with Balabhadra, and stayed awhile at the place where he had spent so much time in the past."

(Harivansha Purana, Bhavishya Parva, Chapter–129, Shloka–15)

यशोदा नन्दगोपश्च कृष्णदर्शनलालसौ।
गोवर्धनगतं श्रुत्वा वासुदेवं सहाग्रजम्।।
नवनीतं च दधि च पायसं कृसरं तथा।
वन्यं पुष्पं महाराज मयूरांगदमेव च।।
बल्लवैरपरैः सार्धं गोपिभिश्च समन्ततः।
जग्मतुः सहसा प्रीतौ गोवर्धनमथो नृप।।

"Yashoda and Nanda would always yearn to see Krishna, so when they heard that Krishna had arrived with his elder brother to the Govardhana Hill, they were elated. Taking a few cowherds and milkmaids who had gathered, they went to the Govardhana Hill carrying butter, curd, *kheer,*[42] *khichri,*[43] wild flowers and armlets made of peacock feathers."

(Harivansha Purana, Bhavishya Parva, Chapter–130, Shloka–1-3)

Comment: However, this incident is not mentioned in any other text including the Mahabharata.

42. Sweet milk porridge
43. A dish consisting of mainly rice and split pulses

180. Who was Ghantakarna and when and how did he meet Krishna?

The Harivansha Purana mentions the story of a devil named Ghantakarna, who lived in the Himalayan forests. Once, when Krishna was headed towards Badrinath, he met Ghantakarna on the way; in response, Ghantakarna tried to extend his hospitality to Krishna:

विहस्य विकृतं भूयः... x ...यत्नस्ततः प्रीतोऽस्मि मांसप।।

"The devil, guffawing monstrously, rushed forth with the corpse of a Brahmin, who was just killed. He took a ghastly-looking piece of that hairy meat, cut it into two pieces, and washed one piece diligently with water. Then, he placed it in a beautiful pot and stood before Krishna with folded hands and said, 'This food is fit for you, kindly accept it. It is a fresh, high-quality, edible corpse of a pious Brahmin. The scriptures prescribe this food for us devils. So, if there is no defect in it, then please accept it.'

Shri Krishna was extremely pleased with him and thought, 'Oh! His deep affection and compassion for a guest like me is so evident in his demeanour.' With these thoughts, Shri Krishna said, 'O Cannibal! This meat cannot be used everywhere nor can it be given to everyone. That which you are calling a high-quality body of a Brahmin cannot even be touched by people like me. O Cannibal! May you be blessed! I am very pleased with your hospitality. Because your mind is pure and you have made great efforts for it, consider that I have accepted this raw meat of yours.'"

(Harivansha Purana, Bhavishya Parva, Chapter–83, Shloka–1-13)

In several Puranas and the Mahabharata, Ghantakarna has been described as a Gana, a being in the service of Shiva. Here too, Krishna's meeting with Ghantakarna took place on the way leading to Shankara. Hence, it can be inferred that in the Harivansha Purana, this story was possibly created only to highlight the reprehensible appearance and food habits of Shiva and those in his service, and depict them as contemptible. In Chapter 45 of the Mahabharata's Shalya Parva, the names of Shiva's Ganas are given; but there is no mention of this story. However, it does mention the name of Ghantakarna. Shloka 41 of Chapter 50 of the Agni Purana mentions the name of Ghantakarna, and he is described as the destroyer of sin and disease (***घण्टाकर्णोऽष्टदशदोः पापरोगं विदारयन्***). Ghantakarna's name is also found in the Skanda Purana. Thus, almost all the Puranas revolving around Shiva have mentioned Ghantakarna.

181. From whom did Krishna acquire the Sudarshan Chakra?

According to the Mahabharata, it was Shiva who gave the Sudarshan Chakra (discus) to Krishna:

यत्तद्भगवता पूर्वं दत्तं चक्रं तवानघ।
जलान्तरचरं हत्वा दैत्यं च बलगर्वितम्॥
उत्पादितं वृषांकेन दीप्तज्वलनसन्निभम्।
दत्तं भगवता तुभ्यं दुर्धर्षं तेजसाऽद्भुतम्॥

Sage Upamanyu said to Krishna: "In the past, the Chakra with the fiery radiance that Shiva had granted you, after killing the conceited demons living under the water, was created by Shiva himself and thereafter given to you. That weapon is extraordinarily radiant and invincible."

(Mahabharata, Anushasan Parva, Chapter–14, Shloka–76-77)

Since these chapters of the Mahabharata are embellished, replete with all sorts of Puranic errors, such evidence is not reliable.

182. Did Krishna's sons also enter into numerous marriages?

While polygamy surprises people and raises questions today, it was a highly common practice in the past. Oftentimes, it was seen as a sign of prosperity, splendour and social prestige. According to the details found across various Puranas, the list of marriages of the more well-known children of Krishna is as follows:

i) Pradyumna: Mayawati (Shambarasura's maid), Shubhangi (daughter of his uncle, Rukmi), Prabhavati (daughter of an Asura named Vajranabha)

ii) Saamba: Lakshmana (daughter of Duryodhana), Gunavati (Prabhavati's cousin), Rama (daughter of Kumbhand or Kushmand, minister of Banasura)

iii) Aniruddha: Rochana (granddaughter of Rukmi, brother-in-law of Krishna), Usha (daughter of Banasura)

Additionally, in the palaces of the princes of Dwarka, many women lived as concubines, who also symbolised splendour. For instance, after the abduction of Aniruddha, the women of his palace start mourning:

ततोऽनिरुद्धस्य गृहे रुरुदुः सर्वयोषितः।
प्रियं नाथमपश्यन्त्यः कुरर्य इव संघशः।।

"All the women living in the palace of Aniruddha, missing their beloved lord's presence, flocked together and started wailing like terns[44] ."

Comment: It is clear from the shlokas above that in those days, there were no social restrictions regarding women or marriages.

183. From where did Krishna acquire the famous bow called Sarang?

According to the evidence found in the Mahabharata, it was Narakasura who possessed the bow called Sarang, which was acquired by Krishna after killing him:

निर्जित्य नरकं भौममाहृत्य मणिकुण्डले।
षोडश स्त्रीसहस्राणि रत्नानि विविधानि च।।
प्रतिपेदे हृषीकेशः शार्ङ्गं च धनुरुत्तमम्।

Vaishampayan said: "After killing the local king, Narakasura, when Shri Krishna retrieved Aditi's gem-studded earrings from his palace and took control of the 16,000 women and several kinds of gems, he also acquired a bow of superior quality called Sarang."

(Mahabharata, Udyoga Parva, Chapter–158, Shloka–8-9)

184. Did Krishna conduct the Rasa in Dwarka as well?

According to the Harivansha Purana, Krishna organised the Rasa in Dwarka on a ship in the open sea. This Rasa abounded in food and liquor, along with singers, musicians and a bevy of beauties, who added to the heady atmosphere. This Rasa is described in Chapter 89 of the Vishnu Parva of this Purana. The Rasa was attended by Krishna and his wives along with Balarama and Revati, Arjuna and Subhadra, Satyaki and other close relatives with their wives. The author of this Purana, resorting to exaggeration, has also included Sage Narada in this celebration. The inhabitants of Dwarka had also joined this celebration in droves. This can be called the Great Rasa, if compared to the Rasa that Krishna had performed with the milkmaids in Vrindavan.

(Harivansha Purana, Vishnu Parva, Chapter–89)

44. A water bird

However, this Rasa is neither mentioned in the Mahabharata nor in any other Purana. Notably, the description of this Rasa in this entire chapter dwells more on the consumption of liquor than anything else. It seems as if the author's intention in this chapter was only to emphasise the availability and consumption of liquor. The food served during that Rasa was both vegetarian as well as non-vegetarian:

पोर्शानि चान्ये शकलानि तत्र ददुः पशूनां घृतमृक्षितानि।
सामुद्रचूर्णैरवचूर्णितानि चूर्णेन मृष्टेन समारिचेन॥
कट्वांकशूलैरपि पक्षिभिश्च घृताम्लसौवर्चलतैलसिक्तैः।
मैरेयमाध्वीकसुरासवांस्ते पपुः प्रियाभिः परिवार्यमाणाः॥

"The meat of animals and birds (words underlined in the shlokas above) was also served to the Yadavas by frying it in ghee."

(Harivansha Purana, Vishnu Parva,
Chapter–89, Shloka–60, 62)

185. Did Kansa really have Vasudeva and Devaki imprisoned?

To answer this question, it is essential to first divide the texts into two groups. Let the first group comprise texts which contain details such as the divine prophecy made during Vasudeva and Devaki's marriage, Kansa's readiness to kill Devaki, and Kansa's order to imprison Vasudeva and Devaki right after he had honoured and pampered Vasudeva. This group of texts includes the Bhagavat Purana, Vishnu Purana, Brahmavaivarta Purana, Padma Purana, Garga Samhita and others. All these texts describe Vasudeva and Devaki's imprisonment. But there is another group of texts which contains absolutely no mention of their imprisonment. In this group, one can include the South Indian version of the Mahabharata and the Harivansha Purana. The popular, North Indian version of the Mahabharata, with commentary by Neelkantha, does not even mention the birth of Krishna and his childhood. But its South Indian version describes Krishna's birth and his escape to Gokul in a single shloka:

वासुदेवस्ततो जातं बालमादित्यसंनिभम्।
नन्दगोपकुले राजन् भयात् प्राच्छादयद्धरिम्॥

Grandsire Bhishma says: "O King Yudhishthira! Then, Vasudeva, fearing Kansa, hid his newborn child Krishna, who was radiant like the sun, in the house of Nanda, the cowherd."

(South Indian Mahabharata, Sabha Parva, Chapter–52, Shloka–17)

On the other hand, in the description given in the Harivansha Purana, there is no mention of Vasudeva and Devaki being imprisoned, but it states that the royal family was asked to collectively keep a watch over them. Enraged by Narada's warning, Kansa said to the ministers who were his well-wishers:

सोऽज्ञापयत संरब्धः सचिवानात्मनो हि तान्।
यत्ता भवत सर्वे वै देवक्या गर्भकृन्तने॥

Vaishampayan says: "Janamejaya! Brimming with anger, Kansa commanded the ministers who were his well-wishers, 'All of you get ready to destroy Devaki's womb.'"

प्रथमादेव हंतव्या गर्भास्ते सप्त एव हि।
मूलादेव तु हंतव्यः सोऽनर्थो यत्र संशयः॥

Kansa said: "Starting from the first child, all seven children should be eliminated. When in doubt, it is essential to destroy the potentially disastrous thing from its very root."

देवकी च गृहे गुप्ता प्रच्छन्नैरपिरक्षिता।
स्वैरं चरतु विश्रब्धा गर्भकाले तु रक्ष्यताम्॥

"Devaki can safely and fearlessly live in her own chamber as per her wish, protected by covert guards. But when she becomes pregnant, she should be kept under special supervision."

मासान् वै पुष्पमासादीन् गणयन्तु मम स्त्रियः।
परिणामे तु गर्भस्य शेषं ज्ञास्यामहे वयम्॥

"My women must start counting the months of her pregnancy, right from her menstruation. When the time comes for the delivery, we will handle the rest of the task."

वसुदेवस्तु संरक्ष्यः स्त्रीसनायासु भूमिषु।
अप्रमत्तैर्मम हितै रात्रावहनि चैव हि।
स्त्रीभिर्वर्षवरैश्चैव व्यक्तव्यं न तु कारणम्॥

"Servants who are my well-wishers should be on the alert night and day and take good care of Vasudeva in the gynaeceum filled with women. Women and eunuchs should also keep a close watch on him, but they should not reveal the reason behind this to him."

(Harivansha Purana, Vishnu Parva, Chapter–2, Shloka–1-5)

In the shlokas given above, there is a discussion on the secret surveillance of Vasudeva and Devaki, and such conspiracies were quite the norm in the corridors of royal palaces for centuries, which is actually closer to reality. Therefore, it can be said that the subsequent writers of the Puranas have attempted to exaggerate the original story by making extensive embellishments to this simple act of royal spying and turning it into a hyperbolic account peppered with a celestial prophecy, drawing out of swords, imprisonment, shackles, miracles and torrential rain.

186. Was there a conflict between Krishna's wives?

Almost all the Puranas describing the incidents related to Krishna's life tell the story of the planting of the Parijat tree in Satyabhama's courtyard. However, the underlying, unrelenting tug of war between Rukmini and Satyabhama, and the rancour between the two wives is described in detail only in the Harivansha Purana. Apart from the conflict between these two women, there is no mention of any kind of tension or jealousy between Krishna's other wives. The tug of war between Rukmini and Satyabhama represents true human nature, especially the nature of a woman. So, even if we discard the exaggeration made in the story, it can be inferred that at least some of it was real.

In the Harivansha Purana, this story has been extended to twelve chapters, out of which the first three chapters describe the jealousy between these two wives and Krishna's distress on account of it. According to the story described in this Purana, while Krishna had gone on a trip to the Raivataka Mountain, a sage gave Krishna a flower from the Parijat tree, which he subsequently gave to Rukmini who was sitting nearby. Rukmini immediately put it in her hair bun. Seeing Rukmini pleased with the flower, that sage (Narada) apprised them of the numerous specialties of the flower. However, this created a problem, for, Rukmini's maids were standing nearby during this conversation, and some of them were Satyabhama's spies. On returning to Dwarka, those maids gave Satyabhama an exaggerated account of the entire incident. *(Harivansha Purana, Vishnu Parva, Chapter–65).* And that was it! Satyabhama was overcome with jealousy. After some time, when

Krishna went to her quarters, he had to face a torrent of taunts and reproachful remarks:

किमत्र बहुनोक्तेन हृदयं वेद्मि तेऽच्युत।।
वाङ्मात्रमेव पश्यामि माधुर्यं सम्प्रयुज्यते।
मयि स्नेहश्च कृतकस्तवान्यत्र न कृत्रिमः।।
ऋजुस्वभावां भक्तां च सर्वथा पुरुषोत्तम।
अवजानासि जानन् मां कैतवीं वृत्तिमास्थितः।।

Satyabhama said: "Lord! What more can I say; I now know the kind of person you are. I notice that you only whisper sweet nothings to me. Your love for me is superficial. But that is not the case with the others; your love for them is real and natural. Krishna! My nature is simple and I truly love you, but in spite of knowing this, you cheat and trick me, and you neglect me."

(Harivansha Purana, Vishnu Parva, Chapter–66, Shloka–49-51)

The remaining chapters of this Purana describe how Krishna fought a terrible battle with Indra to obtain the Parijat tree so that he could pacify Satyabhama. Verily, this story is the height of exaggeration! This incident has been described in its own style in every Purana related to Krishna, but there is no mention of it in the Mahabharata.

187. What relation did Krishna have with Indra?

According to the Puranic beliefs, Sage Kashyap had two wives: Aditi and Diti. The sons born to Aditi were called Devatas, and those born to Diti were called Daityas or Asuras. Among the sons of Aditi such as Indra, Surya, Vamana—an incarnation of Vishnu—and others, Indra was the eldest and Vamana, the youngest. So, when the original Mahabharata of Veda Vyasa underwent extension and the Puranas began to be penned one after the other, Krishna, on account of his great feats, was declared to be an incarnation of Vishnu; and since Vamana was younger than Indra, Krishna was also addressed in some texts as Indranuj (younger brother of Indra) and Upendra, which is the same as younger brother of Indra.

There could possibly be another reason behind this. Indra is said to be the presiding deity of the Vedas and is also considered to be the protector of the Vedas, Aryas and Yajnas. But the Vedas talk about a battle between Indra and Krishna, which has been mentioned at various points in this book too. Therefore, it may also be an attempt by the scholars of the Vaishnava sect who consider Vishnu to be the creator of the world, to establish harmony between Indra and Krishna. But despite this effort, there are several occasions, even in the Puranas, wherein Krishna and Indra are on the verge of a battle, which the authors of the Puranas have tried to justify in various ways, in accordance with the beliefs of their respective sects.

188. Did Yudhishthira's Rajasuya Yajna lead to any adverse effect?
This question has been raised in the Harivansha Purana. Arjuna's grandson, Parikshit had died of snake bite. Enraged by this, his son Janamejaya organised a Serpent Yajna in which innumerable snakes were sacrificed in the fire. After the completion of the Serpent Yajna, Janamejaya conducted the Ashwamedha Yajna, which was also attended by Veda Vyasa, who was his ancestor and the 'Seer' of the entire Kaurava and Pandava dynasty. On this occasion, during a conversation, Janamejaya asks Veda Vyasa:

अनुमान्य तु सर्वज्ञं... X...बुद्धिमन्तश्च्युता नयात्।

"O Lord! You are omniscient. With your permission, I am posing a question to you. I feel that the Rajasuya Yajna is the cause of the destruction of the Kauravas. Considering the tragic end of the kings in the Mahabharata war, this is what I believe. Now, I am of the opinion that the Rajasuya was conceived only for war. It is said that in ancient times, Soma had performed the Rajasuya Yajna, and after this Yajna, there ensued a war called Tarakamaya. Then, Varuna performed that Yajna, and at the end of his Great Yajna, there was a fierce battle between the Gods and Asuras which destroyed everything. Then, King Harishchandra conducted this Yajna, at the end of which there was an epic war called Adibak, which proved to be devastating for the Kshatriyas. Then, my ancestor, the supreme King Yudhishthira organised an insuperable Yajna which was terrible like fire, the beginning of which became the cause of the Mahabharata war. So, why did you not put an end to the ritual of this great Yajna called Rajasuya, which was the root cause of this universally destructive war?

You are the Grandsire of all our ancestors, you are the knower of the past and the future; you are the protector of our clan and the one who gave birth to our ancestors. Then, how did the wise Pandavas go astray from the righteous path in spite of the presence of a leader like you?"

(Harivansha Purana, Bhavishya Parva, Chapter–2, Shloka–14-23)

Responding to Janamejaya's long question in just two shlokas, Veda Vyasa said:

कालेन विपरीतास्ते तव पूर्वपितामहाः।
न मां भविष्यं पृच्छन्ति न चापृष्टो ब्रवीम्यहम्॥
सामर्थ्यं च न पश्यामि भविष्यस्य निवर्तने।
परिहर्तुं न शक्या हि कालेन विहिता गतिः॥

Veda Vyasa said: "O Janamejaya! Your ancestors, the Pandavas, had attained a mental state that was against the urges of Time. They did not ask me anything, and neither do I give unsolicited advice. Besides, I do not see in anyone the power to alter the future. For, it is impossible to alter the course that Time has ordained."

(Harivansha Purana, Bhavishya Parva, Chapter–2, Shloka–24-25)

189. Was Krishna an incarnation of God, the way the entire world believes today?

In the Mahabharata, Krishna himself says that just like other humans, he too is a normal human being:

अहं हि तत् करिष्यामि परं पुरुषकारतः।
दैवं तु न मया शक्यं कर्मकर्तुं कथंचनः॥

Krishna says: "O Arjuna! I can do only as much as a person can do to the best of his ability, or I can make an effort to do as much. There should not be any expectation of a miracle from me. It is not possible for me to avert or alter in any manner what destiny has ordained."

(Mahabharata, Udyoga Parva, Chapter–79, Shloka–5)

The Vishnu Purana mentions this fact in the following manner:

नाहं देवो ना गन्धर्वो न यक्षो न च दानवः।
अहं वो बांधवो जातो नैतच्चिन्त्यमितोऽन्यथा॥

Addressing a gathering of cowherds in Vrindavan, Krishna says: "Dear cowherds! I am neither a god, nor a Gandharva, nor a Yaksha nor a Danava. I have been born amongst you as your brother. So, you should not have some other thoughts about this."

(Vishnu Purana, Part–5, Chapter–13, Shloka–12)

The Harivansha Purana states something similar:

मन्यन्ते मां यथा सर्वे भवन्तो भीमविक्रमम्।
तथाहं नावमन्तव्यः स्वजातीयोऽस्मि बान्धवः॥

Krishna says to the cowherds: "Do not disrespect me by considering me as formidable and mighty. I am your brother from this same community."

(Harivansha Purana, Vishnu Parva, Chapter–20, Shloka–11)

Comment: Krishna generally considered himself to be a normal, regular human being. But yes, in the Gita, he had also called himself the God of Gods. So, Krishna presented himself in the form that was required at any given time. This was the most prominent feature of his personality.

190. Was Krishna a Vedic deity?

In the Vedas, Krishna is depicted not as a deity but the chief of the cowherd community that lives in the forests near the banks of the Yamuna river, and an enemy of Indra, the chief of the Vedic deities:

अव द्रप्सो अंशुमतीमतिष्ठदियानः कृष्णो दशभिः सहस्रैः।
आवत्तमिन्द्रः शच्या धमन्तमप स्नेहितीर्नृमणा अधत्त॥

"On the banks of the river Anshumati (Yamuna), there lived an Asura called Krishna who launched an attack with 10,000 troops. Indra cleverly overwhelmed the Asura who created the ruckus. Thereafter, Indra destroyed the violent army of Krishnasura for the benefit of humans."

(Rigveda, Mandala–8, Sukta–85, Mantra–13)*
*(*Supplementary Edition, Sukta–96)*

It is clear from the Vedic description quoted above that Krishna was not a Vedic deity, but was opposed to Vedic tradition and beliefs.

191. Was Krishna's childhood as pleasant as it is depicted in the texts?

If this question is answered through the lens of a present-day scenario, its underlying meaning can be understood easily. In today's era of advanced communication networks, if an incident occurs in a village or town, a multitude of news reporters rush to the scene and create so many stories that the original incident simply vanishes in the glut of reports. Thereafter, even an efficient police force has to slog for months to investigate and dig out the truth. Now, it has been 5,000 years since Krishna's arrival on earth. In all these years, millions of storytellers have narrated stories about Krishna. Furthermore, huge barriers like the words *'avatar'* and *'leela'*[45] have suppressed the truth about him in such a manner that the less said about it the better. Today, people believe that since Krishna was an *'avatar'*, all his joys and sorrows were part of his *'leela'* or divine play.

It is true that all the Puranic texts have been written with the belief that Krishna was God. But these very texts also contain facts which give us a glimpse of the reality, and to recognise them, one needs to have a keen eye for research and investigation, and some amount of prudence too. The occupation of Nanda and his associates was animal husbandry, so they used to set up hamlets in fodder-rich forests and live there. Now, one can easily imagine how the life of human beings must have been in the forests 5,000 years ago. Add to this the arduous task of relocating after every five to ten years, which was unavoidable. When Krishna was about eight years old, Nanda and his companions had to migrate from Gokul and take refuge in Vrindavan *(Harivansha Purana, Vishnu Parva, Chapter–8-9; Bhagavat Purana, Skandha–10, Chapter–11; Garga Samhita, Vrindavan Khanda, Chapter–1)*. The reason behind this was, the forest had dried up due to the large-scale exploitation of its greenery by the cowherds. And because of the lack of food and water in the now barren forest, wild animals had also begun to invade the hamlet looking for prey.

Krishna's life in Vrindavan was not trouble-free either. He had to tackle feral bulls, monkeys, cloudbursts as well as floods in the Yamuna River, apart from snakes and demons. And if all this was not enough, Kansa's manoeuvres added to his woes. In light of all this, just imagine the kind of childhood Krishna must have led! Ignoring all these struggles of Krishna, people who worship Krishna's idol today, think that his childhood was divine and ethereal. Well, isn't it silly to ignore the truth so blatantly?

Thus, if you read the ancient texts written about Krishna's life after

45. Divine play

removing words such as *'avatar'* and *'leela'* from your mind, then you would understand how he had lived his life amidst a slew of struggles.

192. Why is Vrindavan called 'Vraj'?

'Vraj' is a Sanskrit word used both as a verb and a noun. When used as a verb, it means - to keep moving, to go, to travel, and so on. When used as a noun, it means - the place where abundant fodder is available for cattle, pasture, meadow, and so on. Since Nanda and his companions were cattle ranchers, and that was their sole occupation, the word 'Vraj' is used in both verb and noun form in the context of Nanda and his community. As a verb, 'Vraj' is used to denote the community's constant movement, that is, its relocation to a new region every 10–20 years, or migrating to various regions as per the availability of fodder. Speaking in modern parlance, they led a nomadic lifestyle.

On the other hand, Nanda's community used the word 'Vraj' as a noun for any area where sufficient fodder was available for their animals, without expending extensive effort. Therefore, in the scriptures, Gokul is called 'Vraj' and so is Vrindavan:

तस्माद् वनं नवतृणं गच्छन्तु धनिनो व्रजाः।
न द्वारबन्धावरणा न गृहक्षेत्रिणस्तथा।
प्रशस्ता वै व्रजा लोके यथा वै चक्रचारिणः।।

"The cowherd community must go to the forest that is endowed with the wealth of Vraj, that is, pasture, to a region where fresh, new grass is available. The 'Vraj' where doors have been built, that have been fenced, where permanent houses have been built and cultivation has begun, is not considered good in our world. The 'Vraj', or the cowherds' hamlet, which keeps moving from one place to another, free from any bondage, akin to uninhibited swans, is the best."

(Harivansha Purana, Vishnu Parva, Chapter–8, Shloka–19)

I hope this single shloka quoted above has made the meanings of 'Vraj' as a verb and a noun absolutely clear.

193. Was the youngest Pandava, Sahadeva, married in Dwarka?

This entire story is found in the Harivansha Purana, while no mention of it is found in any other Purana. Pradyumna, Krishna's eldest son, had abducted Prabhavati, the daughter of an Asura king named Vajranabha, and had also killed Vajranabha when the latter had objected to the alliance. This story has been narrated in detail in this book too, in response to another question. In light of this incident, Nikumbha, Vajranabha's brother, who was also extremely powerful, was yearning to wreak vengeance. For this purpose, he began hovering around Dwarka with the idea of abducting a young woman, as a tit for tat for the abduction of his brother's daughter.

In Dwarka, Bhanu, the eldest son of Krishna and Satyabhama, had a large palace, which was normally under heavy security. Bhanu had a beautiful daughter called Bhanumati. When Nikumbha saw Bhanumati, he decided to target her and lay in wait for the right opportunity. As soon as he chanced upon the opportunity, he abducted her and escaped. Consequently, pandemonium broke loose in the palace; and on hearing the commotion, when the alerted Yadava soldiers conveyed the news to Krishna, he immediately left to chase the Asura along with Arjuna—who was staying in Dwarka at the time—and his eldest son Pradyumna. After waging a long battle, he killed Nikumbha and rescued his granddaughter Bhanumati. However, when they returned to Dwarka, a fresh problem reared its head. Everybody began to wonder, who would marry a girl who had been abducted by someone. All the members of Krishna's family were caught up in this turmoil when one day, Sage Narada happened to arrive in Dwarka. When he heard about this problem, he said to Bhanu, the girl's father:

एवं भानुमती वीर सहदेवाय दीयताम्।
श्रद्धानः स शूरश्च धर्मशीलश्च पाण्डवः॥

Narada said: "O valiant Bhanu! Heed my advice and marry your daughter Bhanumati to Sahadeva, because the son of Pandu, Sahadeva, is faithful, valiant and virtuous."

(Harivansha Purana, Vishnu Parva,
Chapter–90, Shloka–75)

आनीतः सहदेवश्च प्रेषितचक्रपाणिना।
विवाहे तदा वृत्ते सभार्यः स पुरीं गतः॥

Vaishampayan said: "Then, Shri Krishna called Sahadeva and when the wedding rituals were completed, he sent him off with his wife, and he thus left for his kingdom."

(Harivansha Purana, Vishnu Parva, Chapter–90, Shloka–77)

So, the two Pandavas, Arjuna and Sahadeva, had married into Krishna's family.

194. What do the texts state about the grandeur of Dwarka?

Sporadic descriptions of Dwarka's appearance are found in one or two shlokas in various Puranas and the Mahabharata. But they do not provide the real picture of the city. However, a detailed account of it is found in one entire chapter of the Harivansha Purana. This chapter offers a detailed description of the expanse of the city, its structure and the various colours of the palaces of Krishna's queens. As the people who read the Puranas are aware, just like the other Puranas, there are exaggerations galore in this Purana too. However, readers can use their discretion to fathom the gist of it. The only benefit of reading this chapter is that most of the facts related to the architecture of Dwarka city can be found in one place. So, let us learn about Dwarka through the words stated in this Purana:

अप्रमेयां महोत्सेधामगाधपरिखायुताम्।
प्राकारवरसम्पन्नां सुधापाण्डुरलेपनम्।।

Vaishampayan said: "The expanse of Dwarka city was difficult to measure. It was built at a great height too, and was surrounded by deep trenches. The beautiful ramparts enhanced its appearance. The walls of Dwarka were coated with lime to make them look bright."

(Harivansha Purana, Vishnu Parva, Chapter–98, Shloka–25)

तीक्ष्णयंत्रशतघ्नीभिर्हेमजालैश्च भूषिताम्।
अयसैश्च महाचक्रैर्ददर्श द्वारकां पुरीम्।।

"I saw Dwarka city adorned with sharp instruments, *Shataghni*[46] and gold nets. It was adorned with huge discs of iron."

(Harivansha Purana, Vishnu Parva, Chapter–98, Shloka–26)

अष्टयोजन विस्तीर्णामचलां द्वादशायताम्।
द्विगुणोपनिवेशां च ददर्श द्वारकां पुरीम्।।

"Dwarka city had a width of 8 yojana (96 km) and a length of 12 yojana (144 km), so its entire area was 96 yojana. The area around it was twice its size, which was 192 yojana. Shri Krishna feasted his eyes on that

46. An ancient canon-like weapon

insuppressible Dwarka city."

(Harivansha Purana, Vishnu Parva, Chapter–98, Shloka–28)

अष्टमार्गमहारथ्यां महाषोडशचत्वराम्।
एवं मार्गपरिक्षिप्तां साक्षादुशनसा कृतम्।।

"There were eight major thoroughfares to enter that city and sixteen major crossroads. Thus, Dwarka city, enhanced by its various roads, was built according to the strategy of Shukracharya himself."

(Harivansha Purana, Vishnu Parva, Chapter–98, Shloka–21)

स्त्रियोऽपि यस्यां युद्धेरन् किमु वृष्णिमहारथाः।
व्यूहानामुत्तमा मार्गः सप्त चैव महापथाः।।

"Women could also fight a war in that city, and as for the great warriors of the Vrishni clan, could one really doubt their valour? It has excellent streets for the brigades of troops as well as seven large roads."

(Harivansha Purana, Vishnu Parva, Chapter–98, Shloka–30)

दावाग्निज्वलितप्रख्यैर्निर्मितैर्विश्वकर्मणा।
आलिखद्भिरिवाकाशमतिचन्द्रार्कभास्वरैः।।

"The magnificent buildings built by Vishwakarma used to shine and glow like the flames of a forest fire. It seemed as if they were etching a golden line in the sky. Their radiance was greater than that of the sun and the moon."

(Harivansha Purana, Vishnu Parva, Chapter–98, Shloka–37)

The golden palace of Rukmini:

प्रसादं चैव हेमाभं सर्वभूतमनोहरम्।।
मेरोरिव गिरेः शृंगमुच्छ्रितं कांचनं महत्।
रुक्मिण्याः प्रवरं वासं विहितं विश्वकर्मणा।।

"That golden palace was a delight for all beings. Its high peaks were overlaid with gold, due to which they were shining like the peak of Mount Meru. Vishwakarma had built that excellent palace for Rukmini."

(Harivansha Purana, Vishnu Parva, Chapter–98, Shloka–42-43)

The white palace of Satyabhama:

सत्यभामा पुनर्वेश्म यदावसत पाण्डुरम्।
विचित्रमणिसोपानं तद् विदुर्भोगवानिति।।

"The palace in which Satyabhama resided was white in colour. Its stairs were overlaid with strange types of gems."

(Harivansha Purana, Vishnu Parva, Chapter–98, Shloka–43)

Jambavati's palace with large flags:

स च प्रासादमुख्योऽथ जाम्बवत्या विभूषितः
प्रभयाभ्यभवत् सर्वांस्तानन्यो भास्करो यथा।।

"Jambavati used to grace the main building on which huge flags were hoisted. Like the sun, it was eclipsing all the other palaces with its glory."

(Harivansha Purana, Vishnu Parva, Chapter–98, Shloka–46)

The golden palace of Satya:

जाम्बूनद इवादीप्तः प्रदीप्तज्वलनो यथा।
सागरप्रतिमोऽतिष्ठन्मेरुरित्यभिविश्रुतः।।
तस्मिन् गान्धारराजस्य दुहिता कुलशालिनी।
गान्धारी भरतश्रेष्ठ केशवेन निवेशिता।।

"Krishna had the daughter of the king of Gandhara, Satya, residing in a palace that was as radiant as the Jambunada gold and a raging fire, which was as vast as the sea, and which was well known by the name of Meru."

(Harivansha Purana, Vishnu Parva, Chapter–98, Shloka–48-49)

The lotus-coloured palace of Bhadra:

पद्मकूल इति ख्यातं पद्मवर्ण महाप्रभम्।
सुभीमाया महाकूटं वेश्मातिरुचिरप्रभम्।।

"The building, which had the colour of the Padmakool lotus, which was radiant, as high as a mountain peak, and shining with a pleasant glow, was the abode of Subhimadevi (Bhadra)."

(Harivansha Purana, Vishnu Parva, Chapter–98, Shloka–50)

The palaces of Lakshmana and Mitravinda:

सूर्यप्रभस्तु प्रासादः सर्वकामगुणैर्युतः।
लक्ष्मणाया नृपश्रेष्ठ निर्दिष्टः शार्ङ्गधन्वना।।
वैदूर्यमणिवर्णाभः प्रासादो हरितप्रभः।
यं विदुः सर्वभूतानि परमित्येव भारत।।
वासं तं मित्रविन्दाया देवर्षिगणपूजितम्।
महिष्या वासुदेवस्य भूषणं तेषु वेश्मसु।।

Vaishampayan said: "O King! The palace, with its desirable qualities and radiance like the sun, was chosen by Shri Krishna as the abode of Lakshmana. And the palace which was effulgent because of its green colour and possessed the glow of the cat's eye stone, which all people considered to be excellent, was the abode of Mitravinda."

(Harivansha Purana, Vishnu Parva, Chapter–98, Shloka–51-53)

One aspect that a reader finds missing in this chapter of the Harivansha Purana is the description of the palace of Kalindi, another wife of Krishna. Nevertheless, based on the descriptions given above, it is evident that the architecture of Dwarka city was a benchmark in itself even during that ancient period, and was also unique across the entire expanse of Aryavarta at that time.

195. How many times was the disastrous game of dice held in the royal court of Hastinapur?

According to the Mahabharata, it was played twice in the assembly of the Kauravas. The first time, when Yudhishthira lost everything—including himself, his four brothers, the kingdom as well as Draupadi—to Shakuni in the game, Draupadi was severely humiliated in a packed assembly at the instigation of Duryodhana and Karna. At that time, Draupadi kept demanding answers to her questions, but no one in the assembly had answered even one of her questions or given her a fair answer. Then, after Duryodhana's own brother, Vikarna, and Vidura expressed their strong objection to the sordid proceedings, Dhritarashtra consoled Draupadi and permitted her to ask for a boon:

वरं वृणीष्व पाञ्चालि मत्तो यदभिवाञ्छसि।
वधूनां हि विशिष्टा मे त्वं धर्मपरमा सती।।

Dhritarashtra said: "Daughter-in-law Draupadi! You are the best and most virtuous woman among all my daughters-in-law. You may ask for a boon as per your wishes."

(Mahabharata, Sabha Parva, Gita Press Edition, Chapter–71; South Indian Mahabharata, Chapter–93, Shloka–27)

ददासि चेद्वरं मह्यं वृणोमि भरतर्षभ।
सर्वधर्मानुगः श्रीमानदासोऽस्तु युधिष्ठिरः।।
मनस्विनमजानन्तो मैवं ब्रूयुः कुमारकाः।
एतं वै दासपुत्रेति प्रतिविन्ध्यं ममात्मजम्।।

Draupadi said: "O King! If you grant me a boon, then I demand that Yudhishthira, who abides by righteous conduct, should be set free from servitude so that no other prince can call my son Prativindya the son of a servant."

(Mahabharata, Sabha Parva, Gita Press Edition, Chapter–71; South Indian Mahabharata, Chapter–93, Shloka–28-29)

एवं भवतु कल्याणि यथा त्वमभिभाषसे।
द्वितीयं ते वरं भद्रे ददानि वरयस्व ह।
मनो हि मे वितरति नैकं त्वं वरमर्हसि॥

Dhritarashtra said: "Kalyani! Your wish shall be fulfilled. Courteous lady! Now, you may demand a second boon. I feel the urge to grant you the boon, because you do not deserve just one boon."

(Mahabharata, Sabha Parva, Gita Press Edition, Chapter–71; South Indian Mahabharata, Chapter–93, Shloka–30)

Comment: The sentiment behind the remark "You do not deserve just one boon" is that 'just one boon is not enough to compensate for the humiliation that you had to endure.'

सरथौ सधनुष्कौ च भीमसेनधनञ्जयौ।
यमौ च वरये राजन्नदासान् स्ववशानहम्॥

Then, Draupadi said: "O King! As my second boon, I demand that Bhimsen, Arjuna, Nakula and Sahadeva along with their chariots and bows and arrows should be freed from servitude."

(Mahabharata, Sabha Parva, Gita Press Edition, Chapter–71; South Indian Mahabharata, Chapter–93, Shloka–31)

तथाऽस्तु ते महाभागे यथा त्वं नन्दिनीच्छसि।
तृतीयं वरयास्मत्तो नासि द्वाभ्यां सुसंस्कृता।
त्वं हि सर्वस्नुषाणां मे श्रेयसी धर्मचारिणी॥

Dhritarashtra said: "O Fortunate One! You are the joy of your clan. Your wish shall be fulfilled. Now, you may ask for a third boon. You are the best among all my daughters-in-law and abide by righteous conduct. I feel that just two boons are not enough to truly honour you."

(Mahabharata, Sabha Parva, Gita Press Edition, Chapter–71; South Indian Mahabharata, Chapter–93, Shloka–32)

लोभो धर्मस्य नाशाय भगवन्नाहमुत्सहे।
अनर्हा वरमादातुं तृतीयं राजसत्तम॥

Draupadi said: "O Lord! Greed is the destroyer of virtue, so now I do not desire another boon. O Jewel among Kings! I do not have the right to demand a third boon."

(Mahabharata, Sabha Parva, Gita Press Edition, Chapter–71; South Indian Mahabharata, Chapter–93, Shloka–34)

Comment: During that period, people in superior positions and elders were referred to as Lord or God. That is why in the above shlokas, Draupadi uses the word 'Bhagavan' to address the king of Hastinapur and her father-in-law's brother, Dhritarashtra.

पापीयांस इमे भूत्वा सन्तीर्णाः पतयो मम।
वेत्स्यन्ति चैव भद्राणि राजन्पुण्येन कर्मणा॥

In the above shlokas, Draupadi, despite her unprecedented humiliation in that packed assembly, did not display greed or take undue advantage of the opportunity presented to her. On the contrary, she demonstrated great equanimity and steadfastness by saying, "O King! My husbands had fallen into servitude and were in great trouble. But now, they are free from it. So, with their efforts, they will themselves achieve the goal of their own well-being."

(Mahabharata, Sabha Parva, Gita Press Edition, Chapter–71; South Indian Mahabharata, Chapter–93, Shloka–36)

Then, Dhritarashtra returned to Yudhishthira all the wealth and the kingdom, saying:

अजातशत्रो भद्रं ते अरिष्टं स्वस्ति गच्छत।
अनुज्ञाताः सहधनाः स्वराज्यमनुशासत॥
इदं चैवावबोद्धव्यं वृद्धस्य मम शासनम्।
मया निगदितं सर्वं पथ्यं निःश्रेयसं परम्॥
वेत्थ त्वं तात धर्माणां गतिं सूक्ष्मां युधिष्ठिर।
विनीतोऽसि महाप्राज्ञ वृद्धानां पर्युपासिता॥
यतो बुद्धिस्ततः शान्तिः प्रशमं गच्छ भारत।
नादारुणि पतेच्छस्त्रं दारुण्येतन्निपात्यते॥

Dhritarashtra said to Yudhishthira: *"Ajatshatro!*[47] May you be blessed with all that is good! By my command, you may go to your capital city without any hurdles, with the wealth that you had lost, and rule your kingdom efficiently. This is the command of this old man. There is one more thing you must pay attention to. All the things I say will be for your benefit only. Dear Yudhishthira! You know the subtle undercurrents of righteousness and virtue. You have humility and you have revered the

47 A person who has no enemy

elders. Where there is wisdom, there is peace. O Bharata! Calm down, that is, forget what has just happened. The axe never hurts a stone or iron; people use it on wood only."

(Mahabharata, Sabha Parva, Gita Press Edition, Chapter–73; South Indian Mahabharata, Chapter–95, Shloka–2-5)

When Dhritarashtra was sending off Yudhishthira with all the wealth and the kingdom, Dushasana was taken by surprise. In fact, he felt as if the ground beneath his feet was slipping away. So, he rushed to Duryodhana who was sitting with his ministers. On reaching there, Dushasana said to his brother:

दुःखेनैतत्समानीतं स्थविरो नाशयत्यसौ।
शत्रुसाद्गमयद्रव्यं तद्बुध्यध्वं महारथाः॥

Dushasana said: "O Great Warriors! You should know that our old father is destroying the great wealth that we had obtained after so much trouble. He has returned all the money to those very enemies."

(Mahabharata, Sabha Parva, Gita Press Edition, Chapter–74; South Indian Mahabharata, Chapter–96, Shloka–4)

Realising the gravity of the matter, Duryodhana's group did not say anything to Dhritarashtra, but they started contemplating a move that could not be countered immediately. They devised a plan, according to which, Duryodhana's group began to collectively and individually instil fear in the mind of Dhritarashtra, by saying that Arjuna was the biggest threat to the peace and happiness of Duryodhana and Hastinapur, and that it was impossible to win against him in a face-to-face war. They told him that Arjuna was the strength of all the Pandavas, so it was impossible to control the Pandavas without destroying him. But Arjuna was invincible! Hearing this, Dhritarashtra advised Duryodhana that he should live in harmony with Arjuna and the other Pandavas, but Duryodhana, expressing his fear, said:

गृहे गृहे च पश्यामि तात पार्थमहं सदा।
शरगाण्डीवसंयुक्तं पाशहस्तमिवान्तकम्॥
अपि पार्थसहस्राणि भीतः पश्यामि भारत।
पार्थभूतमिदं सर्वं नगरं प्रतिभाति मे॥
पार्थमेव हि पश्यामि रहिते तात भारत।
दृष्ट्वा स्वप्नगतं पार्थमुद्भ्रमामि विचेतनः॥

अकारादीनि नामानि अर्जुनत्रस्तचेतसः।
अश्वाक्षराम्बुजाश्चैव त्रासं सञ्जनयन्ति मे॥

Duryodhana said: "Father! Even when I am at home, I see Arjuna with his bow and arrows, ready to shoot at me. I am so terrified that I see thousands of Arjunas all around me! It seems to me that this entire city is brimming over with Arjunas. Father! I see Arjuna when I am alone and I see him in my dreams too, and I feel delirious and appalled. I am now so terrified of Arjuna that even words starting with 'A' such as *Ashva* (horse), *Akshar* (letters of the alphabet) and *Ambuj* (a water-borne flower) frighten me in a similar manner."

(South Indian Mahabharata, Sabha Parva, Chapter–97, Shloka–64-66)

Duryodhana also added that the Pandavas had stormed off in rage, because they (Duryodhana and his group) had humiliated them to a great extent. Hence, it was foolish to think that they would forget the manner in which Draupadi was humiliated here. They would surely gather forces and wreak vengeance on all of us by attacking Hastinapur. Duryodhana said to Dhritarashtra that if he wanted to ensure the safety of his sons and Hastinapur itself, then the only way to achieve that was to incapacitate them and render them totally helpless. Thus, a game of dice should be held once again, but this time, there would be no wagering of kingdom or wealth. Instead, the loser would have to undergo twelve years of exile with his family, in addition to one year of incognito exile. Duryodhana said that if he lost, he would go to the forest with his family, but the rest of his brothers would stay in Hastinapur. But if Yudhishthira lost, all the Pandavas would have to go to the forest due to their bond with Draupadi. Then, after thirteen years, the Pandavas would have become so weak that they would not demand their kingdom, and even if they do, they (the Kauravas) would defeat them easily.

(Mahabharata, Sabha Parva, Gita Press Edition, Chapter–74, Shloka–1-23)

Duryodhana and his group instilled such fear in Dhritarashtra's mind that he was shaken to the core. In that fearful state, Dhritarashtra said:

तूर्णं प्रत्यानयस्वैतान् कामं व्यध्वगतानपि।
आगच्छन्तु पुनर्द्यूतमिदं कुर्वन्तु पाण्डवः॥

"Dear Son! Even if the Pandavas have gone far, if you wish, call them immediately. Let all the Pandavas come here and gamble again with this new stake."

(Mahabharata, Sabha Parva, Gita Press Edition, Chapter–74, Shloka–24; South Indian Mahabharata, Chapter–97, Shloka–87)

This new order of Dhritarashtra was opposed by all the dignitaries of Hastinapur. Among those protesting were Duryodhana's mother Gandhari, Duryodhana's brother Vikarna, stepbrother Yuyutsu, Grandsire Bhishma, Drona, Vidura, Somdutta, Bahlik, Kripacharya and others. However, Dhritarashtra did not pay heed to anyone. On the other hand, the Pandavas had travelled far in the direction of Indraprastha, but a courtier rushed and caught up with them on the way and called them again, citing Dhritarashtra's orders. Thereafter, when all the players were ready to play the game, Shakuni said:

अमुञ्चत्स्थविरो... X ...पुनर्द्यूतमेहि दीव्यस्व भारत॥

"O King Yudhishthira! It was good that our old king has returned all the wealth to you. Now, there will be only one stake in the game—if you beat us, then all of us will go into exile wearing deer skin. After spending twelve years in exile, we will also undergo one year of incognito exile. If we come face to face with you during this incognito exile, then this condition will be repeated and we will have to once again begin with twelve years of exile. And if you lose, the same condition will apply to you. You will also have to undergo normal and incognito exile along with Draupadi and the other four Pandavas. O Yudhishthira of the Bharata clan! Come with this resolve, and gamble with us by throwing the dice again."

(Mahabharata, Sabha Parva, Gita Press Edition, Chapter–76; South Indian Mahabharata, Chapter–98, Shloka–9-15)

Then, in spite of being warned by everyone present in the assembly to not play, Yudhishthira agreed to play the round of gambling in order to obey his uncle, Dhritarashtra. And once again, he lost the game. In the details provided above, only a few selected shlokas have been included as required. If readers wish to learn about the entire situation that played out at the time, they can read the chapters that have been mentioned herewith.

196. Who were Krishna's parents?

As everyone is aware, Vasudeva's son Krishna was born from Devaki. She was the youngest daughter of Devak, the brother of King Ugrasen of Mathura. During her marriage, an untoward event had occurred, because of which her cousin Kansa had become her bitter enemy. Consequently, all of Devaki and Vasudeva's marital dreams were shattered and buried in captivity. They even had to sacrifice seven of their children! Thereafter, several attempts were simultaneously made to save the eighth child, Krishna; and he was successfully saved too, proving the Hindi proverb, 'The one protected by God cannot be killed by anyone.' To read a detailed account of this, you can read my book 'I am Krishna' published in six volumes. One clear benefit of reading this book is, you will not have to scan one Purana after another. All the Puranas have been written by various people in different eras, and all those authors have tampered with the facts to propagate their views and philosophy, because of which, very often, readers are either confused or they get caught up in one of them. The reason behind this is, the subtle quality of prudence is not developed enough in everyone to enable them to discern what the reality is. But the book mentioned above has been penned after a thorough and comparative research. As a matter of fact, several details about Krishna's birth and his parents have already been provided in this book, in answer to other questions. So, reading this book from beginning to end is bound to satisfy those who seek answers to such questions. To answer your question briefly, the parents who gave birth to Krishna were Devaki and Vasudeva, and the parents who raised him were Yashoda and Nanda.

197. Who were Krishna's friends?

Krishna's life was not just inundated with enemies; he also had several great friends, who went on to become the epitomes of friendship and will remain so in the future too. However, a remarkable feature of Krishna's personality is that those who were hostile to him hated him wholeheartedly, and those who were his friends, those who had even the slightest glimpse of his true inner nature, remained totally and wholeheartedly devoted to him all their lives.

There is hardly any description of Krishna's childhood and his antics during this period, in the Mahabharata. And in the one that has commentary by Neelkantha, which is popular in North India, there is not even a single shloka about it; however, the Puranas are flooded with such descriptions. But the problem is that, very often, these Puranas have addressed his friends as mere cowherds. And the few names that have been given, vary in each Purana, that is, different names have been mentioned in different texts. Moreover, not a single one of Krishna's companions from Gokul or Vrindavan appears in his later life. So, one is compelled to conclude that the list of his friends begins from those in Mathura. Of course, if one considers Krishna's elder brother Balarama as his friend, then it can be said that his friend Balarama was with him right from Gokul and Vrindavan till his death. Here are the names of some of Krishna's prominent friends who were associated with him in Mathura and in his later life, and who were dedicated to him throughout their lives.

i) Uddhava - He was Krishna's cousin, who lived in Mathura with his parents. Similar to Krishna, he did not have to dwell in and roam the forests; he grew up in the urban culture of Mathura and was formally educated too. Furthermore, he was a respected councillor in Kansa's court and was also considered a confidant of King Kansa. The proof of this being that Uddhava's name was suggested along with Akrura's and Vasudeva's when it was decided to bring Krishna and Balarama from Vrindavan. This incident is also described in this book, and need not be repeated here. Krishna's first meeting with Uddhava was in Mathura. When Uddhava went to Vrindavan at the behest of Krishna, no one could recognise him there.

ii) Satyaki - His real name was Yuyudhan, but as he was the son of Satyak, he has been mostly called Satyaki in Sanskrit texts. In fact, he became famous by the name of Satyaki. A valiant warrior, he too belonged to Krishna's Vrishni clan. Similar to Uddhava, he too was a selfless friend of Krishna. Whenever warriors had to be dispatched on the toughest of expeditions, Satyaki was the first person Krishna relied on. Whenever an enemy attacked Dwarka in the absence of Krishna, Satyaki used to be on the front line with the soldiers. Furthermore, when Dwarka's armed forces got divided in the Mahabharata war, Krishna had to stand alone on one side, while his Yadava army of Dwarka was on the enemy's side, since it was assigned to Duryodhana's side. That being the case, it was Satyaki's duty to fight on behalf of Duryodhana. But he had distanced himself and his soldier sons from Dwarka's army so that he could avoid spending even a single moment in separation from Krishna. He, along with his sons, had chosen to fight only on behalf of the Pandavas. This is a rare example of the inseparable and devoted friendship between Krishna and Satyaki, which is difficult to find anywhere else in history.

iii) Ugrasen - Although he was senior to Krishna by two generations, he was more of Krishna's friend than his maternal grandfather. This becomes clear if one scans all the texts available today. Ugrasen was greatly impressed with Krishna's selflessness at the time of Kansa's slaying. He had handed over the kingdom of Mathura to Krishna, but instead of accepting it, Krishna had crowned Ugrasen himself as the king. In return, a grateful Ugrasen continued to repay the debt of this favour done unto him throughout his life. Of course, it is a different matter that Krishna's stature had skyrocketed in the blink of an eye because of his proximity to an experienced king like Ugrasen, but Krishna's own unique insight and efforts had also played a major role in this rise in stature. A tremendous rapport underlined the relationship between the grandfather and grandson, so much so that when all the eminent inhabitants of Mathura were hell-bent on getting Krishna expelled from the city due to their fear of Jarasandha, Krishna's grandfather Ugrasen found a way to save his beloved grandson, even under such difficult circumstances. He sent Krishna and Balarama to the ashram of Sage Sandipani where Jarasandha could not launch an attack even if he wished to. Krishna too did not take long to return this favour of his maternal grandfather, and he once again crowned Ugrasen as the king of Dwarka, a kingdom which Krishna had established solely on the strength of his own power. The point worth noting here is, there was no dearth of elders in Krishna's family; for instance, his father Vasudeva and his elder brother Balarama were very much present. But Krishna preferred his maternal grandfather over anyone else. This too is a unique and shining example of a friendship between a maternal grandfather and grandson.

iv) Arjuna - Even a book that is several thousand pages long will not suffice to describe the friendship between Krishna and Arjuna. They were akin to one soul in two bodies. Evidence of their friendship can be found in several places in this book itself. Many people even say that it was only because of Arjuna that Krishna chose to support and protect all the Pandavas. At many places in the Mahabharata, Krishna himself declares that he and Arjuna have committed to lay down their lives for each other. You will find some examples of this in this book as well. Krishna had such faith in his cousin and inseparable friend Arjuna that he did not even desist from getting his own sister abducted by Arjuna. This is the reason why, for centuries, the Avatarists[48] have been so impressed by the friendship of Krishna and Arjuna that they have termed them as Nara-Narayana, that is, the twin-brother avatar of Vishnu.

v) Sudama - This story of friendship that bridges the gap between poverty and affluence is available in only three texts: Bhagavat Purana, Brahmavaivarta Purana and Garga Samhita. In these three texts, it is stated that Sudama, a friend from Krishna's gurukul, visited Dwarka once with the desire to put an end to his destitution, and Krishna, in his own unique style, made him wealthy, without bringing it to Sudama's knowledge.

vi) Daruka - After Krishna's arrival in Mathura, Daruka had joined Krishna's group of friends along with Uddhava, Satyaki and others. Daruka was a valiant warrior as well as one of the best charioteers of Aryavarta during that period. That is why when Krishna became the crown prince of Dwarka, Daruka was officially appointed as his trusted security guard, a charioteer of high calibre, and an intimate friend. Daruka turned out to be the most fortunate among Krishna's friends, as he got the opportunity to be with Krishna till the latter's final moments.

198. What was Dwarka's governance and administration like?

Almost all the Puranas as well as the Mahabharata are silent about the governance and administration of Dwarka. A brief but important factual description is found in one place only, in the Harivansha Purana, based on which one can infer the kind of governance system that was in place in the kingdom. All modern scholars use the same shlokas to describe

48. Those who believe in 'avatars', deities who have descended on the earth in an incarnate form or some manifest shape (an incarnation of a god)

the administrative skills of Krishna. Here are those significant shlokas of the Harivansha Purana:

मर्यादाश्चैव संचक्रे श्रेणीश्च प्रकृतीस्तथा।
बलाध्यक्षांश्च युक्तांश्च प्रकृतीशांस्तथैव च॥
उग्रसेनं नरपतिं काश्यं चापि पुरोहितम्।
सेनापतिमनाधृष्टिं विकद्रुं मन्त्रिपुंगवम्॥
यादवानां कुलकरान् स्थविरान् दश तत्र वै।
मतिमान् स्थापयामास सर्वकार्येष्वनन्तरान्॥
रथेष्वतिरथो यन्ता दारुकः केशवस्य वै।
योधमुख्यश्च योधानां प्रवरः सात्यकिः कृतः॥
विधानमेवं कृत्वाथ कृष्णः पुर्यामनिन्दितः।
मुमुदे यदुभिः सार्द्धं लोकस्रष्टा महीतले॥

Vaishampayan said: "Shri Krishna laid down rules and laws for everyone. He also established proper regulations for merchants, common people, army generals and public administrators. He made Ugrasen the king of Dwarka, and appointed Sage Sandipani, the great scholar of Kashi, as the head priest. He appointed Anadhrishti as the army general and Vikadru as the Prime Minister. The wise Shri Krishna established an advisory council to advise him in all tasks, and chose ten elders from various clans of the Yadavas for this purpose. The great charioteer, Daruka was appointed as the personal charioteer of Shri Krishna. The best among warriors, Satyaki was appointed as the commander-in-chief of the army. Thus, Krishna, whose every deed was commendable, established this administrative system and began to live happily with the Yadavas."

(Harivansha Purana, Vishnu Parva, Chapter–58, Shloka–79-83)

Nothing more than this can be found in the Puranas about the administrative system of Dwarka. But the shlokas quoted above are proof of an efficient administrative system, while also demonstrating Krishna's administrative proficiency.

199. By calling Krishna the strength of the Pandavas, was there a plan to kill him in the Mahabharata war?

Evidence found in the Mahabharata states that during the war, a plan was hatched to kill Krishna, in order to debilitate the Pandavas. The veils shrouding this secret were lifted when Ghatotkachha was killed by Karna, and due to this, a pall of gloom had descended not just on the Pandava camp but on the Kaurava camp too. The only person who was happy with the death of Ghatotkachha was Krishna! Delving into the reason behind this, in the camps of Kurukshetra, while Krishna was engaged in alleviating the grief of the Pandavas, Sanjaya, who had arrived in Hastinapur to convey the news from the battlefield to Dhritarashtra, had to hear complaints, accusations and counter-accusations. The cause of the deep anguish that had gripped the Kaurava camp was the fact that Karna's rare weapon, which he could use only once, and which he had reserved for use on Arjuna, had to be deployed on Ghatotkachha because the circumstances demanded it. Pained by this development, Dhritarashtra spoke in an infuriated tone:

विरोधी च कुमन्त्री च प्राज्ञमानी ममात्मजः।
यस्यैव समतिक्रान्तो वधोपायो जयं प्रति।।
स वा कर्णो महाबुद्धिः सर्वशस्त्रभृतां वरः।
न मुक्तवान्कथं सूतताममोघां धनञ्जये।।
तवापि समतिक्रान्तमेतद्गावल्गणे कथम्।
एतमर्थं महाबुद्धे यत्त्वया नावबोधितः।।

"My son Duryodhana opposes everyone and considers himself to be the most intelligent of all. His ministers are not good either. That is why he has lost the opportunity to employ this infallible measure that would have killed Arjuna and ensured our victory. O Charioteer! Karna is very intelligent; why did he himself not deploy that unerring, powerful weapon on Arjuna? O Sanjaya, supremely wise son of Gavalgan! Why did you forget to advise Karna in this regard?"

(Mahabharata, Drona Parva, Chapter–182, Shloka–17-19)

दुर्योधनस्य शकुनेर्मम दुःशासनस्य च।
रात्रौ रात्रौ भवत्येषा नित्यमेव विकत्थना।।
श्वः सर्वसैन्यानुत्सृज्य जहि कर्ण धनञ्जयम्।
प्रेष्यवत्पाण्डुपाञ्चालानुपभोक्ष्यामहे ततः।।

Then, Sanjaya said to King Dhritarashtra: "O King! Every night, Duryodhana, Shakuni, Dushasana and I used to urge Karna to forget about the rest of the enemy army, and concentrate only on Arjuna and kill him. We used to tell him that we would then use the Pandavas and the Panchalas like servants."

(Mahabharata, Drona Parva, Chapter–182, Shloka–20-21)

अथवा निहते पार्थे पाण्डवान्यतमं ततः।
स्थापयेद्यदि वार्ष्णेयस्तस्मात्कृष्णो हि हन्यताम्॥
कृष्णो हि मूलं पाण्डूनां पार्थः स्कन्ध इवोद्गतः।
शाखा इवेतरे पार्थाः पाञ्चालाः पत्रसंज्ञिताः॥
कृष्णाश्रयाः कृष्णबलाः कृष्णनाथाश्च पाण्डवाः।
कृष्णः परायणं चैषां ज्योतिषामिव चन्द्रमाः॥

Sanjaya informed Dhritarashtra that they further said to Karna, "If you think that after Arjuna is killed, Krishna will make another Pandava confront you, then kill Krishna himself. Krishna is the very root of the Pandavas, Arjuna is like the trunk above, the other sons of Kunti are the branches, and the Panchala soldiers are the leaves. Krishna is the refuge, strength and protector of the Pandavas. Just as the moon is the primary basis for the constellations, Krishna is the greatest support of the Pandavas."

(Mahabharata, Drona Parva, Chapter–182, Shloka–22-24)

तस्मात्पर्णानि शाखाश्च स्कन्धं चोत्सृज्य सूतज।
कृष्णं हि विद्धि पाण्डूनां मूलं सर्वत्र सर्वदा॥

The other Kauravas including Sanjaya and Duryodhana said: "Therefore, O Karna! Forget the leaves, branches and the trunk; just cut off the root. Always and in every respect, consider Krishna as the root of the Pandavas."

(Mahabharata, Drona Parva, Chapter–182, Shloka–25)

हन्याद्यदि हि दाशार्हं कर्णो यादवनन्दनम्।
कृत्स्ना वसुमती राजन्वशे तस्य न संशयः॥
यदि हि स निहतः शयीत भूमौ
यदुकुलपाण्डवनन्दनो महात्मा।
ननु तव वसुधा नरेन्द्र सर्वा
सगिरिसमुद्रवना वशं व्रजेत॥

Sanjaya says regretfully: "O King! If Karna had killed Krishna, the scion of the Yadavas, then this whole earth would have been under his control, there is no doubt about that. O King! If the great soul Krishna, who is the joy of the Yadava clan and the Pandavas, had been killed by that powerful weapon and had fallen in the battlefield, then this entire earth, including the mountains, seas and forests, would have been under your control."

(Mahabharata, Drona Parva, Chapter–182, Shloka–26-27)

Thus, we can see that Krishna was not absolutely safe in that cataclysmic war. He was faced with thousands of dangers too, but all of them came to naught, and the result of the war was exactly what he intended it to be. After all, he was not addressed as 'Jai Shri Krishna' (Victory to Shri Krishna!) without any reason.

200. What details are mentioned about the offspring of the Pandavas in the scriptures?

In the scriptures, one can find very little systematic description regarding the children of the Pandavas. Not much has been said about them even in the world's most voluminous book, the Mahabharata. In the Puranas, especially the newly created ones, fictional stories have been copiously propagated in a few places like the story of Barbareek in the Skanda Purana. Well, I will not confuse you with fictional stories, but I am referring to those texts whose major portions have been considered by scholars to be more or less authentic. So, among the early Puranas, Vishnu Purana is counted, and in this Purana, one finds the following details about the offspring of the Pandavas:

तेषां द्रौपद्यां पञ्च पुत्रा बभूवुः।
युधिष्ठिरात् प्रतिविन्ध्यः भीमसेनात् सुतसोमः श्रुतकीर्तिरर्ज्जुनात् शतानीको
नकुलात् श्रुतकर्मा सहदेवात्।
अपरे च पाण्डवानामात्मजाः तद्यथा यौधेयी
युधिष्ठिराद् देवकं पुत्रमवाप।
हिडिम्बा घटोत्कचं भीमसेनात् पुत्रमवाप।
काशी च भीमसेनादेव सर्वगं पुत्रमवाप।
सहदेवाच्च विजया सुहोत्रं नाम पुत्रमवाप।
रेणुमत्याश्च नकुलोऽपि निरमित्रमजीजनत्।
अर्ज्जुनस्याप्युलूप्यां नागकन्यायामिरावान् नाम पुत्रोऽभूत्।
मणिपुरपतिपुत्र्याश्च पुत्रिकाधर्मेण बभ्रुवाहनं
नाम पुत्रमर्जुनोऽजीजनयत्।।
सुभद्रायांचार्भकत्वेऽपि योऽसावतिबलबलपराक्रम
समस्तातिरथविजेता सोऽभिमन्युरजायत।।

Sage Parashara said, "Those five Pandavas had only five sons from Draupadi:
Draupadi and Yudhishthira's son - Prativindya
Draupadi and Bhima's son - Shrutsen
Draupadi and Arjuna's son - Shrutakirti
Draupadi and Nakula's son - Shrutanik and
Draupadi and Sahadeva's son - Shrutakarma
Apart from these, there were several more sons from the other wives of the Pandavas:

- Yudhishthira had a son named Devak from a wife named Yaudheyi.
- Bhimsen had a son named Ghatotkachha from a wife named Hidimba, and a son named Sarvag from a wife named Kashi.
- Sahadeva had a son named Suhotra from a wife named Vijaya.
- Nakula had a son named Nirmitra from his wife Renumati.
- Arjuna had a son named Irawan from Ulupi, Babhruvahana from Chitrangada, and Abhimanyu from Subhadra. Abhimanyu was incredibly powerful and prevailed over his enemies, right from his childhood."

(Vishnu Purana, Part–4, Chapter–20, Paragraph–11-12)

201. Did Duryodhana suddenly try to imprison Krishna at the palace of Hastinapur or was it a pre-planned conspiracy?

This incident occurred when Krishna was about to reach Hastinapur as an envoy of peace, and a heated debate had taken place in Dhritarashtra's royal court on the matter of how to welcome him. Then, Duryodhana, on hearing the discussions between Dhritarashtra and Vidura, expressed his thoughts, saying that Krishna could never be lured away from the Pandavas, so there was no need to honour him by gifting him wealth:

यदाह विदुरः कृष्णे सर्वं तत्सत्यमच्युते।
अनुरक्तो ह्यसंहार्यः पार्थान्प्रति जनार्दनः।।
यत्तत्सत्कारसंयुक्तं देयं वसु जनार्दने।
अनेकरूपं राजेन्द्र न तद्देयं कदाचन।।
देशः कालस्तथाऽयुक्तो न हि नार्हति केशवः।
मंस्यत्यधोक्षजो राजन्भयादर्चति मामिति।।
अवमानश्च यत्र स्यात्क्षत्रियस्य विशांपते।

न तत्कुर्याद्बुधः कार्यमिति मे निश्चिता मतिः॥
स हि पूज्यतमो लोके कृष्णः पृथुललोचनः।
त्रयाणामपि लोकानां विदितं मम सर्वथा॥
न तु तस्मै प्रदेयं स्यात्तथा कार्यगतिः प्रभो।
विग्रहः समुपारब्धो न हि शाम्यत्यविग्रहात्॥

Duryodhana said: "Father! Whatever Vidura has said about Shri Krishna, who never wavers from his values, is true. Shri Krishna harbours a special affection for Kunti's sons, so he can never be lured away from them. O King! You desire to welcome him with so much wealth, but you must not do that at all. It is not that he does not deserve it, but the time for such things has now passed. Your gesture will give Krishna the impression that we are worshipping him in this manner out of fear. Father! I do not support any idea that is humiliating for the Kshatriyas. And when the conflict has already begun, such display of love by way of this hospitality will not pacify him either."

(Mahabharata, Udyoga Parva, Chapter–88, Shloka–1-6)

Then, Grandsire Bhishma objected to Duryodhana and said, "O King! Whether one honours Krishna or not, remember that he will never tolerate humiliation. So, the entire royal court must patiently listen to all that he has to say. Whatever he says will be ethical and for the benefit of everyone's prosperity and welfare only." Duryodhana then objected to his advice:

न पर्याप्तोस्मि यद्राजञ्श्रियं निष्केवलामहम्।
तैः सहेमामुपाश्रीयां यावज्जीवं पितामह॥
इदं तु सुमहत्कार्यं शृणु मे यत्समर्थितम्।
परायणं पाण्डवानां नियच्छामि जनार्दनम्॥
तस्मिन्बद्धे भविष्यन्ति वृष्णयः पृथिवी तथा।
पाण्डवाश्च विधेया मे स च प्रातरिहैष्यति॥
अत्रोपायान्यथा सम्यङ् न बुद्ध्येत जनार्दनः।
न चापायो भवेत् कश्चित् तद् भवान् प्रब्रवीतु मे॥

Duryodhana said: "Grandsire! Now, there is no possibility of me enjoying all this wealth along with the Pandavas all my life. You should forget all these things now, and listen to me as I tell you about the great task I have decided to accomplish this time. When Krishna, who is the greatest support of the Pandavas, arrives here, I will imprison him. When he is imprisoned, all the Yadavas, several kingdoms of this planet, and the Pandavas too will come under my command. According to the information received from the messenger, Shri Krishna will arrive tomorrow morning. Therefore, advise me only on the best measures that can be taken regarding this matter, the precautions that need to be taken so that Krishna does not get wind of this plan, and anything else that helps me accomplish my secret task without hindrance."

(Mahabharata, Udyoga Parva, Chapter–88, Shloka–12-15)

It is clear from Duryodhana's outspoken statement quoted from the Mahabharata above, that the plan to imprison Krishna was devised long before he had reached Hastinapur. Duryodhana was not foolish to impulsively capture Krishna, but rather, it was his well-planned move.

202. Did Dhritarashtra ever try to split Krishna from the Pandavas?

It is true that Dhritarashtra had tried to do something like this before the war. According to the Mahabharata, when the messenger informed the royal court of Hastinapur that Krishna was arriving as an envoy of peace and would set foot in the city by next morning, the sly Dhritarashtra said something to the principal secretary of the kingdom, Vidura, while giving him instructions about welcoming Krishna. On hearing Dhritarashtra's words, Vidura was perplexed and he wondered if the king had gone insane. Here is what Dhritarashtra had said:

He said, "O Vidura! I have received information that Shri Krishna is arriving here tomorrow. He is the leader of the Yadavas and is also a great person. His reception should leave nothing to be desired. Hearken to how I will extend my hospitality to Shri Krishna right before your eyes. I will give him sixteen gold chariots, pulled by four beautiful horses of the same colour, brought from the Bahlik kingdom. I will give him eight rollicking elephants, 100 young maids laden with gold ornaments, as many male servants and 18,000 soft blankets made of sheep's wool. I will gift him soft deer hide from China, as many as he wants. I have a radiant gem, and a chariot drawn by mules that can travel 14 *yojanas*[49] in a day. I will gift him both. I will give eight times more food than the average to all the servants and vehicles that accompany Krishna. Thousands of well-groomed prostitutes will walk

49. 1 yojana equals approximately 12 kilometres

on foot to receive him. Apart from them, all the daughters-in-law and daughters of the inhabitants who do not want to be veiled can also go. The palace of Dushasana is grander than that of Duryodhana, so arrangements should be made to accommodate Shri Krishna in that palace. All the gems that Duryodhana and I possess are kept in the adjoining chamber. Out of these, Krishna should be given all the gems that he wishes to take."

(Mahabharata, Udyoga Parva, Chapter–86)

On hearing this, Vidura may have been stunned for a moment, but he soon realised Dhritarashtra's intentions. Then, he said to King Dhritarashtra, "O King! You are a generous-hearted, charitable person and now you are old too, so all this is certainly in keeping with your reputation. But, Your Majesty, you must be simple."

आर्जवं प्रतिपद्यस्व मा बाल्याद्बहु नीनशः।
राजन् पुत्रांश्च पौत्रांश्च सुहृदश्चैव सुप्रियान्।।

Vidura said: "O King! You must adopt simplicity. Do not destroy your son, grandson and relatives by foolishly resorting to craftiness."

(Mahabharata, Udyoga Parva, Chapter–87, Shloka–5)

न तु त्वं धर्ममुद्दिश्य तस्य वा प्रियकारणात्।
एतद्दित्ससि कृष्णाय सत्येनात्मानमालभे।।
मायैषा सत्यमेवैतच्छद्मैतद्भूरिदक्षिणा।
जानामि त्वन्मतं राजन्गूढं बाह्येन कर्मणा।।

He continued: "I swear by my body and truth that you do not wish to give all these things to Shri Krishna as your righteous duty or in order to please him. O Charitable King! I speak the truth; this is merely your guile and wile. I understand your intention hidden behind this superficial behaviour of yours."

(Mahabharata, Udyoga Parva, Chapter–87, Shloka–7-8)

अर्थेन तु महाबाहुं वार्ष्णेयं त्वं जिहीर्षसि।
अनेन चाप्युपायेन पाण्डवेभ्यो विभेत्स्यसि।।
न च वित्तेन शक्योऽसौ नोद्यमेन न गर्हया।
अन्यो धनञ्जयात्कर्तुमेतत्तत्त्वं ब्रवीमि ते।।

Vidura said: "You want to lure the mighty Shri Krishna to your side by showering him with gifts, and by doing this, you are hoping that you will lure him away from the Pandavas. But O King! Let me give you a glimpse of the reality. You cannot split Shri Krishna from Arjuna by gifting him wealth, or through any other measure, or by criticising."

(Mahabharata, Udyoga Parva, Chapter–87, Shloka–10-11)

Thus, it is clear from the shlokas of the Mahabharata quoted above that Dhritarashtra had certainly made the wily move of trying to buy Krishna with his wealth and render the Pandavas helpless, but Vidura exposed his intentions right away, in the packed assembly.

203. What assurance did Krishna give Draupadi before heading to Hastinapur as an envoy of peace?

Krishna met the five Pandavas and Draupadi before leaving for Hastinapur as an envoy of peace, and tried to glean what each of them was thinking. So, he first spoke to Yudhishthira, who emphasised on the need to establish a treaty. Bhima and Arjuna also chose treaty as the first preference. However, Nakula, differing from his three elder brothers, put the entire onus on Krishna and said, "O Krishna! Pay no heed to the indecisiveness of these three. Everything in this world is subject to circumstances. So, arrive at a decision that you think is appropriate after gauging the situation and using your discretion. Our mindset has been changing according to the situation. What we had thought at the time of exile changed after that period was over; and what we had thought while living with King Virata as refugees has also changed now. And we do not know what thoughts we might harbour in the near future either. So, you need not act according to what any of us say. You yourself must take a decision after gauging what time demands *(Mahabharata, Udyoga Parva, Chapter–80)*. These words spoken by Nakula indicate his high intelligence and philosophical outlook. And perhaps that is why, in many places in the Mahabharata, he has been called the most intelligent of the five Pandavas.

On the other hand, unlike the rest of the Pandavas, Sahadeva was opposed to the idea of establishing peace talks. He only wanted war! Sahadeva even said that if righteousness is dear to Yudhishthira, Bhima and Arjuna, they could abide by it. He, however, rejected such righteousness and only wanted to fight Duryodhana. On hearing him, Satyaki, a friend of Krishna and the principal warrior of Dwarka, supported Sahadeva and posed a question, "Krishna, have you forgotten how enraged you were on seeing these Pandavas wear the hide of animals in the forest, and how you were raring to take up arms against Duryodhana that very moment?"

Now, it was Draupadi's turn, the most prominent member of the Pandava family. The very Draupadi, who had withered on hearing the words of Yudhishthira, Bhima and Arjuna, cheered up the moment she heard Sahadeva and Satyaki, and stood in front of Krishna with her hair in both hands:

यथावध्ये वध्यमाने भवेद् दोषो जनार्दन।
स वध्यस्यावधे दृष्ट इति धर्मविदो विदुः।।

Draupadi said: "O Janardana! Just as one commits a great sin by killing one who does not deserve to be killed, the one who spares a person who deserves to be killed also incurs a sin; the wise men know this."

(Mahabharata, Udyoga Parva, Chapter–82, Shloka–18)

नन्वहं कृष्ण भीष्मस्य धृतराष्ट्रस्य चोभयोः।
स्नुषा भवामि धर्मेण साऽहं दासीकृता बलात्।।
धिक्पार्थस्य धनुष्मत्तां भीमसेनस्य धिग्बलम्।
यत्र दुर्योधनः कृष्ण मुहूर्तमपि जीवति।।
यदि तेऽहमनुग्राह्या यदि तेऽस्ति कृपा मयि।
धार्तराष्ट्रेषु वै कोपः सर्वः कृष्ण विधीयताम्।।

She continued indignantly: "O Krishna! According to the prescribed laws, I am the daughter-in-law of both Grandsire Bhishma and Dhritarashtra, and yet I was forced to become a maid right before their eyes. O Krishna! In such a situation, if Duryodhana remains alive even for a moment, then the bow of Arjuna and the strength of Bhima be damned! O Krishna! If you consider me worthy of this, and if you have my best interests at heart, then you should direct all your fury at the sons of Dhritarashtra."

(Mahabharata, Udyoga Parva, Chapter–82, Shloka–30-32)

अयं ते पुण्डरीकाक्ष... x ...द सस्वरं बाष्पगद्गदम्।।

She then went on to say: "O lotus-eyed Krishna! Over there, you may do whatever you wish to, with the desire of a treaty with enemies, but in that moment, just remember these tresses that were pulled by Dushasana. If Bhima and Arjuna have begun to speak of a treaty, akin to cowards, then pay no heed to them! My old father will fight against the enemies with his supremely valiant sons. My five mighty sons will also fight a war against the Kauravas under the leadership of Abhimanyu. How will I find peace until I see the severed dark arm of Dushasana rolling in the soil? O Friend! I have spent thirteen years suppressing this fierce anger, and today, when I heard Bhima talk about a treaty, it was heart-rending. Today, they have forgotten my humiliation and are talking about righteousness." Even as she was saying this, Draupadi choked up.

(Mahabharata, Udyoga Parva,
Chapter–82, Shloka–36-42)

तामुवाच महाबाहुः केशवः परिसान्त्वयन्।
अचिराद् द्रक्ष्यसे कृष्णे रुदतीर्भरतस्त्रियः॥
एवं ता भीरु रोरुत्स्यन्ति निहतज्ञातिबान्धवाः।
हतमित्रा हतबला येषां क्रुद्धाऽसि भामिनी॥
अहं च तत्करिष्यामि भीमार्जुनयमैः सह।
युधिष्ठिरनियोगेन दैवाच्च विधिनिर्मितात्॥

Krishna then assured Draupadi and said: "O Krishnaa! You will soon see other women of the Bharata clan weeping in this manner. O Bhamini! The women of those wicked men—our opponents who are the target of your fury—will also cry in the same manner when their family members, brothers-in-law, friends and armies are killed. Driven by the command of King Yudhishthira and the invisible plan devised by the Creator, I, along with Bhima, Arjuna, Nakula and Sahadeva, will do what you desire."

(Mahabharata, Udyoga Parva, Chapter–82, Shloka–44-46)

204. Did the kings fighting on behalf of Duryodhana in the Mahabharata war wish to wreak vengeance on Krishna?

A reference has been made in a section in the Mahabharata that shows the mentality of the rival kings of the time. When Krishna had gone to Hastinapur as an envoy of peace, despite going to Duryodhana's house, Krishna turned down his invitation to dine with him, and had dined at Vidura's house instead. While resting after his meal, he had a conversation with Vidura; and according to Vidura, it was rather futile for Krishna to come to Hastinapur as an envoy of peace and attempt to establish a treaty. In the course of the conversation, Vidura tells Krishna about the kings who had chosen to side with Duryodhana:

सर्वे चैते कृतवैराः पुरस्तात्त्वया राजानो हृतसाराश्च कृष्ण।
तवोद्वेगात्संश्रिता धार्तराष्ट्रान्सुसंहताः सह कर्णेन वीराः॥

Vidura says: "O Krishna! All those who are in favour of Duryodhana are kings who were hostile to you in the past, and whom you had vanquished and humiliated. These people have come to seek refuge with Dhritarashtra's sons as they fear you, and are raring to show their valour by associating with Karna."

(Mahabharata, Udyoga Parva, Chapter–92, Shloka–25)

The shlokas quoted above may not apply to all the kings, but the statement made by Vidura is true in the case of most of the kings. It can be said that a majority of the kings gathered in the name of an ethical war had actually assembled to fight an unethical war to wreak vengeance on Krishna.

Other Bestsellers by **Deep Trivedi**

I am The Mind

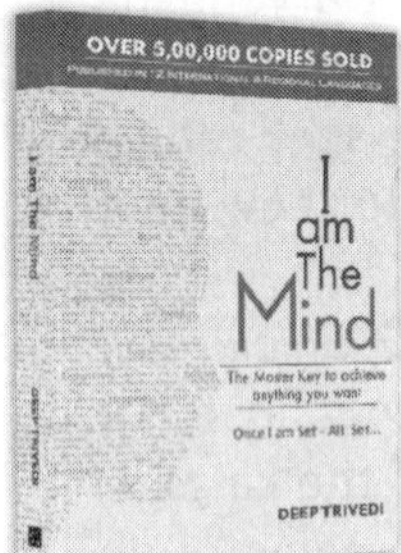

Grasp the power of the mind and make it work to your advantage. With over 5 lakh copies sold Nationally and Internationally, the book has been translated in 12 languages worldwide.

Available in English, Hindi, Gujarati, Marathi and other international & regional languages

3 Easy Steps To Win At Life

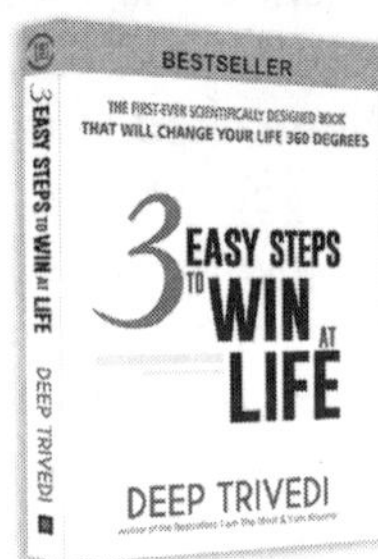

The first-ever scientifically designed book with 50+ day-to-day practical applications that will change your life 360 degrees.

Available in English, Hindi, Gujarati, Marathi

101 All Time Great Stories

Stories are the best medium to communicate profound thoughts and teachings of great men. Penned in a lucid manner, these interesting short stories will surely transport you into the world of great men, artists and philosophers.

Available in English, Hindi, Gujarati, Marathi

I am Krishna

Written in a riveting style, this complete biography of the multi-faceted personality, Krishna, is an unputdownable book. Read the fascinating account of Krishna's life story to understand his psychology, for it alone will help change your life forever.

Available in English, Hindi and Gujarati in individual volumes as well as a complete book set

Available at **www.aatmanestore.com**, all leading book stores, e-commerce sites and Deep Trivedi app in e-book and audio book format